Volume 5
THE G. STANLEY HALL LECTURE SERIES

G. STANLEY HALL, 1844–1924

Volume 5
THE G. STANLEY HALL LECTURE SERIES

Edited by
Anne M. Rogers
&
C. James Scheirer

1984 HALL LECTURERS

Anne Anastasi
Douglas W. Bloomquist
Jerome Kagan
N. Dickon Reppucci
Duane M. Rumbaugh

AMERICAN PSYCHOLOGICAL ASSOCIATION
WASHINGTON, D.C.

99980

Published by the American Psychological Association, Inc.
1200 Seventeenth Street, N.W., Washington, DC 20036
Copyright © 1985 by the American Psychological Association.
All rights reserved.

ISBN: 0-912704-92-6
ISSN: 8756-7865

Copies may be ordered from:
Order Department
American Psychological Association
P.O. Box 2710
Hyattsville, MD 20784

Printed in the United States of America

CONTENTS

PREFACE   1
Anne M. Rogers and C. James Scheirer

COMPARATIVE PSYCHOLOGY: PATTERNS IN ADAPTATION   7
Duane M. Rumbaugh

THE HUMAN INFANT   55
Jerome Kagan

PSYCHOLOGICAL TESTING: BASIC CONCEPTS AND COMMON MISCONCEPTIONS   87
Anne Anastasi

PSYCHOLOGY IN THE PUBLIC INTEREST   121
N. Dickon Reppucci

TEACHING SENSATION AND PERCEPTION: ITS AMBIGUOUS AND SUBLIMINAL ASPECTS   157
Douglas W. Bloomquist

PREFACE

Since 1980 the G. Stanley Hall Lecture Series has sought to bring the best thinking in the field of psychology to the attention of the undergraduate instructor. The annual series consists of five lectures, each devoted to a different topic commonly covered in the introductory psychology course, presented at the annual meeting of the American Psychological Association (APA) and subsequently published as a single, bound volume. Each lecturer is asked not only to present the latest developments concerning the topic, but effective and intriguing ways to teach the topic to undergraduates as well.

This book, the fifth volume of the Hall Series, includes the five lectures presented at the 1984 meeting of the APA in Toronto, Canada. The distinguished authors and their topics are Duane M. Rumbaugh, comparative psychology; Jerome Kagan, developmental psychology; Anne Anastasi, psychological testing; N. Dickon Reppucci, public policy; and Douglas W. Bloomquist, perception and sensory processes. These authors were chosen, after a lengthy selection process, for their mastery of a particular content area, their strong interest in teaching psychology, their experience in teaching introductory psychology, and their understanding of the special problems inherent in teaching introductory psychology.

The instructor of the introductory psychology course faces an ever more formidable task. As the field of psychology splits into more and more specialty areas, it is hardly plausible for a single instructor to attempt to stay current in the many areas surveyed by the introductory course. Yet it is the introductory course that gives most college students, including future psychologists, their first taste of psychology. For those who do not major in the field, the course may be their only systematic exposure to the science and the profession.

These were the issues faced by the APA Committee on Undergraduate Education (CUE) at its meeting of March 1979. As the group responsible for implementing APA's concerns with the undergraduate curriculum, CUE recognized the plight of the introductory course instructor, who may teach 20 to 25 topics within a single course, and looked for ways to be of practical assistance.

The result was a proposal for a lecture series that would consist of 25 lectures, each covering a different topic, presented over a five-year period. Twenty topics were identified as the common subject matter of the introductory course, and four of these were scheduled each year. The fifth lecture each year was to examine a special topic chosen to reflect contemporary interest. To be sure that these lectures reached those for whom they were intended, a two-step process was proposed: The five lectures would be presented at the annual meeting of the APA, and would then be published as an annual APA separate.

The parent board of CUE, APA's Education and Training Board, considered and approved the proposal. Many other groups and individuals contributed to the final shape of the proposal as it worked its way through the APA governance structure: the Committee on Continuing Education, the Board of Convention Affairs, the Division of Teaching of Psychology, and a number of individuals who were leaders in undergraduate psychology education. The series was reauthorized by the APA Board of Directors at its June 1983 meeting for a second cycle commencing in 1985.

In the first paper in this volume, Duane M. Rumbaugh takes a broad look at the field of comparative psychology and makes the case for its potential as an integrative framework for the science of psychology. He begins by exploring the phenomenon of animal behavior, particularly the relative contributions of instinct and learning to behavior. He looks closely at the concepts of ethology and fixed-action patterns and the consequences these can produce. He gives examples of how their senses permit animals to be sensitive to important stimuli in the environment, opening the door to the possibility of behavior stimulated by the environment rather than exclusively by instinct.

Rumbaugh devotes a major portion of his paper to the concept of cognition, the mechanisms of learning, memory, perception, thinking, and language, specifically as these pertain to animals and their behavior. This discussion illuminates such concepts as categorical learning, the feature-positive effect, the serial-position effect, the numerical attributes of stimuli, and the implications of spatial learning and memory studies. Rumbaugh urges further study of how organisms integrate independently learned units of information to a constructive advantage.

Are primates capable of language? Rumbaugh focuses his discussion of the intelligence of primates by considering recent research, particularly with chimpanzees, in which the ability of primates to use the symbols and even the syntax of language is being explored. Rumbaugh builds the case that chimpanzees have the capacity for a fundamental aspect of language—the ability to use arbitrary symbols representationally. Observing that these studies reveal much about the processes of language acquisition, which we could not learn by observing the more rapidly maturing human child, Rumbaugh brings the paper back to his original assertion: Comparative psychology can provide an integrative framework for the entire field of psychology.

Jerome Kagan examines cognitive processes in the human infant as well as the soundness of the hypothesis that insight into early development enables us to predict or at least to understand pathology or other manifestions in the human adult. Kagan identifies and closely considers three questions that dominate theory and research on the topic of infant cognitive processes: What does the infant perceive and what form do these representations take? What is the role of maturation in the development of cognitive functions? What are the consequences of these emerging functions for the child's emotional and social behavior?

The discussion of the development of retrieval memory and the appearance of fears between the ages of 6 and 12 months leads to an examination of the concept of attachment. Specifically, Kagan looks at the assumption that caregiving conditions make the infant more or less vulnerable to anxiety, an assumption that psychological theorists of the past fifty years have built upon to imply that an insecure attachment to the biological mother renders the child vulnerable to psychological symptoms indefinitely.

Raising the concept of temperament, Kagan notes that studies during this century have focused on variations in environmental experiences rather than on the possibility of temperamental differences among infants. Kagan finds evidence of temperamental differences in the infant's characteristic behavioral reaction to unfamiliar people, objects, and situations. He concludes with a summary of his own current work, a longitudinal study of two cohorts of children, which focuses on their behavioral and physiological reactions to unfamiliar peers of the same age and sex. There is evidence that inhibition and lack of inhibition are moderately stable traits possibly influenced by biological processes that predispose some children in one direction or the other.

What is it, Anne Anastasi begins her paper by asking, that test users, test takers, and undergraduates in general should know about contemporary psychological testing? Anastasi reviews the basic concepts of testing as well as recent developments in order to answer this question. She also looks at some of the most prevalent popular misconceptions about testing, which she believes lead to the misuse of tests and to the misinterpretation of test scores. To demonstrate how sophisticated concepts and methodologies can be presented at a simple level, Anastasi discusses her own ways of teaching such topics as standard deviation, factor analysis, and item response theory.

Anastasi leads us through the steps to be taken to answer the fundamental question, "How can I evaluate or judge a test?" Some knowledge of the major steps in test construction and the principle psychometric features of tests, she argues, is a prerequisite to the proper evaluation of a test. Instructors of undergraduate psychology are urged to familiarize themselves with the psychometric features of tests and with general sources of information about tests. She explores major concepts relevant to test evaluation.

Anastasi next moves in for a closer look at two statistical procedures involved in test construction: item analysis and factor analysis. Both qualitative and quantitative item analysis are considered. The concepts of validity generalization and differential validity are explained, and their implications for the practical utilization of validity data are considered. The importance of differential validity when tests are used for classification rather than selection purposes, and its connection to test bias issues, are noted. Anastasi observes that test misinterpretation and misuse commonly arise from misconceptions, not about the statistics of testing alone, but about the psychological behavior that tests are designed to measure. To illustrate, Anastasi cites examples from the area of ability testing, particularly examples of differences between aptitude and achievement testing.

In the fourth paper, N. Dickon Reppucci explores a subject that has only recently emerged as one of importance to psychologists: public policy and the field of psychology. Noting that his topic is rarely covered in the undergraduate introductory psychology course, Reppucci takes as his primary objective to provide a framework for a psychology in the public interest. He does so by discussing the public policy process and by providing examples of psychological research and the roles played by psychologists in the realm of public policy. He defines public interest psychology as a perspective that considers research to have acquired value when its findings are used to promote human welfare, and quotes William Bevan's argument for a conception of psychology that would consider the social, political, and economic contexts within which that research takes place.

For the purposes of this paper, Reppucci limits his discussion of psychology in the public interest to the use of psychology specifically in relation to public policy. He examines ways in which the products and methods of psychology have had an impact on public policy in recent years. Reppucci discusses the roles that psychologists play in public policy: the expert witness, the translator and consultant, the researcher or policy evaluator, the agency or program administrator, the activist-collaborator, and the social engineer.

Next, Reppucci analyzes the public policy process as a series of five interrelated stages: problem identification and definition, policy formation, policy adoption, policy implementation, and policy impact. He notes that underlying this framework there are subtle but important social and emotional elements. Once we are aware of the complexity of the public policy process, we are ready to ask what psychology can contribute. Reppucci concludes with a discussion of the subtle and difficult business of distinguishing scientific knowledge from beliefs and values, but makes the case that this difficulty should not prevent psychology's contributing to the public policy arena the knowledge that it has to offer.

In the fifth and final paper, Douglas W. Bloomquist focuses his discussion around three issues: introducing sensation and perception in the introductory course, ambiguous figures, and subliminal advertising, an applied aspect of subliminal stimulation. Noting that the subject of sensation and perception is not as inherently interesting to many students as are other areas within psychology, Bloomquist suggests that teachers begin by demonstrating why perceptual phenomena are really psychological rather than biological in nature as a first step toward eliciting enthusiasm from students.

Bloomquist suggests as a beginning such provocative questions as: When is a sound not a sound? Does light contain color? Is sugar really sweet? Bloomquist discusses the distinction between the concepts of sensation and perception, and provides ways to illustrate the distinction. He explores how Dallenbach's "puzzle picture" can be used to intrigue students while introducing them to the complexities of the process of perception. To stimulate students' interest and to show them how they take their perceptual experiences for granted, Bloomquist identifies and demonstrates some of the problems in perception with which psychologists deal.

Ambiguous figures are figures that generate alternate visual perceptions. Ambiguous figures are fun, Bloomquist observes, but they are also the subject of serious research by psychologists who seek to understand perceptual processes and the factors that influence which aspects of the figures we perceive. He reviews selected studies and a number of ambiguous figures drawn from the psychological literature and from art.

The topics and mode of presentation of the five papers in this fifth volume of the G. Stanley Hall Lecture Series differ. One author examines a few trends in detail, whereas another author broadly surveys the topic. Some authors give substantial recommendations for classroom activities and demonstrations; others do not. Still, these papers have much in common. They are more than mere reviews. They are integrative accounts of the literature that place each topic in the context of an introductory course, a context that limits what can be taught.

This volume originated with the selection of the G. Stanley Hall Lecturers, a task accomplished by a special advisory committee composed of Ludy T. Benjamin, Jr., Deanna G. Chitayat, Clyde A. Crego, Janet R. Matthews, Charles G. Morris, and R. Steven Schiavo. Their work is greatly appreciated.

The editors also wish to thank Deanna Cook, who guided this volume through the many stages to publication.

Anne M. Rogers
C. James Scheirer

DUANE M. RUMBAUGH

COMPARATIVE PSYCHOLOGY: PATTERNS IN ADAPTATION

DUANE M. RUMBAUGH

Duane M. Rumbaugh received his PhD from the University of Colorado in 1955. Currently he is Regents' Professor, Chair of the Department of Psychology, and Director of the Language Research Center at Georgia State University. He is also an affiliate scientist of the Yerkes Regional Primate Research Center of Emory University. In 1970 he initiated the Lana Project, the first research project on questions of language with apes as subjects for which computer-monitored keyboards were developed. That project has led to the foundation of the Language Research Center of Georgia State University, operated in cooperation with the Yerkes Primate Center. The Language Research Center focuses upon the requisites of language through basic research with apes so as to advance research and instruction with language-deficient humans. The ape research is directed by E. Sue Savage-Rumbaugh and the research with language-deficient humans is directed by Mary Ann Romski.

Dr. Rumbaugh's bibliography lists more than 125 papers, 5 books, and 2 educational films—including the widely used *Survey of the Primates*, written with Austin H. Riesen and Robert E. Lee. He has lectured widely on his research dealing with general learning processes and specifically with apes in language and comparative learning. He is a fellow of the American Psychological Association, of the American Association for the Advancement of Science, and of the New York Academy of Sciences.

Figure 1. A young gorilla captures the spirit of comparative psychology! (Photo by author)

DUANE M. RUMBAUGH

COMPARATIVE PSYCHOLOGY: PATTERNS IN ADAPTATION

Introduction

Comparative psychology, relative to other areas, has not been a clearly defined topic. Consequently, it has received short shrift and has even been totally ignored in introductory psychology courses. Recent developments in the field, however, call for rectification of this state of affairs.

A Framework for Psychology

Comparative psychology has great potential as an integrative framework. Although psychology is the science of behavior, behavior is the subject of other fields as well. I believe that all existing knowledge of

Preparation of this paper was supported in part by the National Institute of Child Health and Human Development and the Division of Research Resources of the National Institutes of Health (NICHD-06016 and RR-00165). I thank the following persons for helpful comments, constructive criticism, and colleagueship: Paul Ellen, Darlene Meador, James L. Pate, Merle Prim, W. K. Richardson, Herbert Roitblat, Mary Ann Romski, R. Barry Ruback, E. Sue Savage-Rumbaugh, and Herbert Terrace. Also, I thank Susan Hall and Judy Sizemore for valuable assistance throughout this effort. Lastly, I thank the APA for the opportunity to contribute to those teachers who have the privilege of teaching introductory psychology in the colleges and universities across the continent.

basic psychological processes and much of what has been learned and will be learned in other behavioral fields, such as animal behavior and sociobiology, should be incorporated into the matrix of comparative psychology. (Beach, 1984, has recently buried the snark and admonishes psychology to get on with it—on with research and theory building in comparative psychology.)

Comparative psychology is more than just research with animals. It is, rather, a perspective, a framework within which to guide the search for similarities and differences in patterns of adaptation and to account for them from within an evolutionary framework. In this chapter I consider comparative psychology in terms of a matrix of five dimensions: species, time, behaviors, basic processes—all in interaction with ecology. I describe the five dimensions using the following examples.

1. *Species.* Primate species differ in terms of their perceptual mechanisms. Arboreal primates are far more likely to be distracted by irrelevant foreground cues in a learning task than are primates that are primarily terrestrial. They also differ qualitatively, as shall be seen, in their transfer of training and learning processes. They differ widely in terms of their social organizational patterns and all other dimensions of traditional interest to psychologists.

2. *Time.* This dimension of the matrix involves development and maturation. The great apes are far more dependent than are rhesus monkeys upon opportunities to learn and to experience while they are infants so far as adult competency in learning, mating, and parenting is concerned.

3. *Behaviors.* Each species has its own behavioral proclivities, contingent upon the interactive consequences of biology and experience. One cannot teach a gorilla to be a chimpanzee or vice versa. Also, anatomy and morphology profoundly influence what behaviors will be manifest and how they will appear.

4. *Basic processes that generate manifest behavior.* For example, animals can see by virtue of different sensory systems. Vipers can see images determined by heat that objects generate. How birds find their way in flight can vary, depending upon what orientation cues are available and reliable. Bats and sea mammals can use sonar for seeing in the dark.

5. *Ecology.* Species, time, and behavior all interact with ecology. Ecology, as used here, includes all contextual variables, natural and contrived. The temperaments, interests, and social tractability of chimpanzees and animals in general are profoundly influenced by the environments within which they grew and within which they function at a given moment. For a chimpanzee to survive in the field, it must be more than just a chimp. It must be one that grew up in the field, during which time it learned how to meet its needs and to take care of itself.

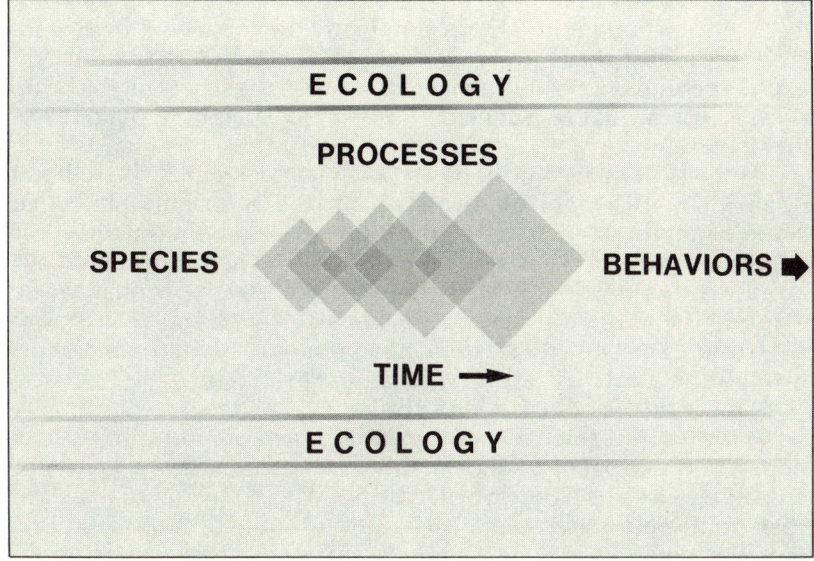

Figure 2. The matrix of comparative psychology

Comparative psychology is, then, a generic area of research. Its integrative potential is great. Because humans are, by virtue of genetics and intellect, conceptualizing creatures, some of us will be comparative psychologists. Our interests will be in patterns of similarities and differences among forms of animal life and how they might be accounted for as patterns of adaptation within an evolutionary framework. In that sense, comparative psychology is an imperative of our genes.

Adaptation

Each animal, at any given moment, is a responding, coping organism that carries the history of its species and its own experience as modulated by the processes of development and maturation. At times it is learning that is salient, whereas at other times social behavior, emotional expression, curiosity, aggression, or altruism is salient. All of these are intertwined and are part of each organism's efforts to but one end—adaptation.

Adaptation is a continuing challenge. It may succeed to varying degrees, but it is never complete. It may fail to varying degrees, but it may never fail completely without dire consequences. To fail completely is to be dead. Behavior interfaces the organism with environmental resources, on the one hand, and protects it from dangers on the other hand (see Beck, 1980; Gottlieb, 1984; Kummer, 1968).

In 1859 Darwin published *On the Origin of Species.* Evolution was not a concept unique to Darwin; others had expressed scientific interest in the fact that life forms changed. Darwin's contribution was that he presented a possible mechanism for change, natural selection, which is differential reproductive success mediated by genetics. How does it work?

Animals can have enormous reproductive potential. Were it not for attrition, offspring from a single pair of flies, for example, would blanket the earth with 191 quintillion descendants in only five months. Fortunately, not all of them survive. Their mortality, however, is neither random nor shared equally. Defective or inadequate offspring die at higher rates. Consequently, some genotypes (sets of cell-based genetic information) have tended to dominate others through their offsprings' survival and reproduction. (See Alcock, 1975, for a further discussion of this topic.)

With natural selection, differential reproduction, differential success in the progeny's survival and reproduction, and the viability of other species are frequently put at risk. This is the case particularly when both species are reliant upon at least one common natural resource of limited amounts. Competition results. There are winners and losers, and which ones reproduce? (See Dawkins, 1976, for a readable book on the genetic view of reproduction.)

None of this is to say, however, that evolution is smart, that it has a plan, or that it knows what it is doing or cares. Perhaps in the most precise sense, evolution selects against, not for, phenotypes. "In short, organisms are what they are because of the history of genetic variations in their ancestors and because none of these antecedent variations impeded their capacity to survive in the particular environments through which they have come in time" (von Glasersfeld, 1980, p. 972). Not all extant attributes of species are current requisites for survival.

Natural selection operates upon individual differences and mutations. Mutations are transmissible changes in the genotype due to natural forces. (The basic taxonomic classification is *species.* Closely related species form *genera,* closely related genera form *families,* and, in turn, families form *orders,* orders form *classes,* and classes form *phyla.*) To the degree that animals are closely related, they share common physical and behavioral traits or attributes. Although species frequently interbreed, with rare exceptions (e.g., Rumbaugh, Wolkin, Wilkerson, & Myers, 1976; Wolkin & Myers, 1980) genera do not. Neither do families or orders.

Toward a Definition of Comparative Psychology

Comparative psychology strives to elucidate patterns of behavioral adaptation within an evolutionary framework. It might sail under various flags and academic registrations, but it always knows its own. Wherever scientific efforts elucidate the processes and profiles of adaptation defined by animal life, one will find the very essence, the grist of comparative psychology. Today the flags under which comparative psychology accrues the units of its science include animal behavior, animal cognition, behavioral biology, ethology, sociobiology, primatology, ape-language research, and, of course, comparative psychology. As stated earlier, knowledge of basic psychological processes and much of the research in other behavioral fields will fall eventually into the matrix of comparative psychology.

There is a long-term, inevitable relation between physiological and comparative psychology. Differences in behavior must reflect differences in neurophysiology. For the present, however, comparative psychology is not dependent upon physiological data for its progress. Riesen (1974) advised that physiological research be more sensitive to comparative data because mechanisms might vary across species. The American Psychological Association's decision to have a separate journal, *The Journal of Comparative Psychology*, has recently been implemented. This well-advised action serves to encourage comparative behavioral research that is not necessarily coupled with physiological correlates or foundations. The physiological portion of what has been *The Journal of Comparative and Physiological Psychology* is now published in its own journal, *Behavioral Neuroscience*. *The Comparative Psychology Newsletter*, edited by Demarest, has been important to the rejuvenation of comparative psychology. The 1984 Grass Instruments calendar, designed by Donald B. Lindsley, provides an interesting and tasteful review of recent major developments in both physiological and comparative research.

The World of Animal Behavior

Humans probably have been intrigued with animal behavior since the early days of hominid evolution (Marshack, 1984). Why did animals behave as they did? How could knowledge of animal behavior be used to enhance the prospects that there would be something to eat? How might an understanding of animal behavior be used to avoid becoming dinner for them? Knowledge garnered by humans has not come easily; it has never come cheaply. It was only after several millions of years of humans' being interested in animals and animal behavior that a scientific understanding began to emerge. The question "What does a given animal or species do?" calls for description. By contrast "Why?" calls for the specification of behavioral requisites.

Learning Versus Instinct

We do not really live in a world in which everything is a dichotomy— either it is this way or it is that way. But human thought tends to force perceptions, conclusions, and attitudes into a dichotomy. Early students of behavior can be said to have done this. Experimental psychologists of the mid-twentieth century emphasized learning to account for behavior (see Catania, 1984, for an excellent undergraduate text with a behavioral perspective). By contrast, the ethologists emphasized instinct, which is not learned but rather controlled by genetics (see Scheller & Axel, 1984, for recent advances), structured by biological events, and triggered or released by relatively specific stimuli, which, from time to time, impinge upon the organism.

What do salmon do when it is time to spawn? We can describe how they swim, scale the cascades, and how they finally return to the small inlet in which they were born. But why do they do this? No one argues that it is because the salmon learned how to get to and from the ocean, which they do but once in a lifetime. It is more probable that their behavior is due to genetics, biology, and critical stimulation from the environment. But it is unlikely that even the behavior of the salmon is totally impervious to the effects of learning. (Most introductory texts have a discussion of genetics, which might be augmented by Thiessen, 1972, and articles such as that by Stebbins, 1984.)

It is now understood, however, that both learned and unlearned factors interact to produce behavior in animals. As was asserted by Thorpe (1972a, 1972b), for example, the homing bird's flight starts with a compass orientation, based on stimulation from probably more than one source, which includes the earth's magnetic field (see Gould, 1980), the bearing and movement of the sun, and possibly locations of stars. Over unfamiliar terrain, this is all that the homing bird has to use; however, familiar visual cues supplant these as the home loft is approached. Thorpe also recounts the flight of a grey-cheeked thrush (*Hylocichla minima*), monitored by a small radio transmitter that it carried. In only a matter of hours it flew 400 miles to its home—despite the changing winds and a thunderstorm that was so severe that the chase plane that was attempting to follow the bird had to turn back!

No behavior is totally divorced from biology; no behavior is totally divorced from experience. Rather, to varying degrees, biology and experience co-act to formulate manifest behavior. (See Bolles, 1975; Jerison, 1973. See also Candland & Nagy, 1969; Capretta & Rawls, 1974; Levine, 1982). Today, the line that differentiates ethology and psychology has become so blurred that one of the most recently constructed laboratories at the National Institutes of Health has been named the Laboratory for Comparative Ethology by an eminent comparative psychologist—the one who is its laboratory chief.

Ethology and Fixed-Action Patterns

Profound as the contributions of Darwin were to the eventual birth of ethology in the twentieth century, they were equally profound for the emergence of comparative psychology, the roots of which are clearly defined even in the nineteenth century (Gruber, 1981). Lorenz founded ethology. His research, together with von Frisch's work on bees and Tinbergen's research on birds, laid the foundation for modern ethology.

Because the concepts from ethology are important in the field of comparative psychology, consideration of research on instinctive behavior is in order. A digger wasp provides a classic example of instinctive patterns. At the time of egg laying, it digs a nest in the ground, with a tunnel to the surface. The wasp paralyzes a caterpillar by stinging it, transports it to the orifice of the tunnel, then leaves it there as it goes underground to check the state of the chamber. If all is well, it then retrieves the caterpillar and moves it down to the chamber. When hatched, the young feed upon it.

This is a very efficient and adaptive pattern—to a limit. It has the limitations of all instinctive patterns. If it is interrupted, compensatory adjustments of significance are unlikely. For example, if the caterpillar is moved while the wasp is underground, checking out the chamber, the wasp takes note. It once again positions it by the orifice of the tunnel and proceeds a second time to check out the underground nest. If the caterpillar is moved a second time while the wasp is rechecking the chamber of the nest, the scenario is repeated. This pattern will be repeated over and over and over just because the location of the caterpillar is slightly altered while the wasp is underground. It is as though the wasp is caught in a behavioral loop from which it cannot break.

Fixed-action patterns. Fixed-action patterns (FAPs) are innate, predictably patterned actions that, in a primed organism, are set into play by stimuli termed *releasers.* Thus, a goose that has laid its eggs is primed to manifest a number of FAPs, such as incubating the eggs and retrieving them if they have rolled from or have otherwise been displaced from the nest. If there is only one specific aspect of a stimulus that is a releaser for an FAP, it might be called a "sign stimulus." Thus, it is the dot on the beak of the adult sea gull that releases pecking by the young birds in the nest, which, in turn, stimulates the regurgitation of food from the adult for the young to ingest. It is the bright white interior of a broken egg's shell that releases removal of the shell from the nest by the black-headed gull, thereby reducing the threat of predation to its young (see Gould, 1982).

FAPs can produce incredible consequences. The weaver bird, for example, builds a distinctive and complex nest. It does this by using a variety of knots and materials to form a complex nest cup, replete with an opening designed to foil entry by predators. At times, FAPs are contingent upon multiple sensory input. Meredith and Stein (1983) reported, for instance, that predation by a cat upon a songbird is under the control of both vision (sight of the bird) and hearing (the bird's songs and movements). One or the other alone is not generally sufficient to trigger predation.

Chiszar (e.g., Chiszar et al., 1982) studied the predation of snakes and reported profound differences. The garter snake, for example, is quite fast and preys on relatively harmless animals, such as worms, small fish, and amphibians. By contrast, the rattlesnake is slow (though when it strikes, it is lightning fast) and preys upon animals that might inflict injury by claws and teeth. The garter snake tends to follow trails scented by would-be prey, which it bites, holds, and consumes. By contrast, the rattlesnake is not initially stimulated to follow the chemical scent of its target prey. Rather, the snake selects a trail used by potential prey and waits in ambush. Generally, only when the prey is within range does it strike. As it does, it is controlled by vision and heat sensors; however, after it strikes, it becomes attracted to chemical stimulation. On the basis of the chemical trail left by the prey, it begins to follow. Hours later it might find that prey, dead and quite safe to eat.

Both genetics and experience seem to determine song patterns in certain birds (Marler, 1972; Thorpe, 1958). Genetics defines the basic template, but it is the hearing of songs at very early ages, well before singing begins, that determines the trills and other nuances of the song to be sung several months later. Auditory feedback that occurs while birds attempt to sing in the first instance also influences the final song's pattern. Nottebohm (1981) has reported obvious and annual structural alterations in the left hemisphere as song learning and singing develop. (Logan & Fulk, 1984, report that mockingbirds, which have no fixed song, respond differently to spring and fall songs. For an excellent film on unlearned behavior, see Reese, 1982.)

Sensory Processes

A basic principle is that the sense organs of a given species are selected so as to be sensitive to important stimuli of the environment. If something is important to adaptation, there will be an organ to sense it. Color vision tends to be important to diurnal animals but not to nocturnal ones, almost certainly because color is difficult to discern in low levels of illumination. If the changing positions of the sun are important, then polarized light might be sensed. Bees, for example, are sensitive to it, and this assists their flights to food locations through the day.

Another important principle is that animals can have backup systems, that is, systems become operational contingent upon what sensory input is optimal. Homing pigeons have keen vision and are sensitive to color. Landmarks are of value. If clouds keep the pigeons from seeing landmarks, other systems, such as the use of magnetic fields, will be emphasized. Some systems are more reliable and error-free than others and, hence, are preferred.

When vision is rendered inadequate, as is the case in deep or murky waters, sound is likely to be relied upon heavily. Although vision might be used primarily at the surface, sea mammals, notably the porpoise and whale, are frequently found to depend heavily upon sound generated from other organisms and upon sonar, which entails the emission of sound waves and then hearing the returning echo (Schusterman, 1981). Similar adaptations have evolved in land mammals, some of which are nocturnal, such as bats. Bats (Griffin, 1958) make their way in flight by emitting sounds from the mouth and by listening to the reflected returns. Once thoroughly familiar with the topography, they can fly about in silence, particularly out and back to the caves where they live. Place a large vertical barrier in their path in familiar terrain, and they will fly into it, whereupon echolocation is activated. Bats are able to echolocate small insects in flight and others that are on leaves. Lest the insects be otherwise at the mercy of the preying bats, several have evolved defensive flight patterns that appear to become erratic just as the sound they perceive from the echolocating bat indicates that a strike is imminent.

The interplay between bats and insects is a good example of the basic principle of measure and countermeasure. Once a predator develops well-coordinated FAPs for obtaining its food, some variant in its prey might prove to have greater than average survival value, and vice versa. And so the cycle goes, reminiscent of the arms race between nations.

Taste and smell can be as important as vision and hearing, depending upon the importance for adaptation and survival. Furthermore, electric fields can be very important, as they are to many sharks, and infrared vision can be of paramount importance to the pit viper, whose separate infrared eyes form an image of the prey through heat-sensitive organs, an image that is projected onto the regular visual display afforded by the optic tectum. This is a good option for seeing in the dark (see Fobes & King, 1982; Stebbins, 1976).

Cognition in Animals

The word *cognition* has various meanings; however, here it is used to refer to mechanisms of learning, memory, perception, thinking, and language that process (e.g., act upon, mediate, structure) information obtained from the environment. The presumed consequence might be that the organism becomes knowledgeable and in an active, initiating manner influences its own behavior and, thus, the consequences of that behavior.

Do Animals Think?

How is it that chimpanzees can learn that television portrays scenarios and provides information about what is going on elsewhere? Chimpanzees can, for example, readily extract a morsel of food that they cannot see directly by watching a television monitor portray the food that they want in relation to the movement of their hands (Menzel & Savage-Rumbaugh, in press). They respond to televised portrayals of where food is cached, where people are hidden, which container holds prized foods, and so forth. They prefer to watch football and wrestling over soap operas and news. They even have their favorite movies, such as "King Kong," and films of old friends and familiar haunts. They also can be reminded to get a can of cola when the manufacturer's advertisement is on television. Why?

G. Stanley Hall (1965), early in this century, called for "a Darwin" who would bring order to the chaos of perspectives and data and provide a comparative perspective of the mind. Do animals have minds? The term is a highly controversial one. When it is used with reference to animals, it is best to presume that the term posits the questions, "Do animals know?" "Do they think?" "Do they have any capacity to initiate behavior other than in direct response to stimuli?"

In his introduction to the book *Animal Cognition,* Terrace (1984; also see Hulse, Fowler, & Honig, 1978) asserts that cognition implies neither consciousness nor mentalism. Rather, it is a model that posits some form of representation to which the animal can refer to guide its choices and behavior. (Terrace also reviews certain data on classical conditioning that possibly suggest a degree of representational learning—blocking, Kamin, 1969; expectancies, Rescorla, 1967; delayed matching, Roitblat, 1980. For an additional examination of the meaning of representation, see Roitblat, 1982.)

Evidence of Cognition

Shimp (1976) reported that pigeons could be queried as to which key was pecked first, second, and third in a given sequence of three pecks.

Different colors of light (red, blue, and white) were used to ask for this information after trials. Shimp reported better than chance performance on all three questions, with the highest accuracy being for the third key pecked.

Olton and Samuelson (1976) and Olton (1978, 1979) demonstrated that in a radial maze, where each arm was baited with food, rats only infrequently reentered arms at the ends of which they had previously eaten in that session. The rats did not exhibit repetitive patterns in exhausting all arms in a given session. If all the food was not consumed in a given arm, the rats did tend to reenter later, as though they remembered that fact (Herrmann, Bahr, Bremner, & Ellen, 1982).

Do pigeons know what they must do to get the task done? Do they know what the task requires of them, despite unpredictable changes in the task? Terrace (1984) reported that if pigeons are taught to peck three stimuli (A, B, C) in a fixed sequence, regardless of the arrangement on the panel, they apparently learn something about the ordinal position in which a given key should be pecked. This was determined by putting the middle stimulus of the series, B, into new sequences for the pigeons to learn—X, B, Y; B, X, Y; and X, Y, B. The pigeons learned the first of these three tasks very rapidly, an indication, according to Terrace, that they knew B's ordinal position apart from other specific keys with which it might be encountered (also see Roitblat, Pologe, & Scopatz, 1983).

Cognition versus behaviorism. Terrace's interest in and support for the development of animal cognition is of note because he was a graduate student of B. F. Skinner, the father of radical behaviorism. A question of interest to comparative psychologists is, how new and how different is Terrace's position now from Skinner's (1938, 1950, & 1953)? Skinner emphasized stimulus control over operant responses and rejected representations. Terrace allows for representations along with the importance of environmental stimuli in control. He argues that to extend "the study of stimulus control to stimuli that the organism generates poses a variety of technical problems. However, from a conceptual point of view, there is no basis at present to distinguish qualitatively between environmental and self-generated stimuli" (1984, p. 20). Radical behaviorism will probably be very reluctant to allow "self-generated stimuli" into an account of behavior. Notwithstanding, the current contest of thought between radical behaviorism and a behaviorism that allows for cognition in the determination of behavior will advance the science of comparative psychology.

Expectancies. Another body of evidence for animal cognition concerns Tolman's (1966, a reprint of his 1936 article) concept of expectancies. In a study reported by Capaldi and Verry (1981), rats were given five runs of a maze on each trial. On either the first or the last run the rats received 20 pellets of food; they received no pellets on the other runs of a given trial. Thus, a rat might obtain 20 pellets on the first run and none on the next four. Or, it might receive no pellets on the first run and then 20 on the fifth run. It was found that if the rats received the 20 pellets on the first run, they ran more slowly on the remaining runs of that trial. If the rats received nothing on the first four trials, they ran more quickly on the last trial. It appears that the rats were running in appropriate relation to whether they had been rewarded on the first run or to whether the pellets were yet to be obtained on the last.

Bever (1984) has sought to differentiate "descriptive reductionism" from "representational reductionism." The former asserts that science should use weak (simple) rather than strong (complex) descriptions and explanations wherever possible. The latter, representational reductionism, asserts that "an animal organizes each newly acquired behavior with the most concrete mechanisms available" (p. 62). Bever proceeds to point out that "descriptive reductionism is not always the correct move" (p. 62). (Animals are probably not aware of Lloyd Morgan's canon in terms of how and what they learn.)

Is it clear that animals have cognitive foundations for that which has been learned? Not really. D'Amato and Salmon (1984) found that cebus monkeys' ability to execute learned conditional discriminations with auditory sounds and visual comparison stimuli was remarkably disrupted simply by turning the house light, in the test apparatus, from off to on. Hulse, Cynx, and Humpal (1984) reported that although starlings, like humans, generalize frequency patterns (i.e., tunes) within the range used in training, they do not do so when the change is in the order of an octave—a change with which humans would have no problem. Although the perception of "primitive rhythm and pitch structure" is demonstrable in starlings, it is constrained relative to that of humans. I, too, have noted that the so-called complex learning-set skills of apes and monkeys are remarkably brittle when the nature of the test apparatus is changed—something that one would not expect if there were really a knowledge base of a human type underlying the mastery manifested by the animals. But that is exactly the point. Animals are not humans. Their cognitions, if extant, are surely both different and more circumscribed than humans'—an important comparative consideration.

Categorical learning. Like the work on expectancies, the study of categorical learning can also be used to support the existence of cognition in animals. As Herrnstein (1984) stated in his review of categorical learning:

> Human language may depend on categorization, but the evidence shows clearly that categorization does not depend upon language.... Categories that are fairly easy to describe physically do not seem to be significantly easier for animals, and may even

be harder, than categories that are hard to describe in those terms. For example, pigeons appear to find patches of colored light a harder category to form than photographs of trees. (pp. 257–258)

Blough's (1984) research has made clear that pigeons' perception of printed letters is much like humans'. This is taken to mean that confusion in the perception of letters (i.e., A vs. R)

is not a function of human verbal learning, of symbol manipulation, of partially uncrossed visual tracts or a convoluted cortex. Since letters are arbitrary forms for pigeons, the results suggest that perception of this sort of form may be a fundamental function of the way that higher nervous systems are constructed. (p. 288)

Feature-positive effect. Hearst (1984) provided an important comparative perspective on the *feature-positive effect*. With a variety of species, including humans, and across a variety of situations, performance is "considerably better when the *presence* of some specific feature of a compound stimulus is the signal for a positive event than when the *absence* of the feature signals the positive event" (p. 328). When conditions are reversed subsequent to initial learning of a feature-positive discrimination problem and where the absence of that once positive cue signals the stimulus to be selected, differences between pigeons and humans become marked. Some humans are able to reverse their choice of cues easily and rapidly, whereas pigeons are not. Humans can formulate a verbal rule to mediate their choices; pigeons cannot and appear to be "unduly controlled by characteristics of and relations between particular external stimuli" (p. 328).

Memory and spatial learning. One of the most robust phenomena to be discovered by studying humans as they attempt to learn and to recall lists of things, such as names, numbers, and pictures, is the *serial position effect*. That is, items at the beginning and at the end of the lists are easier to remember than are those in the middle.

Sands and Wright (1980) devised a clever method for studying the serial position effect in a rhesus monkey. They gave the monkey 10- and 20-item lists of pictures. At the end of each run there was a "probe" picture presented, and the monkey was to declare, through the execution of two different responses, whether it was the same as one of the pictures on the list just seen or whether it was different, in other words, not on the list. Both the monkey and the human were appreciably more accurate if the probe picture had been either near the beginning or near the end of the list rather than in the middle, a remarkable similarity in at least one aspect of memory for two primate forms. (See Sands, Urcuioli, Wright, & Santiago, 1984, for a review.)

An experiment with Lana, the chimpanzee (Buchanan, Gill, & Braggio, 1981), revealed that her free recall and reproduction of lists of up to eight words were remarkably similar to those expected of a young child. In addition, she tended to recall words in clusters, based either on word class or on the colored backgrounds of those words (which were faithful within a class, e.g., all foods and drinks were red, animates were violet, etc.). Interestingly, human data frequently reveal such clustering in memory. (See Medin, Roberts, & Davis, 1976, for more on animal memory.)

The ability to remember where food has been stored provides another example for the possibility of animal cognition. For example, Clark's nutcracker (*Nucifraga columbiana*), a bird that may cache up to 33,000 seeds, is faced with a very interesting challenge. How in the world can the bird subsequently find them, especially when they must do so or die because of the long, harsh winters they must endure in their high, alpine environment? To be able to retrieve food cached at earlier points in time requires that in some manner the bird "check off" sites as food is taken in toto from them, else it would return for something no longer there (Balda & Turek, 1984). This is similar to the Olton effect—rats generally do not return to arms of the maze from which they had exhausted the food.

Also similar are the results of studies reviewed by Kamil (1984) that indicate that nectar-feeding birds shift from flower to flower—new flowers—rather than perseverating in the choice of flowers from which nectar had been previously obtained. Reinforcement theory, in its most straightforward prediction, suggests that the birds should go back again and again to the flowers from which they obtained the reinforcer of nectar. But they did not. Here, then, is still another example of how genetics, it would seem, controls feeding strategies where the amount of nutrients (nectar, in this case) is so small in a given source (a flower) that it would be nonadaptive to return to it to no avail. (For additional discussion of the biological constraints on learning, see Kimble, 1981.)

Spatial learning and memory studies, as done by Olton and Samuelson (1976), have demonstrated that rats can efficiently exhaust all options of the arms in a radial maze to get food baited at the end of each alley. These experiments raise many questions, as is always the case with good research. (It would seem that nothing defines ignorance more clearly than good data, e.g., data raise questions about the unknown, the yet to be discovered.) Was the memory of the rats in this situation analogous to a list, in which each alley was an item on the list, or was it analogous to a map, to which the rat might refer to determine where to go next to get more food?

The short-term memory of humans has a limit of about seven plus or minus two (Miller, 1956). Olton, Collison, and Werz (1977) explored whether rats have a similarly limited short-term memory. They observed rats in mazes that had from 2 through 17 alternatives. The probabilities of correct choices as a function of number of choices revealed no sharp break in the curves as the number of alternatives approximated 7. Rather, as the number of alternatives increased from 2 to 17, there was a steady decay in performance accuracy. Consequently, it must be concluded that (a) this is not a valid test of the rat's short-term memory, which might indeed be limited to about 7 items in certain situations, or (b) it is evidence that the rat's short-term memory is several times greater than that of the typical human, or (c) the learning by the rat in this situation is not at all like a list of items, from which the serial position effect would be expected. (See Roberts, 1984, for more research on this question.)

From an ecological perspective, rats might have evolved a specialized capacity for learning spatial options and their resources. Thus, the rat's ability might well exceed that of humans for this kind of learning and memory. In support of this perspective are data collected by Davenport (see Rumbaugh, 1967) through a maze learning study in which rhesus monkeys and rats served as subjects. The rats were superior to the monkeys; however, the monkeys in other-object discrimination learning studies were clearly superior to the rats. The rat excels at spatial learning; monkeys and humans excel at visual discrimination learning.

If rats' maze learning is spatial, then rats might be able to go from one familiar point to another even over a novel route, if one is but extended to them. Ellen, Parko, Wages, Doherty, and Herrmann (1982) demonstrated that this was the case—rats could use novel routes to go between familiar places. Ellen, Soteres, and Wages (1984) also reported that units of a spatial field, experienced individually and at different times, can, nonetheless, be integrated by the laboratory rat.

Rats are by no means the only spatial learners. Canids, notably wolves (Hall & Sharp, 1978), are known to be able to take novel routes to places, as long as they know where they are and where the destination is relative to where they are. There are reliable reports of the domesticated dog returning to its home, despite its having been taken by car to some new and distant site. Not all dogs do that, of course. But how is it accomplished from time to time?

Spatial learning and memory have been given special attention in this chapter because they address so many important comparative psychological questions and because they can be studied very economically. Fundamentally what is needed is a good idea. Mazes are cheap and laboratory rats might be available. Houses can be viewed as mazes in which the household pet is already oriented. Experiments in which students systematically vary how and what kind of food is placed in various parts of the house can generate high interest in introductory classes.

Menzel (1978) has reported on spatial learning by chimpanzees and how their search behavior is contingent upon their friends' "coming along." The chimpanzees were carried individually about a compound and were shown where food had been, or was, cached. Subsequently, the chimpanzees were able to go to all of the food sites with minimal effort, that is, regardless of the specific point of release, they traversed an efficient route to obtain all of the food. Interestingly, if the chimpanzees were released as a group, with only one of them knowing where the food had been hidden, that chimpanzee was reluctant to go to it unless his companions followed. Thus, leaders can be dependent upon their followers.

Numerical attributes of stimuli. Another facet of animal cognition concerns the numerical attributes of stimuli. Church and Meck (1984) discussed evidence that indicates that "number of successive events (stimuli or responses) can serve as an effective stimulus for behavior, even when all temporal cues are counterbalanced or held constant" (p. 445). Fernandes and Church (1982), for example, trained rats to press one lever if two sounds were presented and to press another lever if four sounds were presented. The duration of each sound and the time between sounds were empirically discounted as variables that controlled the rats' differential responding to the two levers. Accordingly, they concluded that the controlling variable was the number of sequential stimuli, two or four in this study. Other work revealed that there was cross-modal transfer (from hearing to vision) of number. The procedure entailed substituting lights that flashed in lieu of the equivalent numbers of sounds. (See Ettlinger, 1977, for cross-modal research.)

Given that rats have the capacity to use relative numbers of stimuli to determine which response is appropriate, is there evidence that animals can use specific numbers to represent an appropriate quantity of items? Evidence to date is, at best, weak. There is some evidence, however, that chimpanzees can summate two quantities of food items in order to select the greater total given a choice. Sherman and Austin (*Pan troglodytes*), the subjects of many language studies in our laboratory, were given their choice of the left or right pair of food wells, on a tray that contained four wells, with each well containing from zero to four M&M candies or chocolate drops (Rumbaugh, Savage-Rumbaugh, Hegel, & Ivers, 1985). Procedures ensured that their choice of one pair of wells or the other was based on the summation of the items in that pair rather than on which pair had the single well with the greatest number of food items. For example, in the pairing of two and three versus four and zero, the latter pair has the largest number of food items in a single well, but the first pair nets the greater sum. They chose the greater summed value more than 90 percent of the time.

Next, five M&Ms or chocolates were included in the array of numbers to be assigned to the wells. This provided for novel arrays that Sherman and Austin had never seen in prior training and testing (e.g., three and four items in the left two food wells and one and five in the right two food wells). They selected the pair of wells that obtained for them the greater number of food items well above 90 percent of the time. This is not to say, however, that they were adding numbers in the same sense that we add Arabic numbers. Nonetheless, they seemingly evidenced the capacity for summating pairs of quantities to the same conclusion that would be obtained if one were adding in the numeric sense. Whether they can learn to use Arabic numbers in lieu of physical items in varying amounts is the next thing to discover.

Davis and Memmott (1982) reviewed the literature on counting behavior in animals and concluded that although animals can discriminate among numbers of things, there is no strong evidence that they can count. In fact, there is not even any weak evidence of consequence that supports that conclusion. That is not to deny that rodent mothers have ways to keep track of the number of infants in a litter. They do so not by counting, however. They do so by relying on stimuli (ultrasound in the case of the rat) or simply by exhausting the reservoir by retrieving and transporting the young to a nest until the last check reveals that they are all gone.

One cannot predict simplistically from a stimulus–response reinforcement framework the phenomena of learning across all species. Biological constraint and facilitation processes preclude that as an option. Comparative data have had and will continue to have a profound influence upon theoretical perspectives of behavior. (See Seligman & Hager, 1972, for chapters by Garcia and others on earlier research on this topic.)

What About Animal Intelligence?

Introductory students are invariably interested in the issue of animal intelligence. How intelligent is my dog? My cat? Are dogs more intelligent than horses? And what about the porpoise? Isn't it highly intelligent—perhaps as intelligent as humans?

The early history of comparative psychology involved questions about animal intelligence. It has been concluded, however, that this is not an issue that can be constructively addressed, at least for the present (Macphail, 1982). Clearly, there are enough problems with the concept of intelligence across races of humans to discourage either continuing to use the concept or pursuing it amidst the matrix of differences that characterize animal species.

Romanes (1898), one of the early researchers in comparative psychology, was vitally concerned with assessment of animal intelligence and laid the groundwork for the study of it through use of anecdotes (see Wasserman, 1984). Anecdotes have their weaknesses, as is shown in one from McClure (1879) that was obtained "on the authority of a grave and dignified Professor—no less a personage than Prof. Austin, of Cambridge" (p. 134). Austin's account was of a Bornean chap named Tuba, who, in 1864, was missing from his village. His friends put on a search for him and on the fifth day heard his voice and located it as coming from the top of a tree. Indeed, there he was—with a large, female orangutan. After the natives dispatched the orangutan, Tuba recounted his story. He had been out hunting and had stopped to swim. Once back on the river's bank, the orangutan grabbed his arms and forced him to follow her and to climb the tree to her treetop condominium—her nest—where she held him captive for days. During that time, according to Tuba, the orangutan brought him fresh fruit and vegetables and water in a coconut. (Can a young man be safe these days?)

Was Tuba's report true? I do not know, but I will allow that it might have been as reported. There is little but fun to gain by asking whether or not the report by Tuba was truthful or was a rationalization for a prolonged absence that could not be explained without undue embarrassment. There are many reasons, of course, why an orangutan—particularly a female orangutan—might have done what Tuba claimed. Whether intelligence had any justification for the action is a point that is not fruitful to pursue.

Nonetheless, there are many reasons for one to suspect that if thinking can be allowed as a process in humans, it might also be extant in animals—particularly those with large brains relative to the size of their bodies (see Jerison, 1973). Zookeepers, for instance, think that apes think, and they care for them accordingly. Zookeepers do not think that snakes think, and they care for them accordingly. Why?

Research on animal cognition reveals much about factors that determine ways in which various animals seem intelligent. As I have shown, some animals are *biologically smart* by virtue of unlearned behavioral patterns that serve their interests of adaptation very well. Others are *psychologically smart* in that they can learn arbitrary behaviors, even ones that are not necessarily specific to the immediate pressures of survival, such as designing and flying planes, writing novels, and so forth. In fact, human potential in the latter category is so great that its consequences, both direct and indirect, now threaten our survival and that of Planet Earth as well. Consider the threat of the world's using nuclear weapons and the consequences of the pollution produced by our magnificent traveling machines and the lethal wastes casually spewed forth from our nations' manufacturing plants. The threat, as I see it, is not a natural one. In no sense is it a threat of the kind that shaped the evolution of early hominids. It is one generated by intelligence of an extraordinary order that can be both awesome and awful. We, not nature, are responsible for the control of such consequences.

The comparative perspective holds that animals closely related to humans might also have some of those processes that make humans intelligent. What are they? How can they be measured equitably across species? How can they be measured equitably in humans? The answers must await future research and the development of new insights. I offer the perspective that studies of observational learning of arbitrary behaviors and of organisms' abilities to integrate to a constructive advantage independently learned units of information and behaviors will provide important gains in this important area—an area in which current comprehension is very inadequate.

Humans in a Comparative Perspective

The Human Being as a Primate

One of the most important aspects of comparative psychology is that humans are studied not as an isolated species, but as a group that fits on a larger continuum. (See De Waal, 1982; Jolly, 1984; Konner, 1982; Lockard, 1980; Passingham, 1982; Rumbaugh, Riesen, & Lee, 1970; Tanner, 1981; Wilson, 1978.) Humans are primates. The order, Primates, has about 250 species clustered into genera and families. Major groups include the great apes, the lesser apes, Old World monkeys, New World monkeys, and prosimians. An important distinction is to be made between the great apes and monkeys. Apes are frequently, but incorrectly, called monkeys. To do so is akin to confusing zebras with donkeys, violins with banjos, song sparrows with wild geese. Great apes are much more like humans than are the other primates. Consequently, they are uniquely important to an understanding of humans in a comparative perspective.

Within the primate order there is a trend, from the most primitive primates (the prosimians) to the ones with the most highly developed brains, toward increased body size; toward longer gestation, immaturity at birth, time to mature, and life expectancy; and toward standing and walking erect. There is also a host of biological factors that more and more closely approximate those of humans. Chimpanzees, for example, share at least 98 percent (King & Wilson, 1975) of the DNA found in humans. The difference is minimal, although differences in sequences and the control roles of genes make for obvious phenotypic differences (for which some feel grateful).

Within the chimpanzee genus, there are two species, *Pan troglodytes* and *P. paniscus.* The latter, the Bonobo, comes from only a small region in Zaire. The Bonobo is much more like humans than is its cousin, *P. troglodytes,* the common chimpanzee. The social structure of the common chimpanzee is relatively fluid, with various types of groups (all males, mothers with their offspring, mixed-sex groups, etc.) being found. By contrast, the Bonobo has a smaller, more well-defined group in which generally there is one adult male for every female. The sexual behavior of the common chimpanzee is more dependent upon the state of the menstrual cycle than is that of the Bonobo, for which sexual activity is readily stimulated by all kinds of good things—as though to celebrate. The mating pattern of the Bonobo includes gestures (Savage-Rumbaugh, Wilkerson, & Bakeman, 1977), ventral–ventral orientation, and protracted eye contact, behaviors said to be common in human mating but uncommon in other nonhuman primates.

I venture to say that if there were close morphological similarity, particularly facial similarity, our perspective of chimpanzees would be very different than it is now. Everyone would then concentrate upon the question, "Why do they act as they do, given that they appear to be like us?" This question is quite different from the view that I suspect prevails today, namely, "How can the apes' behavior be at all relevant to ours when they appear to be so different from us?"

Although chimpanzees and we humans are interested in different aspects of the world, we must jointly share the majority of sensory experience. The attention, motivations, appetites, and fears of chimpanzees can be brought into close alignment with ours. This is possible only because we are so closely related. When born, chimpanzees are about as dependent as a human child. In particular, the infant *Pan paniscus* tends not to cling and needs cradling from mother for body and head support. They mature in a life-cycle pattern similar to ours. Genetically chimpanzees and humans are more closely related than are sibling species, such as mice and rats.

Their social needs and affective expressions are remarkably similar to ours. An ape raised even for its first two years of life in an impoverished environment, with essentially no social stimulation, will never totally recover behaviorally. Chimpanzees and humans are so dependent upon adequate social environments for the development of social communicative skills, sexual competence, and parental competence, that the dimensions of similarity far outweigh the inevitable and important differences.

The same can be said of chimpanzees' cognitive development. Apes raised in impoverished environments will not fully recover. Although their simple discrimination learning skills remain relatively unscathed, their transfer-of-training and abstractive skills are diminished. The cost of an impoverished environment to apes, even if limited to the first 2 of their 12–15 formative years, will be far greater than will be the cost to rhesus monkeys (*Macaca mulatta*) that are raised in an impoverished environment for the first of their 5–6 formative years. (See Meador, Rumbaugh, Pate, & Bard, in press, for a review.) The same is true for sexual adjustment and parental competence. Primiparous rhesus monkeys reared in social isolation can maintain parental care-giving skills (Harlow & Harlow, 1965), even though their firstborn might not survive from their initial incompetence. For chimpanzees, the recovery of sexual or parental competence, given an impoverished early life, is limited (Davenport & Rogers, 1970).

In sum, chimpanzees are relatively more dependent upon early development than are rhesus monkeys for success in social life. Denied the opportunity to learn these social skills at an early age, chimpanzees will always be behaviorally deficient. The same is true for human beings. (For more on primate socialization see Altmann & Altmann, 1970; Bernstein, Gordon, & Rose, 1983; Fossey, 1982; Fragaszy & Mitchell, 1974; Frederickson & Sackett, 1984; Galdikas, 1981; Goodall, 1963; Hinde, 1979; Kummer, 1968; Levine, 1982; Lewis & Sackett, 1980; Lockard, 1980; Markowitz & Stevens, 1978; Mason, 1979; Nadler, Herndon, & Wallis, in press; Rosenblum & Plimpton, 1979; Sackett, Gunderson, & Baldwin, 1982; Schaller, 1963; Suomi & Immelmann, 1983.)

Comparing Learning Processes Among Primate Species

Are there differences in the quantity and quality of learning abilities of animals? Are these changes, if determined, related to evolution of the central nervous system? (See Jerison, 1973.) There is no question that humans are the most facile learners of all animals if the material to be learned is not fundamental to survival in a biological sense. Seligman (1970) demonstrated that the evolutionary history of species prepares them to learn some things with remarkable facility and also counterprepares them for learning other things, things that might be easy for other species to learn.

Apart from the Seligman perspective, are there differences in the abilities of animals to learn? Problems of testing or measuring equitably the abilities of animals, from diverse taxa, to learn have been so great as to discourage research. Nonetheless, there have been significant gains in tactics requisite to answering this and related questions. The problems of comparative research are simplified if one looks for interactions between species and strategies or processes in learning tasks (Bitterman, 1961).

Rumbaugh and Pate (1984) reported on primates' abilities to transfer operationally defined amounts of learning to test situations. Species were selected so as to offer a range of brain evolution. With progression of the primate brain from the prosimian to the human, there was a general shift in effective transfer, with the prosimians and small monkeys manifesting *negative transfer,* whereas the great apes and humans manifested *positive transfer*. Such a change is clearly a qualitative one along a quantitative dimension (i.e., transfer), reminiscent of Nissen's (1951) and Maier and Schneirla's (1935) assertions that there are qualitative changes in learning associated with brain evolution. Rumbaugh and Pate also reported an interaction between brain evolution and transfer of training ability. The more the prosimians learned (in terms of trials correct), the stronger the negative transfer; by contrast, the more the apes and humans learned, the stronger the positive transfer.

Rumbaugh and Pate also argued that there are qualitative differences in the processes of learning within the primates studied. The paradigm used was one of discrimination-reversal testing. Either the initially correct or the initially incorrect stimulus was deleted after criterion had been achieved on two-choice object-discrimination problems, and a new stimulus was substituted and assigned the cue value of the deleted stimulus. The species with smaller, relatively primitive brains learned as though they had reached criterion, prior to test trials, through stimulus–response associative learning. The species with larger, relatively advanced brains learned as though they had learned about a relation between cues and consequences. Their test behavior suggested that they might well have been inferring what they had to do to get food reward, given that only one or the other of the original stimuli was present and their cue values had been reversed. Although this was not a study in animal intelligence per se, Rumbaugh and Pate did point out that the ability to transfer learning to an advantage (i.e., positive vs. negative transfer) is a hallmark of what humans call intelligence. Thus, the data might bear on the question of animal intelligence.

The data reported by Rumbaugh and Pate were obtained through use of a modified discrimination-reversal learning task, which, in turn, was developed for comparative study out of the learning-set phenomenon demonstrated by Harlow (1949). What is learning set by way of process? Schusterman (1962) demonstrated that chimpanzees could develop high-order learning set as a result of successively learning to a criterion a small number of discrimination problems. Warren (1966, 1974) reported that monkeys, but not cats, developed learning sets as a consequence of that kind of learning. Consequently, there is probably an interaction between species and process involved in learning-how-to-learn, as the learning set phenomenon has been called. (For a further discussion of learning set and recent controversy, see Menzel & Juno, 1982, and Schrier & Thompson, 1984. For more on comparative learning, see Fobes & King, 1982, and relevant chapters in Dewsbury, 1978. For more on learning set mechanisms and the current status of basic learning set methods in comparative research, see Schrier, 1971, 1984. For a fine extension of human developmental stages to comparative studies, see Thomas, 1982.)

Behaviorists who share Skinner's perspective and researchers on primate learning and behavior have had strong differences that now hold the potential for new understandings. Primate behaviorists have frequently held that, as advanced by Kohler and by Yerkes, the great apes are qualitatively different from monkeys and other animals in how they learn and solve problems. Perceptual learning and insightfulness, self-awareness (Gallup & Suarez, 1983), responsivity (Glickman & Sroges, 1966; Parker, 1974), and the like have been the arena from which this argument has been advanced. Epstein, Kirshnit, Lanza, and Rubin (1984) have reported that pigeons can manifest "genuinely novel" behaviors as a result of behavioristic training methods being applied to component parts of "novel" acts. More specifically, they observed that pigeons would peck on a small box in order to move it underneath a toy banana. By standing on the box, they could reach the banana, which they had to peck to get reward. They did so seemingly much as Kohler's chimpanzee, Sultan, "spontaneously" used a tool to get a banana beyond his reach.

Setting aside the fact that Epstein et al. specifically taught the pigeon component parts of the larger action, there would appear to be no difference between them and the chimpanzees. On the other hand, if one obtains such behavior by specific conditioning methods in some species where, by contrast, that behavior is both learned and integrated by the animal on the basis of its own, nonspecific past experience, is there not a difference? Who you are will determine your answer to that question, but the answer to it is not so simple as some would insist. That answer will lead to new understandings. Quite apart from the answer to the stated question, it is of note that the radical behaviorists now allow for the appearance of behaviors not specifically taught, that is, genuinely novel behaviors.

Language and Primates

Are primates capable of language? Are primates capable of speech? Of course, some are. After all, humans are primates. Without question it is our proclivity to learn language readily, particulary speech, and to use it pervasively in communication that, apart from our appearance, sets us apart from other animals. Are primates other than humans capable of language? (See Schiefelbusch & Hollis, 1979, for both classic and current works.) This question has been difficult to address and one that has raised the hackles of scientists. That it has done so indicates that the question is important and that the answer will have impact on perspectives and theories.

What Is Language?

The question "Are primates and animals other than humans capable of language?" has no simple answer, because the main question is "What is language?" We know that adults use language all of the time, but at what point in time can it be said that a child is first using language? When it begins to speak its first words? If so, when a parrot "talks," (Pepperberg, 1981) does it, too, have language? And, what if the child cannot talk? Can it never have language? (See Smith, Newman, & Symmes, 1982, on primate vocal communication.)

The threshold of language has not been clearly defined. This fact permits great confusion, for it allows for the definition of language to be such that no animal other than humans could possibly manifest it. The root of the word, language, is *lingua*, which refers to *tongue*. Many definitions of language would restrict it to speech, which means that apes cannot have language due to the fact that they cannot articulate human speech. The common chimpanzee, *Pan troglodytes*, has practically no voluntary control over its vocalizations. Its vocalizations are primarily for affective or emotive expression. The Bonobo, *Pan paniscus*, has considerable voluntary control in that it can vocalize on a turn-taking basis with humans as if in conversation. Even so, it cannot speak in the human sense.

Then in what sense can species other than humans have language? The perspective held by researchers is that the essence of language is the competent use of symbols—and words are symbols. Thus, if an ape uses either hand signs or geometric configurations, it might be using language—but not necessarily. The crux of the question is, when animals use symbols that resemble humans' use of words, do they know and mean what they are saying?

We live in a day when automated language should help to clarify this important point. Even on the morning that I wrote these lines, I called information for a telephone number. My area code number + 555 + 1212 gave me a human, of that I am sure, for his voice and his expressions were appropriately coordinated with mine. He asked, "City please?" "The name of your party?" I told him. The next voice I heard was clearly that of a computer articulating through the marvels of electronics the number I wished to call. How did I know? Each number was discrete, there was a pause between each one, they did not sound as though they came from a source that knew in a human sense what my question had been in the first place! Place a call through use of a credit card, and the "thank you" of the computer after you have finished entering all digits will give you another prime example. The "thank you" is not that of one person to another. Rather it is as from silicon chip to an automaton from outer space. And, although the voice might be from a silicon chip, we are not automata from outer space. We look for meaning behind the use of symbols, and silicon chips cannot put it there. Can animals? (Can teachers?)

The Ape's Capacity to Use Symbols

Efforts to emulate language in humans through operant conditioning experiments with pigeons (Epstein, Lanza, & Skinner, 1980) are excellent demonstrations of how clever experimenters can be, how tractable the behaviors of pigeons are to the effects of contingencies, and what language is not (Ellen, 1982; Savage-Rumbaugh, 1984; Terrace, in press). Can we know whether or not symbols have any real meaning to apes? I believe that the answer is "yes."

Savage-Rumbaugh, Rumbaugh, Smith, and Lawson (1980) demonstrated that two chimpanzees, Sherman and Austin, were able to classify lexigrams (geometric symbols that function as words) for specific ingestibles and for specific tools (e.g., a screwdriver, lever, string, straw for drinking, key) into generic categories just by looking at the lexigrams. In other words, the chimps could look at a given word-lexigram and through the use of one of two other lexigrams declare whether that word-lexigram was a tool or whether it was a food/drink. This result is analogous to a person asking another to declare whether the name of something is either a tool or ingestible. How can we do thus? How can the chimps do it?

The process whereby it can be done entails representation. Symbols must come to represent things and events not necessarily present in space or time. Therein lies the great power of language to communicate about things that are not present (Savage-Rumbaugh, 1984). We can point to food that we want, we can gesture that we want it or do not want it, we can offer it to others, and so forth. Now, consider trying to communicate needs and ideas with no relevant items present. Without words to refer to each relevant item, we are sorely handicapped. Through the use of iconic gestures we can do better than otherwise, but it is with even arbitrarily structured symbols (either in sound or print) that our communication is greatly facilitated. Abstract concepts, points in time, needs, and fears are particularly difficult to refer to if we do not have words for them.

So, by some process Sherman and Austin were able to conjure a representation for each word-lexigram, make a decision in terms of the question—Was it food/drink or was it a tool?—and then were able to declare their answer through use of other lexigrams. They did so on the basis of trial-1 performance test trials, under conditions that were tightly controlled against inadvertent cuing, and the trials were essentially error-free. There was only one error in 33 test trials: Sherman called the word *sponge* a food—possibly because he would chew off portions of any sponge used for extracting liquids from receptacles, and that was the use to which he had put sponges.

The results of the study by Savage-Rumbaugh, Rumbaugh, Smith, and Lawson (1980) clearly show that chimpanzees have the capacity for a very fundamental aspect of language—the ability to use arbitrary symbols representationally. This is important because the ability to use words to refer to things not necessarily present is the essence of semantics. This very important development serves to justify continued research with apes into questions regarding the nature of language, an effort that was sorely challenged in the late 1970s by a paper from Terrace's laboratory (Terrace, Pettito, Sanders, & Bever, 1979).

Figure 3. Sherman and Austin engaged in their food-sharing task. Sherman is in the process of requesting any of a number of foods and drinks available at the time. Austin watches intently to determine Sherman's request. His task is then to comply with Sherman's request, and then he may have a portion for himself. The chimpanzees exchange roles periodically. The keyboard is portable and computer-monitored. The chimpanzees were in a 55-acre forest when this picture was taken. Although they were on leads, they were untethered. They stayed in close company with the researchers because of social bonding. (One cannot force apes of this size and strength to do anything. Nor do we try.) (Photo by E. Rubert)

The Ape-Language Controversy

Their paper shook confidence about the entire field of ape-language research. Terrace had already reported work from his own chimpanzee project with Nim that evidenced both vocabulary and syntax. But Terrace reversed his position in his 1979 paper and arrived at a number of conclusions, all of which were contrary to the notion that apes had even primitive language skills.

Terrace's main conclusions were that (a) Nim's manual signs for words were to a very worrisome degree imitations of signs made recently by his teachers; (b) chimpanzees' use of signs in other language projects evidenced the same imitation; (c) Nim's stringing of signs failed to add meaning above and beyond that of single words, that is, the strings were not approximations of sentences; (d) Nim failed to take turns in dialogue, as do children, for example, Nim interrupted others a great deal; and (e) Nim was only doing whatever he had to do by way of making signs in order to get what he wanted. Neither Nim nor other signing chimps were talking. Rather, they were simply performing operants, doing tricks. There was no meaning behind their signs.

A heated response followed from those who headed sign language studies with apes, and at that time I was comforted by the fact that neither the Lana Project (Rumbaugh, 1977) nor the Sherman and Austin Project (Savage-Rumbaugh, 1984) employed sign language. (The Yerkes language projects of Lana, Sherman, and Austin had used a computer-monitored, lexigram-embossed keyboard.) Even so, Terrace argued that Lana's sentences could be explained by rote memory—an interpretation that I have had some difficulty appreciating. Lana's initial instruction entailed the mastery of "stock sentences," ones that would activate various vending devices and entertainment systems. True enough, those had been taught to her by operant conditioning procedures, but it was never suggested that these stock sentences initially were other than the product of mindless strings of responses. However, Lana eventually made a number of interesting modifications to them (Rumbaugh, 1977), offering them during interaction with her teachers much as a human carries out his or her part of a conversation.

Thompson and Church (1980) reported that an early corpus of Lana's utterances and sentences could be accounted for by a simple model that called for paired associate learning (e.g., the use of word-lexigrams in association with a variety of exemplars), a limited number (i.e., 6) of stock-sentence frames into which she would substitute a key word, and the contingency as to whether or not a person was present in her room. Terrace gave this report much credence and, in conjunction with other data that he obtained from his pigeon research, concluded that Lana's behaviors were not linguistic.

Research by Straub, Seidenberg, Terrace, and Bever (1979) indicated that pigeons could learn to peck four visual targets (A, B, C, & D) in the correct sequence regardless of their array of presentation. The suggestion was that this was analogous to having Lana elicit "please machine give banana," for example. But I maintain that not only was Lana's ordered use of lexigrams contingent upon incentives and exemplars, but also it did not have to be for ones that were present. And Lana had not just four keys. She had well over a hundred!

Now, subsequently, my colleagues at Georgia State University (Richardson & Kresch, 1983) reported that pigeons can peck three stimulus patterns (i.e., lexigrams) in either of two sequences (A, B, & C vs. A, B, & D, where A, B, C, & D were present on all trials but in varied arrays). These two strings were initially under the control of the background coloration of the keys, where one background color required A, B, & C for reward to be obtained and a second color required A, B, & D. Eventually, the pecking of these two strings was under the control of a light apart from the other keys. It was then the color of that light that signaled which string was correct. This is an important demonstration of how responding to multiple stimuli can become contingent upon something apart from them. Thus, pigeons have firmly placed at least one claw into the domain within which Lana moved with major effect with dozens of exemplars and within varied contexts.

Ape-language research has taught us a great deal about dimensions of language that otherwise never would have been teased out in the study of language acquisition in a normal child, which transpires too rapidly for fine-grained analysis. Ape-language research has also taught us a variety of things unrelated to apes and to language. It has taught us to work harder to retain a sense of community among scientists, particularly when the question under study generates a challenge to the definition of humanity and its origins. It has served to remind us, through hard object lessons, that the press is more probably interested in controversy than in the constructive resolution of controversies. The press is not a patient observer of the scientific process through which there is the sorting out of data and the emergence of changing perspectives—all necessary for progress.

The experiences of scientists with ape-language research should encourage all scientists to be more tentative in what they say, to be more careful about what they commit to paper, to speak with precision, and to listen carefully. These experiences should have reminded everyone by now that no one can prove the null hypothesis. No one should say that apes will never be able to do this or that.

Figure 4. Mulika, a one-year-old pygmy chimpanzee, addresses the challenges of a world of language. (Photo by E. Rubert)

Toward a Mastery of Syntax

But the story does not end here. Lana did far more than punch her keys contingent upon incentives, present or absent. She generated dozens and dozens of strings, many of which came about simply because the potential length of a sentence was increased with a redesign of the keyboard. Pate and Rumbaugh (1983) retested the model defined by Thompson and Church with another (later and larger) corpus of Lana's utterances. Their model was found inadequate to cope with the new data base, because it would have required that Lana have available to her a much larger number of stock sentences (about 135) than the few that she had been taught. It is also significant that Lana sustained an empirical sensitivity to the rules of the Yerkish grammar (von Glasersfeld, 1977) as she generated newer and longer sentences, many of which had apparent communicative value.

Were Lana's sentences clear evidence of syntax? No, but they were evidence of rules of organizing chains of responses where the options (number of keys on the board) are great (over 100). Lana's productions were significantly beyond the disordered strings of Nim's and are, I believe, evidence of a step toward the mastery of syntax as known in human parlance. (Although Lana's strings were but a small step for humankind, they were a giant step for apekind.)

Controversy and new data shift scientists' positions. In a very recent paper, Terrace (in press) pointed up the important contributions of ape-language research to the question, "What is a name?" Although words and names might start as operants, they become more than that. In some manner they come to represent things and events regardless of time. Sherman and Austin have used symbols thus. They can go into a room by themselves, look at an array of foods and drinks (that changes unpredictably across trials), return and state at the keyboard the item that they would like to have, leave once again to go to the array of foods and drinks, then select and retrieve one. The correspondence between what they have stated that they want and what they, in fact, retrieve is better than 90 percent (Savage-Rumbaugh, Pate, Lawson, Smith, & Rosenbaum, 1983).

Sherman and Austin also use their words individually to achieve the same function apparent in the normal child's use of single words, early in language learning. That function is to reduce ambiguity (Greenfield & Savage-Rumbaugh, 1984) and to utter that which is not obvious (e.g., the words they use are ones that provide information to the listener and are not reiterations of the obvious). The selection of word-lexigrams for use serves to clarify matters such as "where," "who," and "which" (where to go, with whom, which food or container, etc.).

In the early years of the recent efforts to investigate questions pertaining to apes and language, the wrong question was at the fore—in the press and in the public's thinking, if not in the perspectives of the scientists involved. The question was "Do the apes have language or don't they?" It could not be answered then, and it is unlikely to be answered now or in the future because there is no concurrence about what minima must exist for it to be said that language exists and is functioning. Where there is a lot of "it," there is no problem, of course; however, when one is dealing with traces and minimal amounts of language, what are the criteria? Individuals may assert their own minima, such as vocabulary and syntax, but even these assertions serve only to define new questions, such as, what are the critical attributes of vocabulary or of syntax? A far more productive question is "What facets of language are to be found in nonhuman forms?" Other related questions are "What are the requisites to them?" and "What are the variables that influence their emergence and competence in use?"

Regrettably, it is well beyond the limits of space in this chapter to deal with all of the developments and issues of apes and language. I assure the reader, however, that there are strong data on hand that make clear that apes have far more capabilities for language than was indicated by the data of the 1970s and early 1980s. They can learn words spontaneously, efficiently, and they can use them referentially for things not present (Savage-Rumbaugh et al., 1980; Savage-Rumbaugh, in press); they can learn words from one another (Savage-Rumbaugh, in press; Fouts, Fouts, & Schoenfeld, 1984); they learn to use their words to coordinate their joint activities and to tell one another things otherwise not known (Savage-Rumbaugh, in press); they can learn rules for ordering their words (Pate & Rumbaugh, 1983; von Glasersfeld, 1977); they do make comments (Greenfield & Savage-Rumbaugh, 1984); they announce their intended actions (Savage-Rumbaugh et al., 1983); they are spontaneous and not necessarily subject to imitation in their signs and not necessarily poor turn-takers in conversation (Miles, 1983); and they are communicative and they know what they are about. To illustrate this last point, in a food sharing situation, where Sherman and Austin took turns in asking for a specific food or drink from an array on a table with the other then serving the requested item, Sherman frequently intervened into Austin's behavior and declared its form and function. Specifically, when Austin appeared not to know the name of an item that Sherman wanted, Sherman took Austin's hand and guided it to the appropriate key on the keyboard, thereby making Austin ask for the food. Sherman then promptly served the food item stipulated thus, giving a piece to Austin and taking one (usually the larger portion) for himself.

As additional evidence that Sherman and Austin know what they are about, they will visually check one another to see if requests are being received and complied with accurately. For example, if

Sherman needs a wrench from Austin, for use in extricating food from a box baited by the experimenter, he will do a double-take when he sees Austin about to give him a key, will recheck and correct his request at the keyboard (if it was in error), will tap on the projector that portrays the word-lexigram for the item requested, and then look at Austin as though to bring his attention to the corrected message of request. In addition, he will not accept the key or other item that Austin would give in error, as dictated by what, in fact, Sherman needed and what he has requested.

And, yes, they do understand, or at least some of them understand, spoken English words. They have even volunteered in the instructional processes of humans as they try to learn new word-lexigrams, known to the ape but not to the human. (Apes have shown their teachers the word for which they were searching on the keyboard.)

Pursuant to the Gardners' re-opening of ape-language research with Project Washoe, the orderly progress of the field was made problematic by the uncritical acceptance of reports by ape-buffs—those who would have the apes given their rights and status as the free people they are not. Desmond (1979) stated it well: "The overriding urge to assist ape in giving man his comeuppance, as if this were a Darwinian imperative, has boomeranged to the detriment of the ape, who is now judged according to an impossible human standard which should never have been set" (pp. 49–50). Now, only five years after Desmond's statements, it is clear that apes have competence for semantics. Apes are in the language domain, a behaviorial domain that is a continuum—not a dichotomy.

Emerging Research Trends

Language learning studies with marine mammals have shed a bright light upon the field of animal language learning research. Herman and his associates (1980; Herman, Richards & Wolz, 1984) have presented convincing data showing that dolphins are adroit at acquiring receptive language skills. They respond with great accuracy to commands given either by hand signs or by computer-generated sounds to carry out a variety of acts, such as to take the hoop from the bottom of the pool (e.g., not the one on the surface) and fetch it to a designated location. In addition, they do thus with novel commands, a strong indication of syntax. Working with sea lions, Schusterman and Krieger (1984) have reported strong corroborating data, with paradigms providing their own unique data. (See Segal, 1983, for tact and mand data from macaque monkeys.)

Recent research also serves to document that monkeys have different vocalizations, although unlearned and not arbitrary, with which they respond to different threats from snakes and birds. Perhaps here was the origin of representational signaling (Gouzoules, Gouzoules, & Marler, 1984). Dolphins have the remarkable ability to mimic sounds (Richards, Wolz, & Herman, 1984), and it appears that well beyond having species-specific songs, birds have esthetic preferences for classical music similar to those of humans. Porter and Neuringer (1984) report that pigeons also discern even novel portions of a symphony from which came the initial discriminative stimulus or signal that reward is to be obtained if a key is pecked. This last study was done as an undergraduate psychology project, a testimony to the contributions that can be made to knowledge through research in comparative psychology.

To conclude, I do three things: (a) summarize briefly comparative psychology in general, (b) give some comparative principles that I think can and should be used in introductory psychology courses, and (c) look to the future of comparative psychology.

Comparative Psychology in Summary

Comparative psychology addresses questions about both how and why species adapt as they do. Adaptation is measured in two ways: by reproductive success across generations and by effectiveness and efficiency of problem solving in the present (e.g., meeting challenges, some of which might threaten survival). The matrix of comparative psychology includes the following dimensions:
1. species (genetics, evolutionary history);
2. time (development and maturation);
3. behavior (patterns thereof as mediated by morphology); and
4. behavioral processes (the psychological and biological foundations of the behavior), which are
5. all in interaction with ecology (the environment).

The field of general psychology will benefit by becoming more comparative. All specializations within psychology would benefit by learning about what comparative psychology has to offer on their topics. (This includes all professional areas.) Comparative psychology is not a method so much as it is a philosophy—a perspective derived from data from various methods and fields. It is not just studying animals. It is not just studying a variety of animals. It is the derivation of an understanding of the whys and hows that provide for diverse patterns of adaptation in animals and humans within an evolutionary framework.

Selected Comparative Principles for the Introductory Course

For the introductory course, there are seven comparative principles that can be used to make the entire course more interesting and to place other topics in an appropriate perspective.

1. Most dimensions of human behavior are best understood by studying their roots, their analogues and homologues in animals. This includes the consequences of early rearing conditions that influence the ability to learn and to transfer with competence as an adult. The more advanced and complex the life form of reference is, the more critical it is that there be opportunities to try to learn, to observe, and to explore and play in contexts appropriate to the species early in life—from birth on. Lacking this, adult forms are, in all certainty, going to be deficient in competence. This generalization holds for the abilities to learn complex tasks, to transfer learning to an advantage, to be socially competent with others, to be emotionally stable, and to be successful in breeding and parenting. Even human behavior is heavily influenced by its biological and evolutionary endowments.

2. Behaviors of species differ because they have been selected for, both by evolution and by their environmental consequences, in order to solve problems, that is, to adapt. This statement holds true for both learned and unlearned behavioral patterns.

3. Similarities in the appearances of animals can be either homologous (based on genetic relatedness) or analogous (based on convergent evolution). The same is true for behaviors.

4. The behavioral adaptations of the more primitive forms of life, such as insects, fish, and birds, are founded primarily in genetics and in highly predictable biological processes. Nonetheless, they, too, can learn to a limited degree.

5. The behavioral adaptations of the more advanced and complex forms of life, such as mammals and notably the primates, are relatively more dependent upon learning. Nonetheless, their behavior and even what they attend to and learn is very much under the influence of biology. It is the totality of the organism, not just its parts, as it interacts with its environment that determines behaviors.

6. It is helpful to view the transition of behavioral adaptations as one from being relatively closed (i.e., heavily dictated by biological factors) to that of being relatively open (with lesser contraints imposed by biological factors). Associated with this transition is the emergence of greater variation in adaptative efforts and behavioral options.

7. It is reasonable to assume that to the degree that there is genetic relatedness among life forms there are similarities in their perceptual and psychological processes. For example, if we hold that humans think, then we should be open to the possibility that some

animals think. Behaviors of humans that lead us to conclude that we think and know should be used as but one point of departure for inquiring into the possibility that other animals do the same.

The Future of Comparative Psychology

Comparative psychology is alive and well. Its stormy history has set the bases for a vigorous and productive recovery (Tobach, Adler, & Adler, 1973). It should draw not only from its own research enterprises for data with which to build its scientific matrix, but also from other fields that include behavioral studies as well. Psychologists have the best prospects of all scientists for filling in the matrix of reference, for they are the ones who know most about the basic processes of behavior—a key dimension in describing and understanding varied patterns of adaptation.

Today, comparative psychology is reminiscent of the proverbial phoenix. It was thought to be dead. But it was not. That perspective was in error, for it is emerging with renewed vigor—from a bed that some, quite in error, thought to be ashes. Comparative psychology today has a story of its own, a story that defines a unique pattern of adaptation in the world of science.

References

Alcock, J. (1975). *Animal behavior: An evolutionary approach.* Sunderland, MA: Sinauer Associates.
Altmann, S. A., & Altmann, J. (1970). *Baboon ecology.* Chicago: University of Chicago Press.
Balda, R. P., & Turek, R. J. (1984). The cache-recovery system as an example of memory capabilities in Clark's nutcracker. In H. L. Roitblat, T. G. Bever, & H. S. Terrace (Eds.), *Animal cognition* (pp. 513–532). Hillsdale, NJ: Erlbaum.
Beach, F. A. (1984). Let's bury the snark. In J. Demarest (Ed.), *Comparative Psychology Newsletter, 4*(2), 1–3. (Available from Monmouth College, W. Long Branch, NJ)
Beck, B. B. (1980). *Animal tool behavior.* New York: Garland STPM Press.
Bernstein, I. S., Gordon, T. P., & Rose, R. M. (1983). The interaction of hormones, behavior, and social context in nonhuman primates. In B. B. Svsre (Ed.), *Hormones and aggressive behavior* (pp. 535–561). New York: Plenum Press.
Bever, T. G. (1984). The road from behaviorism to rationalism. In H. L. Roitblat, T. G. Bever, & H. S. Terrace (Eds.), *Animal cognition* (pp. 61–75). Hillsdale, NJ: Erlbaum
Bitterman, M. E. (1961). Toward a comparative psychology of learning. *American Psychologist, 15,* 704–712.

Blough, D. S. (1984). Form recognition in pigeons. In H. L. Roitblat, T. G. Bever, & H. S. Terrace (Eds.), *Animal cognition* (pp. 277–289). Hillsdale, NJ: Erlbaum.

Bolles, R. C. (1975). *Theory of motivation* (2nd ed.). New York: Harper & Row.

Buchanan, J. P., Gill, T. V., & Braggio, J. T. (1981). Serial position and clustering effects in a chimpanzee's "free recall." *Memory and Cognition, 9*(6), 651–660.

Candland, D. K., & Nagy, S. M. (1969). The open field: Some comparative data. *Annals of the New York Academy of Sciences, 159*, 831–851.

Capaldi, E. J., & Verry, D. R. (1981). Serial order anticipation learning in rats: Memory for multiple hedonic events and their order. *Animal Learning and Behavior, 9*, 441–453.

Capretta, P. J., & Rawls, L. H. (1974). Establishment of a flavor preference in rats: Importance of nursing and weaning experience. *Journal of Comparative and Physiological Psychology, 86*(4), 670–673.

Catania, A. C. (1984). *Learning* (2nd ed.). Englewood Cliffs, NJ: Prentice-Hall.

Chiszar, D., Andren, C., Nilson, G., O'Connell, B., Mestas, J. S., Jr., Smith, H. M., & Radcliffe, C. W. (1982). Strike-induced chemosensory searching in Old World vipers and New World pit vipers. *Animal Learning and Behavior, 10*(2), 121–125.

Church, R. M., & Meck, W. H. (1984). The numerical attribute of stimuli. In H. L. Roitblat, T. G. Bever, & H. S. Terrace (Eds.), *Animal cognition* (pp. 445–464). Hillsdale, NJ: Erlbaum.

D'Amato, M. R., & Salmon, D. P. (1984). Cognitive processes in cebus monkeys. In H. L. Roitblat, T. G. Bever, & H. S. Terrace (Eds.), *Animal cognition* (pp. 149–168). Hillsdale, NJ: Erlbaum.

Davenport, R. K., & Rogers, C. M. (1970). Intermodal equivalence of stimuli in apes. *Science, 168*, 279–280.

Davis, H., & Memmott, J. (1982). Counting behavior in animals: A critical evaluation. *Psychological Bulletin, 92*(3), 547–571.

Dawkins, R. (1976). *The selfish gene.* Oxford, England: Oxford University Press.

Desmond, A. J. (1979). *The ape's reflexion.* New York: Dial Press.

De Waal, J. (1982). *Chimpanzee politics.* New York: Harper & Row.

Dewsbury, D. A. (1978). *Comparative animal behavior.* New York: McGraw-Hill.

Ellen, P. (1982). Direction, past experience, and hints in creative problem solving. *Journal of Experimental Psychology: General, 3*, 316–325.

Ellen, P., Parko, E. M., Wages, C., Doherty, D., & Herrmann, T. (1982). Spatial problem solving by rats: Exploration and cognitive maps. *Learning and Motivation, 13*, 81–94.

Ellen, P., Soteres, B. J., & Wages, C. (1984). Problem solving in the rat: Piecemeal acquisition of cognitive maps. *Learning and Motivation, 12*(2), 232–237.

Epstein, R., Kirshnit, C. E., Lanza, R. P., & Rubin, L. C. (1984). "Insight" in the pigeon: Antecedents and determinants of an intelligent performance. *Nature, 308*, 61–62.

Epstein, R., Lanza, R. P., & Skinner, B. F. (1980). Symbolic communication between two pigeons (*Columba livia domestica*). *Science, 207*, 543–545.

Ettlinger, G. (1977). Interactions between sensory modalities in nonhuman primates. In A. M. Schrier (Ed.), *Behavioral primatology* (Vol. 1, pp. 71–104). Hillsdale, NJ: Erlbaum.

Fernandes, D. M., & Church, R. M. (1982). Discrimination of the number of sequential events by rats. *Animal Learning and Behavior, 10,* 171–176.

Fobes, J. L., & King, J. E. (Eds.). (1982). *Psychology of nonhuman primates.* New York: Academic Press.

Fossey, D. (1982). Reproduction among free-living mountain gorillas. *American Journal of Primatology* (Suppl. 1), 97–104.

Fouts, R. S., Fouts, D. H., & Schoenfeld, D. (1984). Sign language conversational interaction between chimpanzees. *Sign Language Studies, 42,* 1–12.

Fragaszy, D. M., & Mitchell, G. (1974). Infant socialization in primates. *Journal of Human Evolution, 3,* 563–574.

Frederickson, W. T., & Sackett, G. P. (1984). Kin preferences in primates (*Macaca nemestrina*): Relatedness or familiarity? *Journal of Comparative Psychology, 98*(1), 29–34.

Galdikas, B. M. F. (1981). Orangutan sexuality in the wild. In C. E. Graham (Ed.), *Reproductive biology of the great apes: Comparative and biomedical perspectives* (pp. 281–300). New York: Academic Press.

Gallup, G., & Suarez, S. D. (1983). Overcoming our resistance to animal research: Man in comparative perspective. In D. W. Rajecki (Ed.), *Comparing behavior: Studying man studying animals* (pp. 5–26). Hillsdale, NJ: Erlbaum.

Glickman, S. E., & Sroges, R. W. (1966). Curiosity in zoo animals. *Behavior, 26,* 151–188.

Goodall, J. (1963, August). My life among wild chimpanzees. *National Geographic,* pp. 272–308.

Gottlieb, G. (1984). Development of species identification in ducklings: XII. Ineffectiveness of auditory self-stimulation in wood ducklings (*Aix sponsa*). *Journal of Comparative Psychology, 98*(2), 137–141.

Gould, J. L. (1980). The case for magnetic sensitivity in birds and bees (such as it is). *American Scientist, 68,* 256–267.

Gould, J. L. (1982). *Ethology: The mechanisms and evolution of behavior.* New York: Norton.

Gouzoules, S., Gouzoules, H., & Marler, P. (1984). Rhesus monkey (*Macaca mulatta*) screams: Representational signalling in the recruitment of agonistic aid. *Animal Behavior, 32,* 182–193.

Greenfield, P. M., & Savage-Rumbaugh, E. S. (1984). Perceived variability and symbol use: A common language cognition interface in children and chimpanzees. *Journal of Comparative Psychology, 98*(2), 201–218.

Griffin, D. R. (1958). *Listening in the dark.* New Haven: Yale University Press.

Gruber, H. E. (1981). *Darwin on man: A psychological study of scientific creativity.* Chicago: University of Chicago Press.

Hall, G. S. (1965). In C. Strickland & C. Burgess (Eds.), *Classics in education: 23. Health, growth, and heredity.* New York: Teachers College Press.

Hall, R. L., & Sharp, H. S. (Eds.). (1978). *Wolf and man: Evolution in parallel.* New York: Academic Press.

Harlow, H. F. (1949). The formation of learning sets. *Psychological Review, 56,* 51–65.

Harlow, H. F., & Harlow, M. K. (1965). The affectional systems. In A. M. Schrier, H. F. Harlow, & F. Stollnitz (Eds.), *Behavior of nonhuman primates* (Vol. 2, pp. 287–334). New York: Academic Press.

Hearst, E. (1984). Absence as information: Some implications for learning, performance, and representational processes. In H. L. Roitblat, T. G. Bever, & H. S. Terrace (Eds.), *Animal cognition* (pp. 311–332). Hillsdale, NJ: Erlbaum.

Herman, L. M. (1980). Cognitive characteristics of dolphins. In L. M. Herman (Ed.), *Cetacean behavior: Mechanisms and functions* (pp. 363–429). New York: Wiley.

Herman, L. M., Richards, D. G., & Wolz, J. P. (1984). Comprehension of sentences by bottlenosed dolphins. *Cognition, 16*(2), 129–219.

Herrmann, T., Bahr, E., Bremner, B., & Ellen, P. (1982). Problem solving in the rat: Stay vs. shift solutions on the three-table task. *Animal Learning and Behavior, 10*(1), 39–45.

Herrnstein, R. J. (1984). Objects, categories, and discriminative stimuli. In H. L. Roitblat, T. G. Bever, & H. S. Terrace (Eds.), *Animal cognition* (pp. 233–261). Hillsdale, NJ: Erlbaum.

Hinde, R. A. (1979). *Towards understanding relationships*. New York: Academic Press.

Hulse, S. H., Cynx, J., & Humpal, J. (1984). Cognitive processing of pitch and rhythm structures by birds. In H. L. Roitblat, T. G. Bever, & H. S. Terrace (Eds.), *Animal cognition* (pp. 183–198). Hillsdale, NJ: Erlbaum.

Hulse, S. H., Fowler, H., & Honig, W. K. (Eds.). (1978). *Cognitive processes in animal behavior*. Hillsdale, NJ: Erlbaum.

Jerison, H. J. (1973). *Evolution of the brain and intelligence*. New York: Academic Press.

Jolly, A. (1984). *The evolution of primate behavior* (2nd ed.). New York: Macmillan.

Kamil, A. C. (1984). Adaptation and cognition: Knowing what comes naturally. In H. L. Roitblat, T. G. Bever, & H. S. Terrace (Eds.), *Animal cognition* (pp. 533–544). Hillsdale, NJ: Erlbaum.

Kamin, L. J. (1969). Selective association and conditioning. In N. J. Macintosh & W. K. Honig (Eds.), *Fundamental issues in associative learning* (pp. 42–64). Halifax, Nova Scotia: Dalhousie University Press.

Kimble, G. A. (1981). Biological and cognitive constraints on learning. In L. T. Benjamin, Jr. (Ed.), *The G. Stanley Hall lecture series* (Vol. 1, pp. 11–60). Washington, DC: American Psychological Association.

King, M. C., & Wilson, A. C. (1975). Evolution at two levels in humans and chimpanzees. *Science, 186*, 107–116.

Konner, M. (1982). *The tangled wing: Biological constraints in the human spirit*. New York: Harper & Row.

Kummer, H. (1968). *Social organization of Hamadryas baboons*. Chicago: University of Chicago Press.

Levine, S. (1982). Mother-infant relationships: Stress and coping. *Annali Istituto Superiore di Sanita, 18*(2), 223–230.

Lewis, J. K., & Sackett, G. P. (1980). Toward an ontogenetic monkey model of behavioral development. In J. S. Lockhard (Ed.), *The evolution of human social behavior* (pp. 107–123). New York: American Elsevier.

Lindsley, D. B. (1984). *Behavioral neuroscience: Vertebrate brain and behavior.* [Collection of essays to supplement the Grass calendar for 1984 (art work by Trudy Nicholson)]. Quincy, MA: Grass Instrument Co.

Lockhard, J. S. (Ed.). (1980). *The evolution of human social behavior.* New York: American Elsevier.

Logan, C. A., & Fulk, K. R. (1984). Differential responding to spring and fall song in mockingbirds (*Mimus polyglottos*). *Journal of Comparative Psychology, 98*(1), 3–9.

Macphail, E. M. (1982). *Brain and intelligence in vertebrates.* Oxford, England: Clarendon Press.

Maier, N. R. F., & Schneirla, T. C. (1935). *Principles of animal behavior.* New York: McGraw-Hill.

Markowitz, H., & Stevens, V. J. (Eds.). (1978). *Behavior of captive wild animals.* Chicago: Nelson-Hall.

Marler, P. (1972). Song learning and preparedness. In M. E. P. Seligman & J. L. Hager (Eds.), *Biological boundaries of learning* (pp. 336–376). New York: Appleton-Century-Crofts.

Marshack, A. (1984). The ecology and brain of two-handed bipedalism: An analytic, cognitive, and evolutionary assessment. In H. L. Roitblat, T. G. Bever, & H. S. Terrace (Eds.), *Animal cognition* (pp. 491–511). Hillsdale, NJ: Erlbaum.

Mason, W. A. (1979). Ontogeny of social behavior. In P. Marler & J. G. Vandenbergh (Eds.), *Handbook of behavioral neurobiology: 3. Social behavior and communication* (pp. 1–28). New York: Plenum Press.

McClure, J. B. (Ed.). (1879). *Entertaining anecdotes: From every available source.* Chicago: Rhodes & McClure.

Meador, D. M., Rumbaugh, D. M., Pate, J. L., & Bard, K. A. (in press). Learning, problem solving, cognition, and intelligence. In G. Mitchell (Ed.), *Comparative primate biology: Vol. 2. Behavior and ecology.* New York: Alan R. Liss.

Medin, D. L., Roberts, W. A., & Davis, R. T. (Eds.). (1976). *Processes of animal memory.* Hillsdale, NJ: Erlbaum.

Menzel, E. W., Jr. (1978). Cognitive mapping in chimpanzees. In S. H. Hulse, H. Fowler, & W. K. Honig (Eds.), *Cognitive processes in animal behavior* (pp. 375–422). Hillsdale, NJ: Erlbaum.

Menzel, E. W., Jr., & Juno, C. (1982). Marmosets (*Saguinus fuscicollis*): Are learning sets learned? *Science, 217,* 750–752.

Menzel, E. W., Jr., & Savage-Rumbaugh, E. S. (in press). Chimpanzee spatial problem solving using mirrors and televised equivalents of mirrors.

Meredith, M. A., & Stein, B. E. (1983). Interactions among converging sensory inputs in the superior colliculus. *Science, 221,* 389–391.

Miles, H. L. (1983). Apes and language: The search for communicative competence. In J. De Luce & H. T. Wildon (Eds.), *Language in primates.* New York: Springer-Verlag.

Miller, G. A. (1956). The magical number seven, plus or minus two: Some limits on our capacity for processing information. *Psychological Review, 63,* 81–97.

Nadler, R. D., Herndon, J. G., & Wallis, J. (in press). Adult sexual behavior: hormones and reproduction. In G. Mitchell (Ed.), *Comparative primate biology: Vol. 2. Behavior and ecology.* New York: Alan R. Liss.

Nissen, H. W. (1951). Phylogenetic comparison. In S. S. Stevens (Ed.), *Handbook of experimental psychology* (pp. 347–386). New York: Wiley.

Nottebohm, F. (1981). A brain for all seasons: Cyclical anatomical changes in song control nuclei of the canary brain. *Science, 214,* 1368–1370.

Olton, D. S. (1978). Characteristics of spatial memory. In S. H. Hulse, H. Fowler, & W. K. Honig (Eds.), *Cognitive processes in animal behavior* (pp. 341–373). Hillsdale, NJ: Erlbaum.

Olton, D. S. (1979). Mazes, maps, and memory. *American Psychologist, 34,* 583–596.

Olton, D. S., Collison, C., & Werz, M. A. (1977). Spatial memory and radial arm maze performance of rats. *Learning and Motivation, 8,* 289–314.

Olton, D. S., & Samuelson, R. J. (1976). Remembrance of places passed: Spatial memory in rats. *Journal of Experimental Psychology: Animal Behavior Processes, 2,* 97–116.

Parker, C. E. (1974). The antecedents of man the manipulator. *Journal of Human Evolution, 3,* 493–500.

Passingham, R. E. (1982). *The human primate.* San Francisco: Freeman.

Pate, J. L., & Rumbaugh, D. M. (1983). The language-like behavior of Lana chimpanzee: Is it merely discrimination and paired-associate learning? *Animal Learning and Behavior, 11*(1), 134–138.

Pepperberg, I. M. (1981). Functional vocalizations by an African grey parrot (*Psittacus erithacus*). *Z. Tierpsychologie, 55,* 139–160.

Porter, D., & Neuringer, A. (1984). Music discriminations by pigeons. *Journal of Experimental Psychology: Animal Behavior Processes, 10*(2), 138–148.

Reese, E. (Author). (1982). *Imprinting* [Film]. South Hadley, MA: Mount Holyoke College.

Rescorla, R. A. (1967). Pavlovian conditioning and its proper control procedures. *Psychological Review, 74,* 71–80.

Richards, D. G., Wolz, J. P., & Herman, L. M. (1984). Vocal mimicry of computer-generated sounds and vocal labeling of objects by a bottlenosed dolphin, *Tursiops truncatus. Journal of Comparative Psychology, 98*(1), 10–28.

Richardson, W. K., & Kresch, J. A. (1983). Stimulus stringing by pigeons: Conditional strings. *Animal Learning and Behavior, 11*(1), 19–26.

Riesen, A. H. (1974). Comparative perspectives in behavior study. *Journal of Human Evolution, 3,* 433–434.

Roberts, W. A. (1984). Some issues in animal spatial memory. In H. L. Roitblat, T. G. Bever, & H. S. Terrace (Eds.), *Animal cognition* (pp. 425–443). Hillsdale, NJ: Erlbaum.

Roitblat, H. L. (1980). Codes and coding processes in pigeon short-term memory. *Animal Learning and Behavior, 8,* 341–351.

Roitblat, H. L. (1982). The meaning of representation in animal memory. *The Behavioral and Brain Sciences, 5,* 353–372.

Roitblat, H. L., Pologe, B., & Scopatz, R. A. (1983). The representation of items in serial position. *Animal Learning and Behavior, 11,* 489–498.

Romanes, G. J. (1898). *Mental evolution in animals.* New York: Appleton-Century-Crofts.

Rosenblum, L. A., & Plimpton, E. H. (1979). The effect of adults on peer interactions. In M. Lewis & L. A. Rosenblum (Eds.), *The child and its family* (pp. 195–243). New York: Plenum Press.

Rumbaugh, D. M. (1967). The learning and sensory capacities of the squirrel monkey in phylogenetic perspective. In L. A. Rosenblum & R. Cooper (Eds.), *The squirrel monkey* (pp. 256–318). New York: Academic Press.

Rumbaugh, D. M. (Ed.). (1977). *Language learning by a chimpanzee: The Lana project*. New York: Academic Press.

Rumbaugh, D. M., & Pate, J. L. (1984). The evolution of primate cognition: A comparative perspective. In H. L. Roitblat, T. G. Bever, & H. S. Terrace (Eds.), *Animal cognition* (pp. 569–587). Hillsdale, NJ: Erlbaum.

Rumbaugh, D. M., Riesen, A. H., & Lee, R. E. (Authors). (1970). *Survey of the primates* [Film]. Atlanta, GA: Georgia State University.

Rumbaugh, D. M., Savage-Rumbaugh, E. S., Hegel, M., & Ivers, C. (1985). *Summation in the chimpanzee (Pan troglodytes)*. Paper presented at the meeting of the Southeastern Psychological Association, Atlanta, GA.

Rumbaugh, D. M., Wolkin, J. R., Wilkerson, B. J., & Myers, R. H. (1976). A hybrid ape (*Hylobates lar moloch* x *Symphalangus syndactylus*). *Laboratory Primate Newsletter, 15*, 32.

Sackett, G. P., Gunderson, V., & Baldwin, D. (1982). Studying the ontogeny of primate behavior. In J. L. Fobes & J. E. King (Eds.), *Primate behavior* (pp. 135–171). New York: Academic Press.

Sands, S. F., Urcuioli, P. J., Wright, A. A., & Santiago, H. C. (1984). Serial position effects and rehearsal in primate visual memory. In H. L. Roitblat, T. G. Bever, & H. S. Terrace (Eds.), *Animal cognition* (pp. 375–388). Hillsdale, NJ: Erlbaum.

Sands, S. F., & Wright, A. A. (1980). Primate memory: Retention of serial list items by a rhesus monkey. *Science, 209*, 938–940.

Savage-Rumbaugh, E. S. (1984). Verbal behavior at a procedural level in the chimpanzee. *Journal of the Experimental Analysis of Behavior, 41*, 223–250.

Savage-Rumbaugh, E. S. (in press). *Ape language: From conditioned stimulus to symbol*. New York: Columbia University Press.

Savage-Rumbaugh, E. S., Pate, J. L., Lawson, J., Smith, S. T., & Rosenbaum, S. (1983). Can a chimpanzee make a statement? *Journal of Experimental Psychology: General, 112*(4), 457–492.

Savage-Rumbaugh, E. S., Rumbaugh, D. M., Smith, S. T., & Lawson, J. (1980). Reference: The linguistic essential. *Science, 210*, 922–925.

Savage-Rumbaugh, E. S., Wilkerson, B. J., & Bakeman, R. (1977). Spontaneous gestural communication among conspecifics in the pygmy chimpanzee (*Pan paniscus*). In G. H. Bourne (Ed.), *Progress in ape research* (pp. 99–116). New York: Academic Press.

Schaller, G. B. (1963). *The mountain gorilla*. Chicago: University of Chicago Press.

Scheller, R. H., & Axel, R. (1984). How genes control innate behavior. *Scientific American, 250*(3), 54–62.

Schiefelbusch, R. L., & Hollis, J. H. (Eds.). (1979). *Language intervention from ape to child*. Baltimore: University Park Press.

Schrier, A. M. (1971). Extradimensional transfer of learning-set formation in stumptailed monkeys. *Learning and Motivation, 2*(2), 173–181.

Schrier, A. M. (1984). Learning how to learn: The significance and current status of learning set formation. *Primates, 25*(1), 95–102.

Schrier, A. M., & Thompson, C. R. (1984). Are learning sets learned? A reply. *Animal Learning and Behavior, 12*(1), 109–112.

Schusterman, R. J. (1962). Transfer effects of successive discrimination-reversal training in chimpanzees. *Science, 137,* 422–423.
Schusterman, R. J. (1981). Behavioral capabilities of seals and sea lions: A review of their hearing, visual, learning and diving skills. *The Psychological Record, 31,* 125–143.
Schusterman, R. J., & Krieger, K. (1984). California sea lions are capable of semantic comprehension. *The Psychological Record, 34,* 3–23.
Segal, E. F. (1983, November). *Generalized discriminative-response sequences (syntax?) in a Barbary macaque.* Paper presented at the meeting of the Psychonomic Society, San Diego, CA.
Seligman, M. E. P. (1970). On the generality of the laws of learning. *Psychological Review, 77,* 406–418.
Seligman, M. E. P., & Hager, J. L. (1972). *Biological boundaries of learning.* New York: Appleton-Century-Crofts.
Shimp, C. P. (1976). Short-term memory in the pigeon: Relative recency. *Journal of the Experimental Analysis of Behavior, 25,* 55–61.
Skinner, B. F. (1938). *The behavior of organisms.* New York: Appleton-Century-Crofts.
Skinner, B. F. (1950). Are theories of learning necessary? *Psychological Review, 57,* 193–216.
Skinner, B. F. (1953). *Science and human behavior.* New York: Macmillan.
Smith, H. J., Newman, J. D., & Symmes, D. (1982). Primate vocal communication as a model system. In C. T. Snowdon, C. H. Brown, & M. R. Petersen (Eds.), *Primate communication* (pp. 30–49). New York: Cambridge University Press.
Stebbins, G. L. (1984). The flowering of sex. *The Sciences,* May/June, 28–35.
Stebbins, W. C. (1976). Comparative hearing function in the vertebrates. In R. B. Masterton, M. E. Bitterman, C. B. G. Campbell, & N. Hotton (Eds.), *Evolution of brain and behavior in vertebrates* (pp. 107–113). Hillsdale, NJ: Erlbaum.
Straub, R. O., Seidenberg, M. S., Bever, T. G., & Terrace, H. S. (1979). Serial learning in the pigeon. *Journal of the Experimental Analysis of Behavior, 32,* 137–148.
Suomi, S., & Immelmann, K. (1983). On the process and product of cross-species generalization. In D. W. Rajecki (Ed.), *Comparing behavior: Studying man studying animals* (pp. 203–224). Hillsdale, NJ: Erlbaum.
Tanner, J. (1981). *On becoming human.* New York: Cambridge University Press.
Terrace, H. S. (1984). Animal cognition. In H. L. Roitblat, T. G. Bever, & H. S. Terrace (Eds.), *Animal cognition* (pp. 7–28). Hillsdale, NJ: Erlbaum.
Terrace, H. S. (in press). In the beginning was the "name." *American Psychologist.*
Terrace, H. S., Petitto, L. A., Sanders, R. J., & Bever, T. G. (1979). Can an ape create a sentence? *Science, 206,* 891–900.
Thiessen, D. (1972). *Gene organization and behavior.* New York: Random House.
Thomas, R. K. (1982). The assessment of primate intelligence. *Journal of Human Evolution, 11,* 247–255.
Thompson, C. R., & Church, R. M. (1980). An explanation of the language of a chimpanzee. *Science, 208,* 313–314.

Thorpe, W. H. (1958). Further studies on the process of song learning in the Chaffinch, *Fringilla coelebs gengleri. Nature, 182,* 554–557.
Thorpe, W. H. (1972a). Comparison of vocal communication in animals and man. In R. A. Hinde (Ed.), *Nonverbal communication* (pp. 27–47). Cambridge: Cambridge University Press.
Thorpe, W. H. (1972b). Vocal communication in birds. In R. A. Hinde (Ed.), *Nonverbal communication* (pp. 153–176). Cambridge: Cambridge University Press.
Tobach, E., Adler, H. E., & Adler, L. L. (1973). Comparative psychology at issue. *Annals of the New York Academy of Sciences, 22.*
Tolman, E. C. (1966). Operational behaviorism and current trends in psychology. In E. C. Tolman (Ed.), *Behavior and psychological man: Essays in motivation and learning.* Berkeley: University of California Press.
von Glasersfeld, E. C. (1977). The Yerkish language and its automatic parser. In D. M. Rumbaugh (Ed.), *Language learning by a chimpanzee: The Lana project* (pp. 91–130). New York: Academic Press.
von Glasersfeld, E. C. (1980). Adaptation and viability. *American Psychologist, 33*(11), 955–979.
Warren, J. M. (1966). Reversal learning and the formation of learning sets by cats and rhesus monkeys. *Journal of Comparative and Physiological Psychology, 61,* 421.
Warren, J. M. (1974). Possibly unique characteristics of learning by primates. *Journal of Human Evolution, 3*(6), 445–454.
Wasserman, E. A. (1984). Animal intelligence: Understanding the minds of animals through their behavioral "ambassadors." In H. L. Roitblat, T. G. Bever, & H. S. Terrace (Eds.), *Animal cognition* (pp. 45–60). Hillsdale, NJ: Erlbaum.
Wilson, E. O. (1978). *On human nature.* New York: Bantam Books.
Wolkin, J. R., & Myers, R. H. (1980). Characteristics of a gibbon-siamang hybrid ape. *International Journal of Primatology, 1*(3), 203–221.

JEROME KAGAN
THE HUMAN INFANT

JEROME KAGAN

Jerome Kagan received his bachelor's degree from Rutgers University in 1950 and his PhD in psychology from Yale University in 1954. After a short term in the U.S. Army he worked at the Fels Research Institute from 1957 to 1964. Since 1964 he has been a professor at Harvard.

His major research interests focus on cognitive and emotional development in the child during the first six to ten years of life. Major research monographs include *Birth to Maturity*, which is a summary of the longitudinal study conducted at the Fels Research Institute. *Change and Continuity in Infancy* describes basic growth functions during the first two-and-a-half years of life. *Infancy* is a summary of the effect of day care on infants and young children, and *The Second Year* is a monograph describing the emergence of a moral sense and self-consciousness in children during the second year. Kagan's most recent book is a collection of essays entitled *The Nature of the Child*.

Kagan has received the Hofheimer Prize for Research from the American Psychiatric Association and the Wilbur Lucius Cross Medal from Yale University. He is a member of the American Association for the Advancement of Science, the Society for Research in Child Development, the American Psychological Association, and the American Academy of Arts and Sciences.

JEROME KAGAN

THE HUMAN INFANT

Contemporary study of the human infant is addressed to two fundamental questions. The first seeks to discover and to understand the first forms of human learning, cognitive representation, emotion, and action, in the hope that insight into the early forms of these phenomena will inform an appreciation of the adult manifestations. A second question of interest stems from the desire to predict the future. Is it possible to predict the profile of a ten- or twenty-year-old from the profile of reactivity during the first two or three years of life? The possibility that the eras of infancy and later development are connected is at the root of the hope that psychologists will be able to predict future pathology by unraveling the relation between them.

Cognitive Processes in the Infant

Three questions dominate theory and research on cognitive processes in the infant. What do infants perceive, and what form do these initial

This research was supported in part by the John D. and Catherine T. MacArthur Foundation.

representations of experience take? What is the role of maturation in the development of cognitive functions? And what are the consequences of these emerging cognitive abilities for a child's emotional and social behavior? I assume that changes in specific cognitive abilities create the conditions for new emotional experiences and social behaviors, rather than the other way around. As the central nervous system matures new cognitive and motor functions appear as long as the child is in an environment with some variety. The timing of some competencies is remarkably congruent across varied primate species. For example, chimpanzees, orangutans, gorillas, and human infants all begin to crawl at about the same time, namely, at about 5 percent of the time from birth to puberty (Elias, 1984). I use the term *maturation* to refer to the inevitable changes in neurons, transmitters, and synapses that permit a new competency to appear; a psychological competence is not a neurological structure but an emergent phenomenon.

Newborn infants are ready to experience most of the basic sensations—they can see, hear, and smell and are sensitive to pain, touch, and changes in body position. Although all the sensory modalities are not operating at optimal level at birth, they mature very quickly. These sensory capacities permit the young infant to detect the differences between stripes an eighth of an inch wide and a completely gray patch, between vertical and oblique gratings, and between highly contoured and minimally contoured designs. The newborn can discriminate between the musical notes C and C-sharp and the spoken syllables *pa* and *ba,* and is sensitive to the rate of change in sound energy during the first half second of an auditory event.

Methodology

It is now necessary to discuss methodology, for all generalizations are dependent upon the nature of the evidence that is the source of the generalization. Psychologists generally use the simple habituation/dishabituation procedure to determine whether an infant can detect the difference between two events. If, for example, an infant is shown two identical blue cubes until he or she looks away out of boredom and is subsequently shown one of the blue cubes next to a blue sphere, the infant will show more interest in the sphere, implying that the infant detects a difference between the old and the new event. However, my colleagues and I showed ten-month-old infants two identical circles, each containing two horizontal, symmetrically placed black dots. When they became bored with this simple stimulus, some were shown a new pair of circles—one of the aforementioned circles and one with a pair of black dots lying outside the frame. Although infants are capable of detecting a difference between the two stimuli and, therefore, should have looked longer at the circle with the dots outside the frame, they looked equally long at the old and the new stimuli (Linn, Reznick, Kagan, & Hans, 1982).

This result, which can be generalized, reflects a serious problem in inferring a child's knowledge, discriminative ability, or mental states. Although it is legitimate to infer discrimination when an infant dishabituates to a new stimulus, one cannot infer lack of discrimination when there is a failure of dishabituation. A baby who does not dishabituate to a new event may have detected it as different from the prior experience but may have been able to categorize it quickly or not at all. Each procedural probe is only one of many that could be used to access a young infant's psychological ability.

The Schemata

A schema is the first form of the young infant's knowledge and resembles John Locke's conception of the contents of the human mind. The schema is best defined as a representation of experience that bears some relation to the original event. Infants create schemata for what they see, hear, smell, taste, and touch, and these schemata permit recognition of the past. It appears that schemata exist from the first days of life: Newborns who were shown a checkerboard composed of 144 black and white squares showed renewed interest when they were subsequently shown a board with only four squares. This result suggests that they created a schema for the first stimulus and recognized that it had been altered in the second (Friedman, Bruno, & Vietze, 1974).

A schema is not an exact copy of the physical event, for the mind cannot register every feature of an experience. Moreover, succeeding exposures to an event are never identical and because the mind relates the succeeding experience to the earlier one, it probably creates a composite of all similar experiences. The composite is called a *schematic prototype,* and it is a construction. Support for that statement comes from an experiment in which infants were shown a series of schematic faces, with varying distances between the eyes, between the eyes and the nose, or between the nose and the mouth (Strauss, 1979). The children were then shown a face they had never seen, but that represented the average of all the prior faces. Last, they were shown a new face that was not the average and one of the faces they had seen earlier. The children looked longer at the latter two faces than at the face representing the average of all prior faces, suggesting that they regarded the average as the most familiar face, even though they had never viewed it before.

Schemata are created initially on the basis of salient features of a stimulus. For the young infant, prior to the acquisition of symbolic structures, salient visual features are contrast and change, especially black and white contours; movement; color; and number of elements. Intermittent sounds and fast rise times are salient auditory features. The early attraction to contour is probably based on the structure of the central nervous system; the visual cortex is especially responsive to contour (Haith, 1980). Just as the infant responds to an optimal amount of contour in the visual mode, so, too, does he or she show maximal responsiveness to a combination of frequency, rise time, and loudness in the auditory mode. It appears that the rate of change of sound energy in the auditory mode is analogous to the density of contour in the visual mode (Kearsley, 1973).

Young infants perceive colors categorically, as do adults. If a child is habituated on a particular red stimulus and dishabituated on two stimuli that have identical wavelength differences with this original red stimulus, but one dishabituation stimulus falls in the category called "red," whereas the other falls into the category called "green," there is greater dishabituation to the latter (Bornstein, Kessen, & Weiskopf, 1975). Infants also prefer curved lines to straight lines. A child will look longer at a bull's-eye than at a design of equal contour composed of straight lines, and will show greater dishabituation when first shown a straight and then a curved line than if the order of presentation is reversed (Hopkins, Kagan, Brachfeld, Hans, & Linn, 1976).

If infants extract schematic prototypes from experience, they must be attending to the separate dimensions of an event. This possibility implies that they might represent abstract stimulus qualities of experience, and recognize the abstract representation in a modality other than the one that gave rise to the original schema. There is some evidence, albeit controversial, that infants can do this. For example, infants who first hear either a pulsing or a continuous tone, and are then shown both a broken and a continuous line, will look longer at the broken line after they hear the pulsing tone but will look longer at the continuous line after they hear the continuous tone (Wagner, Winner, Cicchetti, & Gardner, 1981). If infants without language can create schemata representing qualities like continuity and discontinuity extracted from auditory and visual experience, then philosophers who have argued for the existence of universals are partially vindicated.

The Discrepancy Principle

During the early weeks of life an infant's attention is captured by the physical qualities of events. But as the child acquires schemata, the relation between these constructions and immediate experience begins to compete with the original power of contour, movement, color, and curvature to attract and to hold the infant's attention. It appears that events that are a partial transformation of existing schemata or their prototypes begin to dominate the infant's attentiveness. These events are called "discrepant."

It is not uncommon in development for one mechanism to dominate the functioning of an organism until its mission is completed and is replaced by or subordinated to another. The partial transformation with the greatest power is a rearrangement of elements, an addition or a deletion of an element, or a change in a dimension that is central to the stored schema. A doll without a head and a doll whose head is placed between its legs represent two such salient transformations for six-month-olds. A doll without ears does not, because ears are not a salient dimension for the schema of a human, at least not for six-month-old babies. Thus, the relation between the duration of sustained attention awarded to an event and its relation to the child's schema is curvilinear (McCall, Kennedy, & Applebaum, 1977).

Events that transform nonsalient elements and events that transform all the central elements elicit less attention and less excitement than do those that transform some, but not all, of the central dimensions. Eight-month-old children with a schema for an adult human will become excited when they see pictures of infants but not when they see pictures of butterflies. Two-year-olds, to whom women and infants have become very familiar, become excited by pictures of butterflies (Reznick, 1982).

It is probably not a coincidence that the discrepancy principle emerges most clearly between eight and twelve weeks of age. This phenomenon must reflect a maturational change, because many other competencies also appear at this time, including the vanishing of the Moro reflex; changes in the scanning of contoured designs, especially the reexamination of similar elements (Bronson, 1982); a decrease in crying, but an increase in babbling; the percentage of quiet sleep; and the appearance of alpha in the EEG. My colleagues and I suggest that one of the new competencies that matures is an ability to recognize the relation of an event in the field to one's schema. Thus, by three months of age, a basic form of recognition memory has become a robust cognitive function.

An infant's emotional state is influenced by the ability or inability to assimilate a discrepant event to its schema. If the event can be assimilated, the infant often shows positive excitement. If the infant cannot, a state of uncertainty is generated. If the infant continues to attempt to assimilate a discrepant event, remains unsuccessful, and, additionally, has no way to deal with the comprehension, a subsequent state is generated. Some psychologists call this state fear or anxiety.

Gunnar, Leighton, and Peleaux (1983) have shown that the ability to predict the appearance of a discrepant event or to make some response to it tends to reduce uncertainty and distress. Thus, if one-year-olds watch a mechanical toy that is regularly activated and inactivated every four seconds, they will show much less fear than if the very same toy moves at irregular and unpredictable times. In a classic experiment, Mast, Fagen, Rovee-Collier, and Sullivan (1980) trained three groups of infants to kick mobiles constructed of two, six, or ten wooden blocks. After learning to produce the kick in order to make the mobile move, all the infants were exposed to a mobile containing only two units. The children who had been originally exposed to the two-unit mobile showed no change in their behavior. But those who experienced a change from a ten- or a six-block mobile to one containing only two blocks cried, suggesting they were upset by the change. I view their distress as a reaction to a comparison of the amount of movement produced by the two-unit mobile in front of them with their schema of the previous day's more exciting experience with the larger mobile.

The Growth of Retrieval Memory

The ability to relate an experience in the present to relevant schemata is one of the important maturing functions of the first year. During the first months of life children show the ability to recognize the past, but, by eight months, there is an improvement in the ability to retrieve the past and to compare past and present on the stage of active memory. Four-month-olds can recognize whether a face in front of them is similar to one they have seen before, but are less able to retrieve the schema for that familiar face while lying alone in their cribs.

A reasonable procedure to evaluate an infant's ability to retrieve a schema is similar to the procedure used to study object permanence. A group of infants was studied longitudinally from eight to twelve months of age in a procedure in which they had to find a toy that was hidden under one of two identical cloths in front of them. However, each infant had to wait one, three, or seven seconds before being permitted to reach for the toy, and an opaque screen separated the child from the toy during the delay. The infants improved steadily in their ability to remember the location of the toy across the four months of observation. No eight-month-old could remember the toy's location when the opaque screen was lowered during a brief one-second delay, but by one year all infants could find the toy when the opaque screen was lowered for three seconds (Kagan, Kearsley, & Zelazo, 1978).

A more compelling example of the role of the maturation of recall memory involves a stage in the growth of the concept of the permanent object. A child is shown two cloths; let me call them A and B. The examiner hides a toy under cloth A (the left and right positions of the toy are counterbalanced) and allows a baby to retrieve it two or three times. After the successful retrievals the researcher hides the toy under cloth B. The puzzling result is that eight- to nine-month-old babies are likely to go to cloth A, even though they saw the toy being hidden under cloth B.

The conditions that reduce this error provide a clue to its origin. If the delay between hiding the toy under cloth B and the opportunity to reach is very short—less than a second—the error is much less likely to occur. Moreover, if the nine-month-old does not make the error with the two-second delay, the error is likely to occur if the delay is increased several seconds. Indeed, throughout the second half of the first year, the experimenter can increase the likelihood of the error simply by increasing the delay between hiding the toy under cloth B and the time when the child is permitted to reach. At eight months, a delay of five seconds is sufficient; by twelve months a delay of ten to twelve seconds is necessary to produce the error (Diamond, 1983).

In addition, the ability to relate the present to the immediate past on the stage of active memory also improves at this time. A demonstration of this maturing competence is revealed in an experiment with eight-, nine-, and eleven-month-old infants. The experimenter used a special mirror that allowed the infant to feel an object that was different from the one he or she was seeing or had just seen. But on other trials, there was congruence between the object that was felt and the object that was seen. If the infants were actively comparing the tactile and the visual information, they should have been more exploratory on the trick trials when the two objects were different than on the regular trials when they were the same. The eight-month-olds did not behave differently on the two kinds of trials. But the older children behaved as if they were puzzled when they saw one object but felt a different one (Bushnell, 1982). In order to experience this state of puzzlement, the children would have to be relating the information from the two senses on the stage of active memory.

The appearance of retrieval memory and the comparison of information on the stage of active memory are associated with a variety of other events, all of which appear to be maturational, including the reaching in the dark for an object that has produced a noise, the inhibition of approach behavior to novelty, avoidance of the deep side of the visual cliff, and the appearance of stranger anxiety and separation anxiety (Kagan, Kearsley, & Zelazo, 1978; Campos, Svejda, Bertenthal, Benson, & Schmidt, 1981). At this stage, deaf children learning sign language first use signs to refer to objects in the environment, a behavior that requires them to relate what is present in their experience to schemata they acquired earlier (Petitto, 1983).

The remarkable uniformity in the appearance of these milestones across different rearing environments suggests that these talents follow orderly changes in the central nervous system, especially maturation of the prefrontal cortex, because this part of the brain is activated when a monkey is presented with a problem in which it must remember under which of two covers a piece of food was hidden.

Memory and Fear

The ability to retrieve and hold schemata in active memory and to relate discrepant events to their sources are cognitive processes necessary for the universal appearance of certain fears that appear during the second half of the first year, especially fear of unfamiliar adults and fear following temporary separation from a parent. The two most common fears have been called stranger anxiety and separation anxiety. If a child cannot assimilate an unfamiliar adult approaching him or her, despite an attempt to do so, and, additionally, has no behavior to deal with the state of uncertainty being generated, the child may cry.

A similar analysis is applicable to separation anxiety. A one-year-old, following departure of the mother, retrieves from memory the schema of the mother's former presence and compares that knowledge with the present in active memory. If the child cannot resolve the inconsistency inherent in the comparison, he or she may become uncertain and cry; this is known as separation anxiety. It is interesting that macaque monkeys that are removed from their mothers become depressed only when they remain in the same cage where they had been with their mothers and, therefore, have some reminder of her earlier presence. If the infants are removed to a new cage they do not show the depression.

The appearance of separation anxiety is the same for children raised in American nuclear families, on kibbutzim in Israel, in Indian villages in Central America, or in orphanages and day care centers (Kagan, Kearsley, & Zelazo, 1978). I believe that the appearance of this fear between eight and twelve months of age is due to the emergence of an ability to retrieve the past and to compare past and present in active memory. The fear recedes after age two because children are then able to understand the event, predict the return of the mother, and issue a useful reaction.

This maturational interpretation is supported by work with monkeys, which reveals that onset of fear to the unusual or unfamiliar depends upon maturation of the brain. Six rhesus monkeys were raised individually with a wooden hobby horse in a restricted environment that permitted visual access to the outside world but no interaction with any living creature. Six other monkeys were raised individually with a dog in an environment that permitted considerably more freedom and playful interaction. Each monkey was placed alone in an unfamiliar environment on a regular schedule and the investigator measured how fearful each monkey became. Heart rate and distress calls were used as the signs of fear. Although the monkeys raised with dogs showed more fear than did those raised with the inanimate toy, both groups of animals showed a major increase in fearfulness between two and four months of age (Mason, 1978).

These findings imply that maturation of specific parts of the brain must occur before novel environments and unfamiliar events will produce fear. It is important to note that this fear emerges without much social experience in the monkeys raised with the wooden toy. The rate of brain and body growth in the monkey is about three to four times that of the human infant. Hence, the comparable developmental era in the child is between seven and fifteen months. This is the interval when fear of strangers and of separation from the mother appear in most human infants, regardless of their form of rearing.

The Infant's Attachments

This discussion of separation anxiety provides a nice bridge to a consideration of the concept of attachment, for in the 1950s and 1960s the infant's emotional bond to the parents was measured by the appearance of separation anxiety. The three behaviors that indicate a special relationship to a caregiver are obvious. First, infants are more easily placated by the adults who care for them than by those who do not, are less distressed by the unfamiliar when in the presence of these adults, and, finally, will approach those adults for play when their mood is gay and for solace when they are distressed. This trio of facts is as replicable as any in psychology and invites a term to name the properties of the infant that will explain why a small number of people can reduce the infant's uncertainty and be sources of pleasure and preferred targets for behavior. The word *attachment* is a good choice because it conveys the idea that the infant has acquired a special emotional relation with those who care for him or her. It appears that an attachment is most likely to develop toward those objects to which the infant displays species-specific responses, like clinging, vocalizing, smiling, holding, and playing. Thus monkeys display clasping reactions toward the ventral surface of their mothers, precocial birds follow their mothers, and human infants hug, vocalize, play, and smile at their mothers.

If the state of attachment is built through interaction with caregiving adults, attachments should vary in their intensity, strength, or quality, depending upon the history of the prior interaction. The assumption that some caregiving conditions could make the infant more or less vulnerable to anxiety as a result of a weak attachment catapulted the concept of attachment to prominence. In the last half of this century, psychological theorists have implied that a weak or insecure attachment to the biological mother renders a young child vulnerable to psychological symptoms.

The strongest statement on the significance of the attachment and love relation between child and parent appears in Bowlby's ambitious trilogy on attachment and loss, in which he claims that loss of a loved person is one of the most intensely painful experiences any human being can suffer. On the final page of *Loss*, Bowlby (1980) tells the reader about the centrality of affectional relationships. He states: "Intimate attachments to other human beings are the hub around which a person's life revolves, not only when he is an infant or a toddler, but throughout . . . adolescence and . . . maturity as well, and on into old age" (p. 442). He argues that an attachment to another person is both instinctive and enduring. And, like other contemporary theorists, he asserts that an insecure attachment during infancy will affect future vulnerability to psychopathology permanently. Although the first of these hypotheses is likely to be true, the other two are controversial.

This idea has not been popular in most societies, either in the present or in the past. The Efe!, a seminomadic group in Zaire, believe that a child will grow best if a woman other than the mother is the first to hold and to nurse the newborn (Tronick, Winn, & Morelli, in press). In eighteenth-century France, over one half of the middle-class infants were sent to wet nurses who cared for several infants at the same time. Although strong public reaction to the high mortality rates among these infants led to a decline in the use of wet nurses toward the end of the nineteenth century, there is no evidence that French mothers worried about the effects of this experience on their infant's attachment or future vulnerability to anxiety. It is only during this century, and especially after Freud's writings, that words like attachment, trust, and dependence became important constructs to apply to the infant, and the proper amount of maternal love became an issue of serious concern.

There are good reasons why Americans in this century have become concerned with the hazards of anxiety in the infant. The geographical mobility that has increased in the United States after World War I forced many Americans to live in communities of strangers whom they felt they could not trust. Second, the combination of an economic depression, the atrocities of World War II, and now possible nuclear catastrophe have created in the average citizen a serious apprehension about the future. I believe these worries have been projected onto the infant. People want to understand why they feel anxious and are drawn to an interpretation that is rooted in experiences in the deep past. The numerous books and magazine articles on attachment of infant to mother and the necessity of skin-to-skin bonding between mother and child in the first postnatal hours are generated by some very strong emotions, suggesting that something more than scientific fact is monitoring the discussion.

Measuring Attachments

A basic methodological issue is measuring the variation in the attachment bond between infant and parent. What metric should be used—intensity, degree of pleasure, speed of approach? Bowlby and Ainsworth chose "degree of security" because, I suspect, feeling secure is salient in the consciousness of the modern West. Had Hume been interested in this idea, he would have probably chosen "degree of pleasure." Because human infants become distressed when they are separated from their mothers, it seems reasonable to conclude that the reaction to separation and reunion with the mother might index the quality of the infant's attachment.

Ainsworth, Blehar, Waters, and Wall (1978) have carefully standardized a procedure they believe measures the degree of security inherent in a child's attachment to the mother. It has come to be known as the Strange Situation. Briefly, infants of between nine and twenty-four months are observed in an unfamiliar laboratory room during a series of three-minute episodes—when they are with their mothers, with a stranger, with the mother and with the stranger, and when alone. The key episodes are those in which the mother leaves the child, once with the stranger and once alone, and returns several minutes later to be reunited with the child. The child's reaction to the mother's departure and return are viewed as providing a sensitive index of the infant's quality of attachment.

In general, children who show mild protest following the departure, seek the mother upon her return, and are easily placated by her (about 70 percent of a typical sample of middle-class, one-year-old American children) are classified as the most securely attached. Infants who do not protest departure and do not approach the mother when she reenters (about 20 percent) are classified as insecurely attached-avoidant. Finally, children who become seriously upset by the departure and who, although seeking contact with the mother, resist her attempts to soothe them (about 10 percent) are classified as insecurely attached–resistant.

Is this procedure a valid index of security of attachment? Some of the important evidence for the validity of the procedure comes from the fact that 18-month-old children who were classified as securely attached became more resilient, curious, and socially adroit with peers than did infants who were classified as insecurely attached (Arend, Gove, & Sroufe, 1979; Waters, Wippman, & Sroufe, 1979). Because a secure attachment is viewed as aiding development, these positive outcomes are regarded as validation for the method of classification. However, there are serious problems that restrain an uncritical enthusiasm for the sensitivity of this method to disclose the nature of the bond between infant and caregiver.

One troublesome fact is that the classifications are not as stable as one might expect. In two independent studies of children observed at both 12 and at either 18 or 19 months, the attachment classification for 40 to 50 percent of the children changed (Thompson, Lamb, & Estes, 1982; Egeland & Farber, 1984). In one of these studies (Egeland & Farber, 1984), 35 of 82 infants who had been classified as insecure at 12 months were classified as securely attached six months later, and 28 of 107 infants, securely attached at the earlier age, were insecurely attached on the second evaluation.

The Influence of Vulnerability and Socialization

However, there are other problems with measuring attachment. One is the child's temperamental vulnerability to becoming uncertain and anxious in the Strange Situation; the other is the degree to which parents socialize their children during the first year to cope with the stress of unfamiliarity. One gains an appreciation of the problems by reflecting on the key behaviors evaluated in the Strange Situation. A one-year-old in an unfamiliar room is left unexpectedly with a stranger or alone. Because the degree of distress shown by the child does influence how he or she will behave when the mother returns and, therefore, whether the attachment will be classified as secure or insecure, it is important to know what factors, other than the historical relationship with the mother, might lead a child to become very upset, mildly upset, or minimally upset.

One factor is the child's vulnerability to becoming anxious in response to unexpected experiences. It is known that infants differ in their vulnerability to anxiety to the unfamiliar (Kagan, Reznick, Clarke, Snidman, & Garcia-Coll, in press). Imagine three groups of infants, each with equally close relationships with their mothers. However, one group is not easily frightened by the unfamiliar, does not cry when the mother leaves, and, therefore, is unlikely to approach her when she returns. These children will probably be classified as "avoidant." Infants who are moderately vulnerable to anxiety are more likely to cry when the mother departs and, therefore, approach her when she returns. But because they are not extremely upset they will be easily placated and most likely classified as "securely attached." Finally, children who are very vulnerable to anxiety will become extremely upset by the departure, and because they are in such an extreme state of upset will push the mother away as they continue to sob. They are likely to be classified as "resistant" or "insecurely attached." Indeed, the best predictor of whether the child will seek contact with the mother when she returns to the room is the degree of crying and upset shown following the mother's departure (Gaensbauer, Connell, & Schultz, 1983).

There is research to show that infants differ in their vulnerability to anxiety. Japanese newborn infants who were classified as resistant at one year were more likely than newborn infants who were classified later as securely attached to cry intensely to the minor frustration of having a nipple removed from their mouths. These same irritable infants also cried more often and more intensely when they were observed in their homes at one and three months of age. When they were seven months old they showed more fear to an adult stranger, and when two years old they were more cautious with an unfamiliar peer (Chen & Miyake, 1982/1983). In the study cited earlier (Egeland & Farber, 1984) minimally alert newborns who were rated as difficult to feed and nurture were most likely to be classified as insecurely attached at one year. Thus it appears that infants classified as resistant-insecurely attached differ temperamentally from securely attached infants from the first days of life.

In a recent comparison of abused and maltreated infants and a control group, 19-month-old infants who showed a great deal of anxiety and distress in a play situation in an unfamiliar room with their mother were most likely to be classified as insecurely attached-resistant in the Strange Situation. This temperamental vulnerability to anxiety was a better predictor of insecure attachment than was the fact of maltreatment (Schneider-Rosen, 1984). This datum implicates the importance of temperament in the child's reaction to the Strange Situation.

It is of historical interest that Ainsworth's first book on attachment, *Infancy in Uganda* (1967), also implicated the importance of temperament, for she noted that insecurely attached babies cried frequently whenever she observed them. They were fussy babies who "cried not just when parted from their mothers but even when with their mothers" (p. 391). Ainsworth's descriptions imply that the children's irritability was a function of their temperament, rather than of the emotional bond to the mother.

A second important factor that influences a child's behavior in the Strange Situation is the degree to which parents socialize their children to control anxiety at the unfamiliar. The child of an attentive and loving mother who has encouraged self-reliance and control of fear is less likely to cry when the mother departs and, therefore, is less likely to approach her when she returns. This child will be categorized, however, as avoidant–insecurely attached. The child whose mother has been protective and less insistent that her child be tough is more likely to cry and, therefore, rush to the mother when she reenters the room. Such a child will be classified as securely attached.

In one study, the mothers of babies who would have been classified as less securely attached had careers outside the home and were less accommodating to their infants' needs, probably because they valued control of fear and self-reliance in their young children. Another way of stating this is to say that these infants were better able to cope with uncertainty when their mothers left them alone. These children might be at a greater advantage in later childhood, at least in our society, than those who cry when the mother leaves. It is likely that both groups of infants are attached, but that one is better able to deal with the uncertainty created by the testing procedure (Hock & Clinger, 1981). This idea is enhanced by studies of West German children living in Bielefeld where nearly half of the one-year-olds were classified as avoidant because they did not greet the mother when she returned to the room (Grossmann, Grossmann, Huber, & Wartner, 1981). The investigators explained that these German children had been encouraged by their parents to control their anxiety.

A basic flaw in the logic of the inferences drawn from the Strange Situation is revealed by the reactions of infant monkeys who were removed from their mothers after an attachment had been established. When the monkey was put in an unfamiliar place following a separation, it showed both an increase in disturbed behavior and a rise in the level of cortisol in the blood. However, if the same monkey was put in a similar environment with familiar animals, it did not show any behavioral signs of distress, but continued to show high levels of cortisol. The high cortisol levels suggest that the infant animal was reacting emotionally to the mother's absence, even though its behavior implied it was not upset. Thus, even though an infant behaves as if he or she is not upset by the loss of the mother in the Strange Situation, that fact alone cannot be regarded as evidence of an insecure attachment (Levine, 1982).

Finally, there is the argument based on reasonableness. The classifications of secure and insecure are based on a child's behavior during two, three-minute episodes in an unfamiliar room. Is it reasonable that a history of interaction between mother and infant comprising more than a half a million minutes in the home would be revealed by six minutes in a laboratory room? I think not, and I am joined by two groups of psychologists who, following exhaustive reviews of relevant research, concluded that this procedure was simply not a sensitive index of security of attachment (Campos, Lamb, Goldsmith, Barrett, & Stenberg, 1983; Lamb, Thompson, Gardner, Charrov, & Estes, 1984). Although the Strange Situation probably does not provide a sensitive index of the quality of attachment, attachment is a useful concept and should not be abandoned. Psychologists are in an unfortunate position because they are convinced that the construct of attachment has utility but do not yet possess sensitive ways to evaluate the subtle variations that exist in this complex human bond.

Temperamental Variation Among Infants

During most of this century explanations of different patterns of social behavior among young children have emphasized variation in environmental experiences and have ignored those infant qualities that psychologists call temperamental. A seminal axiom of the disciplines in which life processes are studied is that the inherent properties of the unit under study make some contribution to the unit's growth as it exploits successive encounters with its surroundings. Whenever a generation of theorists overemphasizes the influence of the surroundings, ignores the endogenous characteristics of the unit, or awards too much power to the unit and not enough to the environment, future generations will make the necessary corrections. The sciences of human behavior are in a transition; the importance of the young child's inherent characteristics, partially revealed through temperamental predispositions, is being recognized. Thomas and Chess (1977), Plomin and Rowe (1979), Rothbart and Derryberry (1981), Carey and McDevitt (1978), and many others have helped to effect this change in attitude. This body of work implies that variations in an infant's characteristics invite different treatments by family members and peers and constrain the growing child's psychological choices.

Inhibition to the Unfamiliar

One fundamental temperamental disposition can be described as a child's initial behavioral reaction to unfamiliar people, objects, and situations. This characteristic is moderately stable and is seen clearly during the transition from infancy to early childhood. One of the most sensitive indexes of this quality is a child's behavior with an unfamiliar peer. One small group of children becomes extremely quiet and vigilant, stays close to the caregiver for a period of five to fifteen minutes, and, even after the period of obvious inhibition passes, rarely approaches the unfamiliar peer. A second, somewhat larger group of uninhibited children begins to play immediately. The former group seems to be a young version of the prototypic introvert; the latter representative of the extravert. These two behavioral styles displayed with unfamiliar children are only the most obvious index of a more general quality, namely, the tendency to display or not to display an initial period of inhibition of speech and play, associated with a retreat to a target of attachment, whenever the child encounters an unfamiliar event. In searching for concise adjectives to capture the differences between the two kinds of children, recognizing that any word distorts what is observed, the words *restrained, watchful,* and *gentle* capture the essence of the inhibited child, whereas *free, energetic,* and *spontaneous* reveal the style of the uninhibited youngster. When an inhibited child throws a ball, knocks down a tower of blocks, or hits a large toy clown, the act is monitored, restrained, almost soft. The same act performed by an uninhibited child seems relaxed and free.

Why are inhibition and lack of inhibition to the unfamiliar stable characteristics during the transition between infancy and childhood? It is possible that maturation of the brain is accompanied by cognitive abilities that permit the child to make inferences about the possible consequences of an unfamiliar event. If a two-year-old attempts to predict what might happen after meeting an unfamiliar person and cannot solve that problem, the child becomes vulnerable to uncertainty. Ten-month-old infants are not mature enough to attempt the inference. Additionally, during their second year, children become better able to remember the past and to compare representations of the past and present over longer periods of time so that if assimilation is not possible, uncertainty may emerge. Finally, during the second year children display their first appreciation of correct and incorrect performance, dysphoric emotion to broken or flawed objects, and empathy with those who are hurt (Kagan, 1981). The realization that one can make a mistake is one potentially important origin of uncertainty and, therefore, of behavioral inhibition.

There are, therefore, good reasons for expecting the emergence, during the second and third years, of individual differences in behavioral inhibition and lack of inhibition with unfamiliar children. Although these behavioral differences are particularly salient during the transition to childhood, the underlying predisposition may be observed throughout the life span, albeit in different manifestations. If the differences in behavioral inhibition among three-year-old children are present during the first months of life, they might be reflected in extreme distress to frustration, quality of sleep, or symptoms indexing physiological arousal, like chronic constipation, allergies, and, perhaps, extreme irritability.

Chen and Miyake (1982/1983) report that newborn infants who react with extreme distress and are not easily placated when a nipple is removed repeatedly from their mouths are likely to become fearful and inhibited during early childhood; those who do not become upset are less likely to show the later signs of fear and inhibition. Lester (in press) and Garcia-Coll (1979), as well as others, have found that behaviors observed during the newborn period predict psychological characteristics that are similar to behavioral inhibition during later infancy. Other investigators have also noted these qualities. Bronson (1970) has commented on the preservation of individual differences in fearfulness, and Emmerich (1964) has found that behaviors resembling inhibition and lack of inhibition were preserved among nursery school children who were observed from the ages of three to five. (See also Halverson & Waldrop, 1976; Simpson & Stevenson-Hinde, in press.)

These qualities can persist into adulthood, for extremely shy and withdrawn preschool children who had been seen in a child guidance clinic were likely, as adults, to choose relatively secure bureaucratic jobs with minimal risk, rather than entrepreneurial vocations with their attendant increase in unpredictability (Morris, Soroker, & Burruss, 1954; see also Coolidge, Brodie, & Feeney, 1964). Furthermore, psychiatrists make a useful distinction between adult patients who are chronic worriers and a much smaller group—less than one percent—who are vulnerable to sudden panic reactions. The latter patients were more likely to be extremely fearful and timid during childhood (Gittelman & Klein, 1984). It appears that a small proportion of extremely fearful, inhibited children are predisposed to be adult panic patients.

The 71 members of the Fels Research Institute's longitudinal study, who were Caucasian and primarily middle-class, were observed and tested from infancy through adolescence and evaluated again as young adults. Of the many individual qualities quantified during the first three years of life, only inhibition and lack of inhibition were preserved across adolescence and young adulthood (Kagan & Moss, 1983). The children who were extremely shy, timid, and fearful during their first three years displayed a coherent cluster of behaviors during the early school years. They avoided dangerous activities, were minimally aggressive, conformed to parental requests, and avoided unfamiliar social encounters. The four boys who were most inhibited during the first six years chose intellectual careers as adults (music, physics, biology, and psychology). The four boys who were least inhibited during the first six years chose more traditional masculine vocations (football coach, salesman, and two chose engineering). Furthermore, the extremely inhibited children became adults who showed more dependency on their love objects and more conscious feelings of anxiety in social situations than did those who were extremely uninhibited as young children.

In another longitudinal study, Kagan, Kearsley, and Zelazo (1978) compared 53 Chinese-American children with 63 Caucasian children as they aged from four to twenty-nine months. Forty-nine of these children were either in full- or part-time day care; 67 were raised at home without surrogate care. The most important result was that the Chinese children, whether raised at home or in the day care center, were consistently more inhibited than the Caucasians during infancy and the transition to childhood. For example, each child was observed in a laboratory setting during which unfamiliar visual and auditory events were presented. During most of the procedures, the Chinese children vocalized and smiled less often than did the Caucasians.

The Chinese were more likely than the Caucasians to cry intensely following temporary separation from the mother and when the 20-month-old children were brought to an unfamiliar room with their mother, a familiar adult, and a stranger, the Chinese children stayed close to their mother for a longer period of time than did the Caucasians. These ethnic differences were most dramatic in children from seven to twenty months of age. Additionally, each mother ranked 16 different personality qualities in her two-year-old, from most to least characteristic. The Chinese parents regarded fearfulness and timidity as more characteristic of their child than did the Caucasian mothers. For example, the Chinese mothers rated the statement "Stays close to mother" as a salient quality of the child, whereas the Caucasian mothers regarded talkativeness, a sense of humor, and emotional spontaneity as more characteristic of their children.

Physiological Correlates

A second important difference between the two groups of children provides a clue to the bases for the inhibition and lack of inhibition. The Chinese children had more stable heart rates while they were processing unfamiliar visual and auditory information than did the Caucasians, and the differences in heart rate variability represented the best preserved dimension across the 26 months of the investigation. This physiological index was much more stable than behavioral qualities like attentiveness, irritability, vocalization, or smiling.

Heart rate variability, as well as absolute heart rate, are regulated by the sympathetic and parasympathetic branches of the autonomic nervous system. Heart rate, blood pressure, and sympathetic activity typically increase during inspiration as vagal tone is inhibited, but decrease with expiration as the vagus is disinhibited. As a result, the heart rate of children and adults at rest usually displays a regular cycle that is yoked to breathing, and the rate is moderately variable over epochs of three to ten seconds. However, when the vagal influence is restrained, the cardiac deceleration that normally accompanies expiration is muted, and heart rate rises slightly and becomes much less variable (Bunnell, 1982).

The mental effort associated with working at cognitive problems is one of the conditions typically associated with the loss of respiratory sinus arrhythmia and an accompanying rise and stabilization of heart rate (Light, 1984). It is a well established fact that under cognitive stress adults show an increase in epinephrine secretion and heart rate, but a decrease in heart rate variability. This phenomenon is often part of a general bodily response to stress that involves release of ACTH from the pituitary, glucocorticoids from the adrenal cortex, epinephrine from the adrenal medulla, and norepinephrine from sympathetic nerves (Axelrod & Reisine, 1984). The involvement of the sympathetic nervous system in this phenomenon is supported by the fact that if the sympathetic nervous system is blocked, for example, by the drug propanolol, the rise in heart rate in response to a cognitive problem is reduced or absent. Thus, because inhibited children are more likely than uninhibited ones to show a rise in heart rate in response to cognitive tasks, greater activity of the sympathetic nervous system is implied. Frankenhaeuser (1979) comments on the existence of major individual differences in the secretion of epinephrine and norepinephrine to stress and the stability of those two reactions: "We may thus conclude that those psychosocial stimuli which are perceived as deviating from the ordinary input level, or which are in some other way incongruous with a person's expectancies based on his [or her] previous experience, are likely to induce changes in sympathetic-adrenomedullary activity" (p. 90).

There are stable individual differences among adults in the tendency to react to cognitive problems with a rise and stabilization of heart rate. Manuck and Garland (1980) tested 19 college men on two occasions about a year apart. Ten men were reactive and showed heart rate increases in response to cognitive tasks, whereas nine men were much less reactive. The tendency to display a rise in heart rate was stable over the 13 months of the study; correlations were about 0.8. Light and Obrist (1983) administered a reaction time task to college males in which winning was made easy, difficult, or impossible. The men who showed a larger increase in heart rate at task onset maintained higher heart rate levels than did those who did not show the initial rise in cardiac rate, leading the authors to posit an individual difference dimension in the ease of sympathetic activation to a cognitive task. If inhibited and uninhibited children differed in the ease with which central nervous system discharge occurred to uncertainty, those with a low threshold for such discharge would be likely to undergo activation of the sympathetic nervous system and display a rise and stabilization of heart rate. This difference in threshold of reactivity of the sympathetic nervous system among humans may be a homologue of similar variation noted in rats (Blizard, 1981) and monkeys (Suomi, Kraemer, Baysinger, & DeLizio, 1981).

Current Research

My colleagues and I are currently studying two cohorts of children longitudinally. One cohort of 46 children has been seen at 21, 48, and 67 months of age and consists of equal numbers of inhibited and uninhibited children. The second cohort of 54 children, half inhibited and half uninhibited, has been seen at 31 and 43 months of age (Garcia-Coll, Kagan, & Reznick, 1984; Kagan et al., in press; Snidman, 1984). The primary index of behavioral inhibition in the third and fourth years is derived from the child's profile of reactions to an unfamiliar peer of the same age and sex. As I indicated earlier, inhibited children wait a long time before they play with toys, talk, or approach another child. Initially, they spend long periods of time close to their mothers while staring at the other child and are unlikely to approach or talk to the peer. As the results so far indicate, differences in behavior, as well as heart rate variability, are preserved to a significant degree. The stability correlations for both behavior and heart rate variability range between 0.4 and 0.6. Because respiration rate exerts an influence on heart rate, it is important to note that even though there is considerable variation in respiration rate—from 18 to 33 cycles per minute—there is no relation between respiration rate and either heart rate or heart rate variability during baseline or cognitive testing, and the two groups do not differ in respiration rate.

Very few uninhibited children have become inhibited during the period of study. About half of the inhibited children remain extremely inhibited, and the other half have changed toward a less inhibited style, but one that is still less spontaneous than that of the typical uninhibited youngster. However, the inhibited children who displayed very stable heart rates at the early ages (21 months in Cohort One and 31 months in Cohort Two) seem to be more likely to remain inhibited than were the inhibited children who had variable heart rates at the initial assessment.

The older inhibited children showed more obvious signs of anxiety and tension while being tested than did the uninhibited children. The inhibited four-year-olds were quiet, looked at the examiner frequently, and more often refused to answer a difficult problem. During the assessment at five-and-a-half years of age, the inhibited children remained quiet and sat with a tense posture of the trunk, often accompanied by small motor movements of the fingers, lips, or tongue. The uninhibited children, by contrast, sat with a relaxed posture or, as the session wore on, displayed restless motor movements of trunk and limbs.

The inhibited five-and-a-half-year-olds seemed to become more uncertain following mild cognitive stress than did the uninhibited youngsters. The basis for this claim comes from a change in errors on a test of recognition memory for pictures of familiar objects. Early in the session each child was shown a set of 24 unrelated pictures and was then tested on a set of 24 pictures, half of which the child had just seen, half of which were new. The child was asked to indicate which pictures were new and which old. After an intervening set of three cognitive procedures intended to be difficult, the child was given a parallel test of recognition memory. More than two-thirds of the uninhibited children showed fewer errors on the second than on the first test, whereas more than two-thirds of the inhibited children showed an increase in errors on the second test. Less stressful cognitive tasks revealed no performance difference between the inhibited and uninhibited children. Because performance on recognition and retrieval memory tests is affected by anxiety, these data imply that the inhibited children became increasingly uncertain over the course of testing.

This suggestion is affirmed by the fact that more inhibited than uninhibited children displayed a rise in heart rate over the trials of most of the cognitive tests. For example, three-quarters of the inhibited children but only one-third of the uninhibited children showed a rise in heart rate while listening to a series of three to six words they had to recall. The two groups also differed in the tendency to show a rise in heart rate over the 24 test items of the recognition memory procedure. On the first administration of recognition memory about one-third of each group showed a small but steady rise in heart rate over the 24 test trials. However, on the second test, 76 percent of the inhibited, but only 23 percent of the uninhibited, children showed a steady rise in heart rate over the 24 trials.

This cardiac acceleration over the course of the second testing, together with the increase in errors, implies a higher level of task-related uncertainty for the inhibited children. This hypothesis is also affirmed in the larger pupillary dilations of inhibited children to mildly difficult cognitive problems. Furthermore, more inhibited than uninhibited children showed a decrease in variability of the pitch periods of single word utterances when spoken under stressful conditions than when the same words were spoken singly under non-stressful conditions.

The hypothesis of higher levels of physiological arousal among the inhibited children is supported by interview data gathered from the mothers of both cohorts. The incidence of symptoms suggestive of higher arousal, such as chronic constipation, allergies, fears, and sleeplessness during the first two years of life was significantly more frequent among inhibited children, especially among those with high and stable heart rates.

It also appears that inhibited four-year-old children may have some conception of their characteristics, for they are more likely to attend to drawings of passive agents than to drawings of active agents. The four-year-old children were shown ten pictures, each illustrating the interaction of an active and a passive figure. The figures were animals, people, or an animal and a person (for example, a woman feeding a child, a man pointing a finger at a woman). The right and left positions of the active and passive agents were counterbalanced.

The coder noted whether the child was looking to the right or to the left during successive fixations of each picture. Inhibited children looked less often at the active than at the passive figures and, when asked to describe the picture, first named the passive rather than the active agent more often in their verbal descriptions. The uninhibited children showed the opposite profile.

When these children were seen at five and one-half years of age, they heard a story supported by twenty pictures about two children—one bold and one fearful. For eighteen of the scenes the two illustrated figures were separated physically so that an observer could code the duration of fixation of each figure. The inhibited children looked significantly less often at the bold figure than did the uninhibited youngsters. Furthermore, the children who had looked more often at the active figures at four years of age were the ones who looked more often at the bold figure at five and one-half years of age. More than 40 percent of the uninhibited, but only 15 percent of the inhibited, children looked at the active figure at age four and the bold figure at five and one-half years of age.

The mothers' descriptions of their children revealed that most were aware of their child's typical style, even though a few mothers of uninhibited children described them as shy and a few parents of inhibited children described them as bold. The correlations between the mothers' descriptions and our behavioral observations averaged about 0.5. My colleagues and I believe that the mothers' rankings were moderately valid in this study because of unusual conditions rarely met in most investigations. First, we were evaluating children who were at the extremes for these behavioral qualities. Second, we had established rapport with the mothers over the several years of the investigation, and perhaps had raised each parent's consciousness about the qualities of inhibition and lack of inhibition.

Summary

The corpus of evidence gathered to date implies that the qualities of inhibition and lack of inhibition are robust and moderately stable traits, even though the underlying predisposition can be expressed in various ways during the transition from infancy to childhood. In infants of less than two years of age, it is seen most clearly in reactions to unfamiliar toys, situations, and adults. In older children, especially those between two and four years of age, the disposition can be seen most clearly in reactions to an unfamiliar child, and in children of between four and six years of age, it is seen in changes in heart rate, motoricity, and behavior with an examiner in a testing situation. No single setting or procedure captures this predisposition across the first five years of life. Thus, as the child ages, it is necessary to look for more subtle expressions of this predisposition.

It is likely that a combination of inhibited behavior, together with a high and stable heart rate to cognitive stress, represents the children who are more extreme on this dimension. About one half of the inhibited children have shown a high and stable heart rate on all assessments, in contrast to about one-fifth of the uninhibited children. Reznick and I (Kagan & Reznick, in press) have shown that among a sample of three-year-olds not selected to be extremely inhibited or uninhibited, those who were highly motivated to master cognitive tasks showed a rise and stabilization of heart rate. Some uninhibited children showed such a heart rate profile in response to cognitive procedures. Thus, a rise and stabilization of heart rate in response to cognitive tasks can reflect motivational involvement rather than the temperamental quality of inhibition to the unfamiliar. It is also possible for a child to behave as inhibited because of socialization rather than of having a lower threshold for physiological arousal to uncertainty. About one third of a behaviorally inhibited group under study has not shown a high and stable heart rate on any of the assessments, and it is possible that their behavioral surface is a result of socialization.

The complete corpus of data suggests that, among young children, inhibition and lack of inhibition to the unfamiliar might be influenced by biological processes that predispose some children to one or the other style. I do not suggest that all shy, timid children—or adults—are born with this temperamental disposition, only that possession of the disposition makes it more likely that a child will develop one of these sets of characteristics. Of course, the environment has an important influence on these psychological attributes. A small group of extremely inhibited children in Cohort One are becoming less inhibited as their parents impose pressure on them to adopt a more bold and less fearful approach to the environmental challenge.

The strongest support for the claim that these two profiles involve inherent biological influences comes from the heart rate and pupillary reactions to mild cognitive stress. The fact that more of the inhibited children consistently show a higher and more stable heart rate and larger pupillary dilations in response to cognitive problems implies a lower threshold for central nervous system discharge to uncertainty. A recent review of the factors controlling autonomic responses suggests that a part of the lateral hypothalamus may be one place where psychological incentives are transduced to become important influences on the autonomic nervous system (Smith & DeVito, 1984). When the paraventricular nucleus of the hypothalamus is stimulated there is a rise in blood pressure and heart rate and an inhibition of reflex bradycardia. These facts suggest that this area of the lateral hypothalamus is one site of control over emotional responsiveness to stressful events. This region has a monosynaptic connection to the intermediolateral cells of the spinal cord and, thence, to the sympathetic nervous system. Perhaps this is one of the significant places where mind meets body, with individuals varying in the ease with which the hypothalamus responds to psychological uncertainty, the ease with which the autonomic nervous system responds to hypothalamic discharge or, perhaps, the threshold for pituitary secretion of ACTH to hypothalamic hormone. In short, there are many places where thresholds could vary as a result of biological differences among organisms.

There is some evidence that ethnic groups may differ in the thresholds within this system. Recall that the Chinese children studied in the day care investigation were more inhibited and had a more stable heart rate than did the Caucasians during the first two-and-a-half years of life. Kleinman (1982) has reported that symptoms of anxiety, panic, and neurasthenia are more frequent among Chinese psychiatric patients than among European and American patient populations. This seemingly odd asymmetry in modal diagnostic category implies, in addition to the role of culture, a possible genetic vulnerability to specific symptoms. This admittedly speculative idea deserves further study.

The view that my colleagues and I currently hold is that a small group of children, no more than 15 percent of the normal population, are born with either a high or low threshold for discharge of the central nervous system and, subsequently, of the autonomic nervous system following encounter with the unfamiliar, the unexpected, or with a psychological challenge. Environmental conditions determine the degree to which this biological tendency will be actualized. It is likely that an unusually benevolent environment that gently promotes an uninhibited coping style might create a socially outgoing demeanor in a child born with a potential for an inhibited temperament. Analogously, an overly stressful environment can create inhibited behavior in a child who is born with a temperamental disposition that favors an uninhibited coping style. Inhibition or lack of inhibition to the unfamiliar is only one of the fundamental temperamental dispositions.

It is likely that future research will reveal that other candidates, like activity level, lability of emotional mood, and even predominant affective states, will prove to be as stable and theoretically significant as the qualities of inhibition and lack of inhibition, with each of these characteristics expressed in different forms during the successive stages of development and each associated with a specific cluster of biological processes. Perhaps the empirical strategy my colleagues and I used will prove useful in investigations of these other characteristics. Rather than study variation in a volunteer sample, we deliberately selected children who belong to extreme groups because we believe that such a strategy facilitates understanding. Psychiatrists and behavioral geneticists interested in the etiology of schizophrenia do not evaluate mood and thought processes in a random sample of children but select youngsters who are the offspring of schizophrenic parents because of the reasonable assumption that the cluster of qualities that define this category do not fall on a continuum. It may be equally advantageous to supplement studies of volunteer groups by selecting children who are at the extremes of qualities like activity, regularity of sleep, irritability to frustration, lability of emotional states, and intensity of expression of anger, sadness, fear, and joy.

This summary of contemporary understanding of the human infant has been necessarily selective, but the choice of topics reflects my view of the foci of interest that are changing most rapidly. The next generation of investigators will pursue with great vigor the maturation of cognitive functions and the intermodal schemata that infants create. These schemata are likely to be critical for language acquisition. The concept of attachment will continue to be seminal, but new procedures for evaluating different qualities of attachment will be invented, and investigators will acknowledge the temperamental qualities of infants and their contribution to the products of environmental experience.

References

Ainsworth, M. D. S. (1967). *Infancy in Uganda.* Baltimore: Johns Hopkins University Press.
Ainsworth, M. D. S., Blehar, M. C., Waters, E., & Wall, S. (1978). *Patterns of attachment: A psychological study of the Strange Situation.* Hillsdale, NJ: Erlbaum.
Arend, R., Gove, F. L., & Sroufe, L. A. (1979). Continuity of individual adaptation from infancy to kindergarten. *Child Development, 50,* 950–959.
Axelrod, J., & Reisine, T. D. (1984). Stress hormones: Their interaction and regulation. *Science, 224,* 452–459.
Blizard, D. A. (1981). The Maudsley reactive and non-reactive strains: A North-American perspective. *Behavioral Genetics, 11,* 469–489.
Bornstein, M. H., Kessen, W., & Weiskopf, S. (1975). The categories of hue in infancy. *Science, 191,* 201–202.
Bowlby, J. (1980). *Attachment and loss: Vol. 3. Loss: sadness and depression.* New York: Basic Books.
Bronson, G. W. (1970). Fear of visual novelty. *Developmental Psychology, 2,* 33–40.
Bronson, G. W. (1982). *The scanning patterns of human infants: Implications for visual learning.* Norwood, NJ: Ablex.
Bunnell, D. E. (1982). Autonomic myocardial influences as a factor determining intertask consistency of heart rate reactivity. *Psychophysiology, 19,* 442–448.

Bushnell, E. W. (1982). Visual-tactual knowledge in 8-, 9 1/2-, and 11-month-old infants. *Infant Behavior and Development, 5,* 63–75.

Campos, J. J., Svejda, M., Bertenthal, B., Benson, N., & Schmidt, D. (1981). *Self-produced locomotion and wariness of heights.* Paper presented at the meeting of the Society for Research in Child Development, Boston, MA.

Campos, J. J., Lamb, M. E., Goldsmith, H. H., Barrett, K. C., & Stenberg, C. (1983). Socioemotional development. In J. J. Campos & M. M. Haith (Eds.), *Handbook of child psychology: Vol. 2. Infancy and developmental psychobiology* (4th ed., pp. 783–915). New York: Wiley.

Carey, W. B., & McDevitt, S. C. (1978). Stability and change in individual temperament diagnoses from infancy to early childhood. *Journal of the American Academy of Child Psychiatry, 17,* 331–337.

Chen, S., & Miyake, K. (1982/1983). Japanese versus United States comparison of mother-infant interaction and infant development: A review. In K. Miyake (Ed.), *Annual Report of the Research and Clinical Center for Child Development* (pp. 13–26). Sapporo, Japan: Hokkaido University.

Coolidge, J. C., Brodie, R. D., & Feeney, B. (1964). A ten-year follow-up study of sixty-six school phobic children. *American Journal of Orthopsychiatry, 34,* 675–684.

Diamond, A. (1983). Behavioral changes between six and twelve months. Unpublished doctoral dissertation, Harvard University, Cambridge.

Egeland, B., & Farber, E. A. (1984). Infant-mother attachment: Factors related to its development and changes over time. *Child Development, 55,* 753–771.

Elias, M. F. (1984, April). *Crawling: An explanation in terms of developmental constraints.* Paper presented at meeting of the International Conference on Infant Studies, New York.

Emmerich, W. (1964). Continuity and stability in early social development. *Child Development, 35,* 311–332.

Frankenhaeuser, M. (1979). Psychobiological aspects of life stress. In P. H. Venables & M. J. Christie (Eds.), *Research in Psychophysiology* (pp. 203–223). New York: Wiley.

Friedman, S., Bruno, L. A., & Vietze, P. (1974). Newborn habituation to visual stimuli. *Journal of Experimental Child Psychology, 18,* 242–251.

Gaensbauer, T. J., Connell, J. P., & Schultz, L. A. (1983). Emotion and attachment. *Developmental Psychology, 19,* 815–831.

Garcia-Coll, C. (1979). *Temperament in early development.* Paper presented at annual meeting of the Interamerican Congress of Psychology, Peru.

Garcia-Coll, C., Kagan, J., & Reznick, J. S. (1984). Behavioral inhibition in young children. *Child Development, 55,* 1005–1019.

Gittelman, R., & Klein, D. F. (1984). Relationship between separation anxiety and panic and agoraphobic disorders. *Psychopathology, 17* (Suppl. 1), 56–65.

Grossmann, K. E., Grossmann, K., Huber, F., & Wartner, U. (1981). German children's behavior toward their mothers at 12 months and their fathers at 18 months in Ainsworth's Strange Situation. *International Journal of Behavioral Development, 4,* 157–181.

Gunnar, M. R., Leighton, K., & Peleaux, R. (1983, April). *The effects of temporal predictability on year-old infants' reactions to potentially frightening toys.* Paper presented at meeting of the Society for Research in Child Development, Detroit, MI.

Haith, M. M. (1980). *Rules that babies look by.* Hillsdale, NJ: Erlbaum.
Halverson, C. F., & Waldrop, M. F. (1976). Relations between preschool activity and aspects of intellectual and social behavior at age seven-and-a-half. *Developmental Psychology, 12,* 107–112.
Hock, E., & Clinger, J. B. (1981). Infant coping behaviors. *The Journal of Genetic Psychology, 138,* 231–243.
Hopkins, J. R., Kagan, J., Brachfeld, S., Hans, S., & Linn, S. (1976). Infants' responsivity to curvature. *Child Development, 47,* 1166–1175.
Kagan, J. (1981). *The second year.* Cambridge: Harvard University Press.
Kagan, J., Kearsley, R. B., & Zelazo, P. R. (1978). *Infancy: Its place in human development.* Cambridge: Harvard University Press.
Kagan, J., & Moss, H. A. (1983). *Birth to maturity.* New Haven: Yale University Press.
Kagan, J., & Reznick, J. S. (in press). Cardiac reaction as an index of task involvement. *Australian Journal of Psychology.*
Kagan, J., Reznick, J. S., Clarke, C., Snidman, N., & Garcia-Coll, C. (in press). Behavioral inhibition to the unfamiliar. *Child Development.*
Kearsley, R. B. (1973). The newborn's response to auditory stimulation. *Child Development, 44,* 582–590.
Kleinman, A. (1982). Neurasthenia and depression. *Culture, Medicine, and Psychiatry, 6,* 117–190.
Lamb, M. E., Thompson, R. A., Gardner, W. P., Charrov, E. L., & Estes, D. (1984). Security of infantile attachment as assessed in the Strange Situation. *Behavioral and Brain Sciences, 7,* 127–171.
Lester, B. M. (in press). A method for the study of change in neonatal behavior. In T. B. Brazelton & B. M. Lester (Eds.), *Infants at risk: Towards plasticity and intervention.* New York: Elsevier.
Levine, S. (1982). Comparative and psychobiological perspectives on development. In A. Collins (Ed.), *Minnesota Symposium: Vol. 15. The concept of development* (pp. 29–53). Hillsdale, NJ: L. Erlbaum.
Light, K. C. (1984). Cardiovascular and renal responses to competitive mental challenges. In J. F. Orlebeke, G. Mulder, & L. J. P. van Doornen (Eds.), *Cardiovascular psychophysiology: Theory and methods.* New York: Plenum Press.
Light, K. C., & Obrist, P. A. (1983). Task difficulty, heart rate reactivity, and cardiovascular responses to an appetitive reaction time task. *Psychophysiology, 20,* 301–312.
Linn, S., Reznick, J. S., Kagan, J., & Hans, S. (1982). Salience of visual patterns in the human infant. *Developmental Psychology, 18,* 651–657.
Manuck, S. B., & Garland, N. F. (1980). Stability of individual differences in cardiovascular reactivity: A 13-month follow-up. *Physiology and Behavior, 24,* 621–624.
Mason, W. A. (1978). Social experience in primate cognitive development. In G. M. Burghardt & M. Bekoff (Eds.), *The development of behavior: Comparative and evolutionary aspects* (pp. 233–251). New York: Garland Press.
Mast, V. K., Fagen, J. W., Rovee-Collier, C. K., & Sullivan, M. W. (1980). Immediate and long-term memory for reinforcement context: The development of learned expectancies in early infancy. *Child Development, 51,* 700–707.
McCall, R. B., Kennedy, C. B., & Applebaum, M. I. (1977). Magnitude of

discrepancy and the direction of attention in infants. *Child Development, 48,* 772–785.

Morris, D. P., Soroker, E., & Burruss, G. (1954). Follow-up studies of shy, withdrawn children: I. Evaluation of later adjustment. *American Journal of Orthopsychiatry, 24,* 743–754.

Petitto, L. A. (1983). *From gesture to symbol.* Unpublished doctoral dissertation, Harvard University, Cambridge.

Plomin, R. A., & Rowe, D. C. (1979). Genetic and environmental etiology of social behavior in infancy. *Developmental Psychology, 15,* 62–72.

Reznick, J. S. (1982). The development of perceptual and lexical categories in the human infant. Unpublished doctoral dissertation, University of Colorado, Boulder.

Rothbart, M. K., & Derryberry, D. (1981). Development of individual differences in temperament. In M. E. Lamb & A. L. Brown (Eds.), *Advances in developmental psychology* (Vol. 1). Hillsdale, NJ: Erlbaum.

Schneider-Rosen, K. (1984). *Study of attachment in maltreated and control infants.* Unpublished doctoral dissertation, Harvard University, Cambridge.

Simpson, A. E., & Stevenson-Hinde, J. (in press). Temperamental characteristics in three- to four-year-old boys and girls in child-family interactions. *Journal of Child Psychology and Psychology.*

Smith, O. A., & DeVito, J. L. (1984). Central neural integration for the control of autonomic responses associated with emotion. *Annual Review of Neuroscience, 7,* 43–65.

Snidman, N. (1984). *Behavioral restraint and the central nervous system: Predicting performance on cognitive tasks from autonomic nervous system activity.* Unpublished doctoral dissertation, University of California, Los Angeles.

Strauss, M. S. (1979). Abstraction of prototypical information by adults and 10-month-old infants. *Journal of Experimental Psychology: Human Learning and Memory, 5,* 618–632.

Suomi, S. J., Kraemer, G. W., Baysinger, C. M., & DeLizio, R. D. (1981). Inherited and experiential factors associated with individual differences in anxious behavior displayed by rhesus monkeys. In D. F. Kline & J. Rabkin (Eds.), *Anxiety: New research and changing concepts* (pp. 179–199). New York: Raven Press.

Thomas, A., & Chess, S. (1977). *Temperament and development.* New York: Brunner/Mazel.

Thompson, R. A., Lamb, M. E., & Estes, D. (1982). Stability of infant-mother attachment and its relationship to changing life circumstances in an unselected middle-class sample. *Child Development, 53,* 144–148.

Tronick, E. Z., Winn, S., & Morelli, G. A. (in press). Multiple caretaking in the niche of human evolution. In T. Field & M. Reite (Eds.), *The psychology of attachment.* New York: Academic Press.

Wagner, S., Winner, E., Cicchetti, D., & Gardner, H. (1981). Metaphorical mapping in human infants. *Child Development, 52,* 728–731.

Waters, E., Wippman, J., & Sroufe, L. A. (1979). Attachment, positive affect, and competence in the peer group. *Child Development, 50,* 821–829.

PSYCHOLOGICAL TESTING: BASIC CONCEPTS AND COMMON MISCONCEPTIONS

ANNE ANASTASI

ANNE ANASTASI

Anne Anastasi obtained an AB degree from Barnard College and a PhD from Columbia University. She taught at Barnard and then at Queens College of the City University of New York, where she was the first chairperson of the psychology department at the newly established college. Next she joined the Graduate Faculty of Arts and Sciences of Fordham University, where she subsequently served two terms as chairperson of the joint graduate and undergraduate psychology departments. She retired in 1979 with the title of Professor Emeritus.

A past president of the American Psychological Association (APA), Anastasi held many other offices, including the presidencies of the Eastern Psychological Association, the APA Divisions of General Psychology, and of Evaluation and Measurement. She is the recipient of the APA Distinguished Scientific Award for the Applications of Psychology, the Educational Testing Service Award for Distinguished Service to Measurement, the American Educational Research Association Award for Distinguished Contributions to Research in Education, the Edward Lee Thorndike Medal for Distinguished Psychological Contribution to Education awarded by the APA Division of Educational Psychology, and the American Psychological Foundation Gold Medal. Her publications include *Psychological Testing, Differential Psychology*, and *Fields of Applied Psychology*, as well as some 150 monographs and journal articles.

ANNE ANASTASI

PSYCHOLOGICAL TESTING: BASIC CONCEPTS AND COMMON MISCONCEPTIONS

As I thought about the purpose of the G. Stanley Hall Lectures and about the audience to which they are addressed, I decided to orient my presentation toward three major objectives. The first objective is to consider what test users, test takers, and undergraduates in general should know about contemporary psychological testing. This rather broad objective covers both an overview of basic concepts and an updating of information. The second is to examine some of the most prevalent popular misconceptions about tests that lead to misuses of tests and misinterpretation of test scores. The third is to illustrate how complex and sophisticated concepts and methodologies can be presented simply and in readily comprehensible terms. I shall illustrate my own efforts to meet the third objective with the treatment of statistical topics, ranging from the standard deviation to factor analysis and item response theory. The three objectives are not segregated into different sections of this paper, but are intermingled within my discussions of appropriate topics.

How to Evaluate a Psychological Test

The fundamental question that a nonspecialist needs to answer about tests is, "How can I evaluate or judge a test?" This question can, in turn, be broken down into more specific questions. First, what kind of information can this test provide about the person who takes it? Second, how good is this test—that is, how well does it meet general standards that apply to all tests? Third, how well does the test fit the particular purpose for which it is to be used?

Much of the information needed to answer these questions can be found in a properly prepared technical manual, which should accompany any test that is ready for operational use. Some of the more responsible test publishers also provide simplified but accurate versions of the necessary information, in order to help technically untrained persons to gain some understanding of particular tests. An outstanding example is the booklet about the Scholastic Aptitude Test entitled *Taking the SAT*, distributed by the College Entrance Examination Board (1983a, 1983b, 1983c), together with the accompanying slide shows for use by counselors in orienting students. Informative brochures have likewise been developed for the Graduate Record Examination and for several other testing programs conducted by Educational Testing Service. A few major commercial publishers have also taken steps to disseminate explanatory materials among test takers and other concerned groups.

Despite the availability of these simplified materials that are designed for the general public, the *test user* cannot properly evaluate a test without having some familiarity with the major steps in test construction and some knowledge of the principal psychometric features of tests, especially as they pertain to norms, reliability, and validity. By test user, as contrasted to test constructor, I mean essentially anyone who has the responsibility either for choosing tests or for interpreting scores and using them as one source of information in reaching practical decisions. Many test users serve both of these functions. Test users include teachers, counselors, educational administrators, testing coordinators, personnel workers in industry or government, clinicians who use tests as aids in their practice, and many others in an increasing number and variety of real-life contexts. Anyone responsible for choosing tests or using test results needs some technical knowledge in order to understand the tests properly. If a test user, in this sense, lacks adequate background for this purpose, he or she needs access to a properly qualified supervisor or consultant. Many current criticisms of tests are actually directed not to the tests themselves, but rather to misuses of tests by unqualified users.

Instructors of undergraduate psychology can serve a dual role in helping to disseminate accurate information about testing and thereby combating misuses and misinterpretation of scores. First, they can contribute through what they transmit to the students in their own classes. Second, they can serve as resource persons to answer special questions that will surely be directed to them, not only by students in general, but also by colleagues, parents, and members of the general public. Therefore, undergraduate psychology instructors, whatever their own fields of specialization, need to know somewhat more about the technical properties of tests than would be required for one or two class periods or even for an undergraduate course in psychological testing.

The instructor should be familiar with general sources of information about tests, such as the *Mental Measurements Yearbooks* (MMY). In addition to providing routine information (publisher, price, forms, age levels), these yearbooks include critical reviews by one or more test specialists and a complete bibliography of published references about the tests. The publication of the MMY is now handled by the Buros Institute of Mental Measurements, located at the University of Nebraska.[1] The ninth MMY is in preparation. Beginning in 1983, the test entries of the MMY, together with the critical reviews, are also being included in the online computer service for the Buros Institute database, which is offered through Bibliographic Retrieval Services, Inc. (BRS). Each month, updates are transmitted to this retrieval service as they become available. BRS coverage has been extended back to 1977, with some retrospective coverage for selected entries. This retrieval service can be obtained by communicating with the yearbook editor at the Buros Institute.

Another important reference is the test standards prepared by the American Psychological Association (APA) in collaboration with two other national associations concerned with testing, the American Educational Research Association and the National Council on Measurement in Education. The first edition was published in 1954; subsequent editions appeared in 1966 and 1974. A fourth edition is now in press. These standards provide a succinct but comprehensive summary of recommended practices in test construction, reflecting the current state of knowledge in the field. The later editions give increasing attention to proper test use and to the correct interpretation and application of test results.

Norms and the Interpretation of Test Scores

There are several psychometric features of tests that a test user should know about. First, there is the concept of norms. A common error among the general public, including undergraduates, is to confuse *percentile scores* with traditional *percentage scores*. The difference, of course, is that the former refer to people and the latter to items.

---

[1]Contact James V. Mitchell, Jr., Editor; Buros Institute of Mental Measurements; University of Nebraska—Lincoln; 135 Bancroft Hall; Lincoln, NE 68588. Telephone: (402) 472-1739.

The latter, moreover, are raw scores, in the sense that they do not carry a built-in interpretation. If a child gets 50 percent correct on an arithmetic test, one cannot judge whether this performance is good, bad, or indifferent. If the difficulty level of the test were altered, the percentage correct that resulted could vary from 0 to 100. By contrast, a 50th percentile score indicates that this child performs like the typical individual of comparable experiential background. This example illustrates why norms are needed in the first place; it is one way to introduce the concept of norms.

Another source of truly prodigious confusion is the IQ. Much of this confusion is associated with the psychological rather than the statistical interpretation of this score, to which I shall return later. In its purely psychometric aspects, the IQ began as a ratio between mental age and chronological age. Although it was used for several decades, this type of score was eventually abandoned because of its many technical deficiencies, including the fact that it did not yield comparable scores at different ages. Moreover, it was applicable only to traits that showed a regular increase with age, and it did not apply at all to adults except through a bizarre sort of logical extrapolation. Thus the ratio IQ was abandoned—well and good! It seems, however, that the term fulfilled a special popular need for magic and for simple answers. Hence was born the deviation IQ, which is nothing more than a standard score with an IQ label attached to it.

Because standard scores in various forms are today the most common type of test score, they need to be explained. This is also a good place to introduce the student to the standard deviation (SD); without an acquaintance with the SD, one cannot go very far in understanding modern psychology. Here let me confess to a strong bias on my part: I draw a sharp distinction between the mechanics of statistical computation and the understanding of statistical concepts. In my statistics courses, I taught both, but the concepts always preceded the computation. In other courses, I taught the concepts only and let the computation go unless it was needed for a special purpose. For this reason, I always presented the basic formulas, which might or might not be followed by the short-cut formulas with labor-saving devices. It has been my observation that when students are taught the short-cut formulas first, such as computing the SD or the Pearson r with raw scores and correction term in lieu of deviations, they usually learn to go through the necessary motions and arrive at an answer. But they rarely understand what they are doing, why they do it, or what the answer means.

In teaching about the SD, I like to begin with our efforts to describe the performance of a group. We start with the mean, which provides a single number that best characterizes the group as a whole. Then we ask what more we want to know about the group, especially if we want to compare it with another group. Pretty soon, the idea of the extent of individual differences (that is, variability) emerges. After working our way through the range and its limitations, someone is bound to come up with the idea of finding the difference between each person's score and the mean. Averaging these differences should tell us something. But unfortunately, the plus and minus deviations add up to zero, because that is one of the properties of the mean. So how do we get rid of those minus numbers? It soon becomes clear that the only mathematically defensible way of doing so is to square each deviation and take the square root of their mean. I used to go through the same sort of process in arriving at the basic formula for the Pearson r, which incidentally, can be logically derived by recognizing the need for standard scores to express the two variables in comparable units.

So much for statistics. Before I leave the topic of norms, let me consider so-called *criterion-referenced tests* (see Anastasi, 1982, pp. 94–98, 419–420). I say "so-called" because the label is a bit confusing. In psychometrics, the *criterion* generally refers to some independent, external measure that the test is designed to predict, such as a direct measure of job performance used in evaluating an applicant selection test. The criterion-referenced tests, however, can be more accurately described as content-referenced. Typically, such tests use as their interpretive frame of reference a specified *content domain* rather than a specified population of persons. The focus is on what the individual can do and what he or she knows, rather than on how the individual compares with others. Several other terms have been proposed by different writers, such as *domain-referenced* and *objective-referenced*. However, criterion-referenced has remained the most popular term. I shall therefore use it in this discussion, even though it is not the most appropriate term.

When first introduced some twenty years ago (Glaser, 1963), criterion-referenced tests were regarded as an alternative to norm-referenced tests, which represented a fundamentally different approach to testing. Actually, criterion-referenced and normative interpretations can in fact be combined to provide a fuller evaluation of the individual's performance on certain types of tests. Several recently developed tests for assessing mastery of specific subject-matter areas do in fact combine both interpretations. This is illustrated by the Stanford Diagnostic Test in reading and in mathematics and by the Metropolitan Instructional Tests in reading, mathematics, and language (both series published by The Psychological Corporation).

Thus far, criterion-referenced testing has found its major applications in education, especially in individualized instructional systems in which testing is closely integrated with instruction. Administered at different stages, these tests are used to check on prerequisite skills, diagnose learning difficulties, and prescribe subsequent instructional procedures. Criterion-referenced tests have also been used in broad surveys of educational accomplishment, such as the National Assessment of Educational Progress (Womer, 1970), and in meeting demands for educational accountability (Gronlund, 1974). Testing for the attainment of minimum requirements, as in qualifying for a driver's license or a pilot's license, also utilize essentially criterion-referenced testing. A related application is in testing for job proficiency where the mastery of a small number of clearly defined skills is to be assessed, as in many military occupational specialties (Maier & Hirshfeld, 1978; Swezey & Pearlstein, 1975).

In general, criterion-referenced tests are most suitable for assessing minimum competency in readily identifiable basic skills. A fundamental requirement for the construction of this type of test is a generally accepted domain of knowledge or skills to be assessed. The selected domain must then be subdivided into small units that are defined in highly specific behavioral terms, such as "multiplies three-digit by two-digit numbers" or "identifies the misspelled word in which the final *e* is retained when adding *-ing.*" Unless the content domain is itself quite narrowly limited, it is difficult to include a representative content sample in the test. Without such careful specification and control of content, however, the results of criterion-referenced testing could degenerate into an idiosyncratic and uninterpretable jumble. The approach is limited chiefly to testing for basic skills in well-established subject-matter areas. While useful in providing supplementary information in such contexts, criterion-referenced testing does not represent a new approach to testing, and its application presents several technical as well as practical difficulties (Angoff, 1974; Ebel, 1962, 1972).

Reliability and Measurement Error

A second major concept relevant to test evaluation is that of reliability (Anastasi, 1982, chap. 5). In psychometric terminology, reliability means consistency of performance. Specifically, it refers to the consistency of the scores obtained by the same persons when reexamined with the same test on different occasions, or with different sets of equivalent items, or under other variable examining conditions. In its broadest sense, test reliability indicates the extent to which individual differences in test scores are attributable to "true" differences in the characteristics under consideration and the extent to which they are attributable to chance errors. In other words, measures of test reliability make it possible to estimate what proportion of the total variance of test scores is *error variance*. The crux of the matter, however, lies in the definition of error variance. Factors that might be considered error variance for one purpose would be included under true variance for another. For example, if one is interested in measuring fluctuations of mood, then the day-by-day score changes on a test of cheerfulness–depression would be relevant to the purpose of the test and would thus be part of the true variance of the scores. If, on the other hand, the test is designed to assess more durable personality traits, the daily fluctuations would fall under the heading of error variance.

This distinction is illustrated by some current tests designed to yield separate measures of traits and states, such as the State–Trait Anxiety Inventory developed by Spielberger and his associates (Spielberger, Gorsuch, & Lushene, 1970). Another example is provided by Atkinson's use of an adaptation of the Thematic Apperception Test (TAT) cards in assessing achievement drive (Atkinson, 1981; Atkinson & Birch, 1978, pp. 370–374). Using a computer simulation, Atkinson demonstrated that it is possible to obtain a construct validity as high as .90, with a reliability across cards as low as .07. According to Atkinson's theory of motivation, the individual responds to the successive cards through a continuous stream of activity, which reflects the rise and fall in the relative strength of different behavior tendencies. When a behavior tendency is expressed in activity, its strength is thereby reduced. Consequently, fluctuations in the expression of a particular drive would be expected in the course of taking the test. If responses are aggregated across cards, however, one can identify individual differences in drive strength that correspond to stable traits over time. In this example, reliability over time, as well as validity, would be high, while internal-consistency reliability would be low.

There could, of course, be as many varieties of test reliability as there are conditions affecting test scores. But in standardized test administration, most irrelevant variance is minimized by controlling the testing environment, instructions, time limits, rapport, and other testing conditions. The kinds of reliability measured in actual practice, therefore, are few. The major sources of error variance arise from time sampling and content sampling. Retest reliability provides a measure of stability over time. If alternate forms are administered on different occasions, the error variance arises from both temporal fluctuations and differences between the specific items or content sampled in the two test forms. Split-half reliability, such as commonly found by analyzing scores on odd and even items, measures only reliability across content samples, or the consistency of performance on two sets of comparable items administered at the same time. This reliability is often labeled a measure of internal consistency of the test.

Another measure of reliability frequently reported in test manuals is that developed by Kuder and Richardson (1937). Again utilizing a single administration of a single test form, the K-R reliability is based on the consistency of responses to all items in the test. This *interitem consistency* is influenced by two sources of error variance: (a) content sampling, as in alternate-form and split-half reliability; and (b) heterogeneity of the behavior domain sampled. The more homogeneous the domain, the higher the interitem consistency. For example, if one test includes only multiplication items, while another comprises addition, subtraction, multiplication, and division items, the former will probably exhibit more interitem consistency than the latter. It can be shown mathematically that the K-R reliability coefficient is actually the mean of all possible split-half coefficients resulting from different splits of a test (Cronbach, 1951).[2] The ordinary split-half coefficient, on the other hand, is based on a planned split designed to yield equivalent sets of items. Hence, unless the test items are highly homogeneous, the K-R coefficient will be lower than the split-half reliability. In fact, the difference between these two coefficients may serve as a rough index of the homogeneity of the test.

The K-R formula is applicable to tests whose items are scored as right or wrong, or according to some other pass-fail system. Some tests, however, may have multiple-scored items. On a personality inventory, for example, the respondent may receive a different numerical score on an item, depending on whether he or she checks "usually," "sometimes," "rarely," or "never." For such tests, a generalized measure is available, known as coefficient alpha (Cronbach, 1951; Novick & Lewis, 1967; for a clear computational layout, see Ebel, 1965, pp. 328–330). Although requiring a little more computational labor, coefficient alpha is interpreted in the same way as the Kuder-Richardson coefficient.

Another source of error variance that has received some attention is *scorer variance*. Most tests provide sufficiently objective and standardized scoring procedures to ensure empirical uniformity of scoring. Certain types of tests, however, leave a good deal to the judgment of the examiner or scorer. This is especially true of clinical instruments employed in intensive individual examinations, as well as projective tests of personality and some creativity tests. For such tests, scorer reliability may be found by having a sample of test papers independently scored by two examiners and correlating the two sets of scores. When several scorers are to be compared, two-way analysis of variance and intraclass correlation may be employed for the same purpose.

The reliability coefficient, however computed, is itself a measure of the percentage (or proportion) of error variance in the test score. This is one case in which a correlation coefficient corresponds directly to a percentage and can be interpreted as such. For example, a reli-

---

[2]This is strictly true only when the split-half coefficients are found by the Rulon formula, based on the variance of the differences between the two half-scores, not when the coefficients are found by correlation of halves and the Spearman-Brown formula (Novick & Lewis, 1967).

ability coefficient of .85 signifies that 85 percent of the variance in test scores depends on true variance in the trait measured and 15 percent depends on error variance (as operationally defined by the procedures followed). This interpretation frequently causes confusion, because students learned in general statistics that it is the square of a correlation coefficient that represents proportion of common variance. Actually, the proportion of true variance in test scores is the square of the correlation between scores on a single form of the test and true scores, free from chance errors. This correlation, known as the index of reliability,[3] is equal to the square root of the reliability coefficient. Hence, when the index of reliability is squared, the result is the reliability coefficient, which can therefore be interpreted directly as the percentage of true variance.

A particularly useful application of test reliability to the interpretation of an individual's test scores is provided by the standard error of measurement (SEM). So important is the SEM for this purpose that the College Board includes data on the SEM and an explanation of its use, not only in brochures distributed to high school and college counselors and the accompanying slide show, but also in the individual score reports sent to students (College Entrance Examination Board, 1983c, 1984a, 1984b). Given the reliability coefficient of a test (r_{tt}) and the standard deviation (*SD*) of its scores obtained on the same group, the SEM can be computed with a simple formula: SEM = $SD \sqrt{1-r_{tt}}$. When so computed, the SEM is expressed in the same units as the test scores. With it, the probable range of fluctuation of an individual's score that resulted from irrelevant, chance factors can be estimated.

More and more tests today are reporting scores not as a single number, but as a score band within which the individual's true score is likely to fall. These score bands are found by employing the familiar normal curve frequencies to establish specified confidence intervals. Thus a distance of ±1 SEM from the obtained score yields a probability of roughly 2:1 (or 68:32) that the individual's true score falls within that range. Similarly, the 95 percent confidence interval can be found by taking ±1.96 SEM; and ±2.58 SEM gives the 99 percent confidence interval.

The use of such score bands is a safeguard against placing undue emphasis on a single numerical score. It is also useful in interpreting differences between scores. The SEM can be used to compute the statistical significance of score differences between persons on the same test or score differences within the individual on different tests. The latter is especially important in score pattern analysis, as on the

---

[3]Derivations of the index of reliability, based on two different sets of assumptions, can be found in Gulliksen (1950, chaps. 2 and 3). See also Guilford and Fruchter (1978, pp. 411–412).

Wechsler scales and on multiple aptitude batteries such as the Differential Aptitude Tests (DAT). The test manuals for such tests now regularly include the data that are needed to identify the smallest score difference corresponding to specified significance levels. Users are cautioned against drawing conclusions from differences that fall below these limits and that may therefore indicate no more than chance fluctuations.

Validity: What Does a Test Measure?

And now I come to test validity, which is undoubtedly the most basic and pervasive feature of any test (Anastasi, 1982, chaps. 6–7). The validity of a test concerns what the test measures and how well it does so. It indicates what can be inferred from test results, and it enables users to judge how well the test meets their particular assessment needs. Obviously, validity relates to all three questions that were cited earlier as the essential elements of test evaluation.

Validity in the Test Development Process

Many test manuals are still organized in accordance with the traditional view that validity is one among several technical properties of a test and that it belongs in the later stages of test development. Certainly that is the impression created as one reads most manuals. For several decades, there has also been a widespread belief that there are three distinct kinds or aspects of validity, namely, content, criterion-related, and construct validity (APA et al., 1974). When first introduced in the 1954 *Technical Recommendations* (APA et al.), this tripartite classification brought some order and uniformity into what was then a rather chaotic approach to test validity. Soon, however, there appeared a tendency to reify the three validities, to apply them too rigidly, and to lean on the labels for support. Initially this rigidity was manifested by the acceptance of content validation as applicable to achievement tests; of criterion-related validation as appropriate for personnel selection and classification and for other essentially predictive uses of tests; and of construct validation as relevant principally to theoretically oriented basic research. Construct validation was looked upon with awe and great respect, but usually kept at arm's length by practical test users. More recently, this tripartite rigidity has taken on another, more global form. There seems to be a compulsion, exemplified in several recent test manuals, to do something—anything—that could be classified under each of the three headings, regardless of the nature or purpose of the test. The results are then reported in three separate, neatly labeled sections. Once the three validities have been ticked off in checklist fashion, there is a relaxed feeling that validation requirements have been met.

In contrast to such rigid approaches, it is now being gradually recognized that validity is built into a test through a wide variety of possible procedures—many more than three. These procedures are employed sequentially, at different stages of test construction (Guion, 1983; Jackson, 1970, 1973). The validation process begins with the definition of the constructs to be assessed. These definitions may be derived from psychological theory, from prior research, or from analyses of real-life behavior domains, as illustrated by functional job analyses or curricular surveys. In psychometric terminology, a construct is a theoretical concept of varying degrees of abstraction or generalizability. It corresponds closely to what is commonly termed a trait. Constructs may be simple and narrowly defined, such as speed of walking or spelling ability, or they may be complex and broadly generalizable, such as abstract reasoning or scholastic aptitude. The formulation of detailed specifications for subtests and test items is guided by available knowledge about the constructs to be included. Items are then written to meet these specifications. Empirical item analyses follow, with the selection of the most effective (i.e., most valid) items from the initial item pool. Other appropriate internal analyses may also be carried out, including factor analyses of item clusters or subtests. The final stage includes validating and cross-validating various scores through statistical analyses against external, real-life criteria.

It should be noted that almost any information gathered in the process of developing or using a test is relevant to its validity. It is relevant in the sense that it contributes to an understanding of what the test measures. Certainly, data on internal consistency and on retest reliability help to define the homogeneity of the construct and its temporal stability. Norms may well provide additional construct specification, especially if they include separate normative data for subgroups classified by age, sex, or other demographic variables that affect test performance. Remember that systematic age increment was a major criterion in the development of early intelligence tests, such as the Stanford-Binet.

Actually, the entire test development process contributes to construct validation, whatever the nature or purpose of the test. If one considers procedures rather than labels, it becomes clear that content analyses and correlations with external criteria fit into particular stages in the process of construct validation, that is, in the process of both determining and demonstrating what a test measures. In a 1980 article, Messick (1980b) argued convincingly that the term validity, insofar as it designates the interpretive meaningfulness of a test, should be reserved for construct validity. He maintained that other procedures with which the term validity has traditionally been associated should be designated by more specifically descriptive names. Thus, content validity could be called content relevance and content coverage to refer to domain specifications and domain representativeness, respectively. Criterion-related validity could be labeled predictive utility and diagnostic utility to correspond to predictive and diagnostic uses. These changes in terminology would help, but it may be some time before the old terms can be dislodged. In the meantime, we should not be misled by rigid applications of the traditional terminology.

Item Analysis

In my rapid overview of test construction stages, I referred to two statistical procedures that call for a closer look in their own right. They are item analysis and factor analysis. Some acquaintance with the basic concepts and techniques of item analysis (Anastasi, 1982, chap. 8; see also pp. 301–304, 410–413) can help test users in their evaluation of published tests. Items can be examined qualitatively, on the basis of their content and form, and quantitatively, on the basis of their statistical properties. Qualitative analysis concerns chiefly content relevance and content coverage. The necessary information for this evaluation is often given in achievement test manuals, in tables that show the number of items falling into different content categories. Items can also be examined with reference to effective item-writing guidelines (Gronlund, 1977; 1981, chaps. 5–7; Hopkins & Stanley, 1981, chap. 9; Thorndike & Hagen, 1977, chap. 7).

Quantitative techniques of item analysis cover principally statistical assessment of the difficulty and the discriminative value of items. The selection of items through these techniques influences both the reliability and the validity of the finished test. For ability tests, *item difficulty* is defined in terms of the percentage of persons who answer the item correctly. In personality inventories, the percentage of persons who answer the item in the keyed direction serves the same function for statistical analysis. In either case, the percentages may be converted to normal curve sigma-distances. The item values are thereby expressed on a scale of approximately equal units, on the assumption that the trait is normally distributed. Items are chosen to fit the specified level and range of difficulty for the particular testing purpose. For most tests, which are designed to assess each person's performance level with maximum accuracy, the most suitable items are spread over a moderate difficulty range around the 50 percent level.

Item discrimination, the second major feature, refers essentially to the relation between performance on an item and standing on the trait under consideration. To investigate this relation, the persons who pass a given item and those who fail it may be compared either on an external criterion or on the total test score. In the initial stages of test development, the total test (or subtest) score provides a first approximation to a measure of the relevant trait or construct. The relation is usually expressed as a biserial correlation for each item.

It is apparent that the item statistics I have been considering are restricted to the samples from which they were derived. For several testing purposes, however, what is needed is item information applicable across samples that differ in ability level. In educational achievement tests, for example, it is advantageous to be able to compare a child's score over several grades on a uniform scale. Another example is provided by large-scale testing programs, such as that of the College Board, that need many equivalent test forms to be administered at different times (Donlon, 1984). It would be unfair to individuals to evaluate their scores in terms of their particular sample, insofar as the performance level of samples tested at different times of the year or in different years varies significantly.

Until recently, the standard procedure employed to provide a comparable scale across samples was some variant of Thurstone's (1925, 1947) absolute scaling. What is required for such scaling is the inclusion of a set of common anchor items in the test forms administered to two samples. By computing the mean and SD of the difficulty values of these anchor items in each of the two samples, a conversion formula can be worked out for translating all the item values obtained in one group into those of the other. A different set of anchor items can be used to link different pairs of groups. Each new form is linked to one or two earlier forms, which in turn are linked to other forms, through a chain extending back to the group chosen as the fixed reference group. For the College Board SAT, this reference group was the sample of approximately 11,000 candidates tested in 1941 (Donlon, 1984). Scales built in this way—from a fixed reference group—are analogous to scales used in physical measurement, in at least one respect. In measuring distance, for example, the foot is a convenient and uniform unit; we do not know nor care whose foot was originally measured to define this standard.

With the increasing availability of high-speed computers, more precise mathematical procedures have been developed to provide sample-free measurement scales for psychological tests (Baker, 1977; Hambleton & Cook, 1977; Lord, 1980; Weiss & Davison, 1981). These procedures were originally grouped under the general title of latent trait models. The basic measure they use is the probability that a person of specified ability (the so-called latent trait) succeeds on an item of specified difficulty. There is no implication, however, that such latent traits or underlying abilities exist in any physical or physiological sense, nor that they cause behavior. They are statistical constructs derived mathematically from empirically observed relations among test responses. A rough, initial estimate of an examinee's ability is the total score obtained on the test. In order to avoid the false impression created by the term, *latent trait,* some of the leading exponents of these procedures have substituted the term *item response theory,* or IRT (Lord, 1980; Weiss & Davison, 1981); this designation is now gaining usage within psychology.

By whatever name they may be called, these procedures utilize three parameters: item discrimination, item difficulty, and a lower-asymptote or "guessing" parameter corresponding to the probability of a correct response occurring by chance. Some simplified procedures, such as the Rasch model (Andersen, 1983; Wright, 1977), use only one parameter, the difficulty level, on the assumption that item differences on the other two parameters are negligible. But this assumption has to be empirically verified for different tests. IRT is gradually being incorporated in large-scale testing programs. For example, beginning in 1982, this model has been adopted for equating scores on the new forms of the SAT, so as to express them on the continuing uniform scale[4] (Donlon, 1984).

One of the most important applications of IRT is to be found in *computerized adaptive testing* (Green, 1983a, 1983b; Lord, 1977; Urry, 1977; Weiss, 1976). Also described as individualized, tailored, and response-contingent testing, this procedure adjusts item coverage to the responses actually given by each examinee. As the individual responds to each item, the computer chooses the next item. If an item is passed, it is followed by a more difficult item; if it is failed, an easier item follows. This will be recognized as the basic testing procedure used in individually administered intelligence tests, such as the Binet. Adaptive testing achieves the same objective in less time, with far greater precision, and without one-to-one administration by a trained examiner.

After each successive item is presented, the computer calculates the examinee's cumulative ability score, together with the error of measurement of that score. Testing is terminated when the error of measurement reaches a preestablished acceptable level. Exploratory research on computerized adaptive testing has been in progress in various contexts. Its operational use is under consideration in several large-scale testing programs in both civilian government agencies and the military services. An example is provided by current efforts to develop a computerized adaptive version of the Armed Services Vocational Aptitude Battery (ASVAB).

---

[4]However, selection of items for inclusion in any one form still currently follows the earlier procedures (i.e., equated difficulty values in terms of fixed reference group and biserial correlation with total score).

Factor Analysis

Factor analysis has been in use for several decades and is familiar to most psychologists. Hence, I shall merely touch upon some procedural highlights and say something about what factors mean. The principal object of factor analysis is to simplify the description of data by reducing the number of necessary variables or dimensions. For example, beginning with the intercorrelations among 20 tests, it may be possible to show that two or three factors are sufficient to account for nearly all the common variance in the set. These are the types of factors identified in such factor-analytic systems as Thurstone's primary mental abilities and Guilford's structure-of-intellect model. If the data are obtained from a sufficiently heterogeneous population, Spearman's *g* factor may emerge as a second-order factor to account for the correlations found among the factors themselves.

All techniques of factor analysis begin with a complete table of intercorrelations among a set of tests (or other variables), known as a correlation matrix.[5] Every factor analysis ends with a factor matrix, that is, a table showing the weight or loading of each of the factors in each test. It is also customary to represent factors geometrically as reference axes, in terms of which each test can be plotted as a point on a graph. This can easily be done if one works with two factors at a time; the results from successive graphs can then be combined mathematically. It should be noted that the position of the reference axes is not fixed by the data. The original correlation table determines the position of the tests only in relation to each other. The same points can be plotted with the reference axes in any position. For this reason factor analysts frequently rotate the axes until they obtain the most satisfactory and easily interpretable pattern. This is a legitimate procedure, somewhat analogous to measuring longitude from, say, Chicago rather than Greenwich.

Often the object of rotation is to approximate simple structure, that is, to describe each test with the minimum possible number of factors. Most factor patterns employ *orthogonal axes,* which are at right angles to each other. Occasionally, the test clusters are so situated that a better fit can be obtained with *oblique axes.* In such a case, the factors themselves will be correlated. It can be argued that meaningful categories for classifying individual differences need not be uncorrelated. For example, height and weight are highly correlated; yet they have proved to be useful categories in the measurement of physique. When the factors are correlated, the intercorrelations among the factors can themselves be factor analyzed to derive second-order factors. This process has been followed in several studies, with both aptitude and personality variables.

[5]A matrix is any rectangular arrangement of numbers into rows and columns.

There are several different methods for carrying out a factor analysis and for subsequent rotation of axes. The resulting factor matrices may look quite different. This has sometimes created the impression that the findings are arbitrary and artificial; occasionally, it has engendered controversies about the "true" solution. Actually, these factor matrices represent alternative and equally applicable ways of describing the same data. It has been shown that different factor solutions are mathematically interchangeable; they can be transformed one to another by computing the appropriate transformation matrix (Harman, 1976, pp. 338–341).

By whatever statistical procedures such factors are found, and however elaborate such procedures may be, we must bear in mind that the factors, like the test scores from which they were derived, are descriptive and not explanatory. The constructs identified through factor analysis do *not* represent underlying entities, causal factors, or fixed personal characteristics. There is an increasing accumulation of evidence showing the role of experiential background in the formation of factors (Anastasi, 1970, 1983a). It is not only the level of performance in different abilities, but also the way in which performance is organized into distinct traits, that is influenced by the individual's experiential history. Differences in factor patterns have been found to be associated with different cultures or subcultures, socioeconomic levels, and types of school curricula. Changes in factor patterns over time have also been observed. These include long-term changes, which may reflect the cumulative effects of everyday experience, as well as short-term changes resulting from practice and other experimentally controlled learning experiences. Research on animals has also yielded suggestive evidence regarding the experiential production of factors through the control of early experiences.

Validity Generalization

In the practical utilization of validity data, there are two important questions that have received increasing attention in recent years. The first pertains to validity generalization. Test manuals commonly report correlations between test scores and various practical criteria, in order to help the potential user in understanding what a test measures. Although a test user may not be directly concerned with the prediction of any of the specific criteria employed, by examining such criteria he or she is able to build up a concept of the behavior domain sampled by the test. If we follow this thinking a bit further, we can see that all test use and all interpretation of test scores imply construct validity. Because tests are rarely, if ever, used under conditions that are identical to those under which validity data were gathered, some degree of generalizability is inevitably involved. Thus, the interpretive meaning of test scores and their practical utilization is always based on constructs, which may vary widely in breadth or generalizability with regard to behavior domains, situations, and populations.

When standardized aptitude tests were first correlated with performance on presumably similar jobs in industrial validation studies, the validity coefficients were found to vary widely (Ghiselli, 1959, 1966). Similar variability among validity coefficients was observed when the criteria were grades in various academic courses (Bennett, Seashore, & Wesman, 1984). Such findings led to widespread pessimism regarding the generalizability of test validity across different situations. Until the mid-1970s so-called situational specificity of psychological requirements was generally regarded as a serious limitation in the usefulness of standardized tests in personnel selection[6] (Guion, 1976). In a sophisticated statistical analysis of the problem, however, Schmidt, Hunter, and their associates (Schmidt & Hunter, 1977; Schmidt, Hunter, & Pearlman, 1981) demonstrated that much of the variance among obtained validity coefficients may be a statistical artifact resulting from small sample size, criterion unreliability, and restriction of range in employee samples.

The industrial samples available for test validation are generally too small to yield a stable estimate of the correlation between predictor and criterion. For the same reason, the obtained coefficients may be too low to reach statistical significance in the sample investigated and may thus fail to provide evidence of the test's validity. It has been estimated that about half of the validation samples used in industrial studies include no more than 40 or 50 cases (Schmidt, Hunter, & Urry, 1976). This is also true of the samples often employed in educational settings to compute validity coefficients against grades in particular courses or specialized training programs (Bennett, Seashore, & Wesman, 1984). With such small samples, criterion-related validation is likely to yield inconclusive and uninterpretable results within any single study.

By applying some newly developed techniques to data from many samples drawn from a large number of occupational specialties, Schmidt, Hunter, and their co-workers were able to show that the validity of tests of verbal, numerical, and abstract reasoning aptitudes can be generalized far more widely across occupations than had heretofore been recognized (Pearlman, Schmidt, & Hunter, 1980; Schmidt, Gast-Rosenberg, & Hunter, 1980; Schmidt, Hunter, Pearlman, & Shane, 1979). The variance of validity coefficients typically found in earlier industrial studies proved to be no greater than

---

[6]Situational specificity has played a different and significant role in both the theory and practice of personality testing (see Anastasi, 1983b; Mischel, 1977, 1979; Mischel & Peake, 1982).

would be expected by chance. This was true even when the particular job functions appeared to be quite dissimilar across jobs. Evidently, the successful performance of a wide variety of occupational tasks depends to a significant degree on a common core of cognitive skills. It would seem that this cluster of cognitive skills and knowledge is broadly predictive of performance in both academic and occupational activities demanded in advanced technological societies.

Differential Validity

The second question of special relevance to the test user concerns differential validity. From a practical standpoint, we should bear in mind that the term *differential validity* is currently used in two different senses, one referring to different criteria, the other to different populations. When the term is used in the first sense, the goal of good test usage is to maximize differential validity; when it is used in the second sense, the goal is to minimize it.

Classification Decisions

Differential validity against separate criteria is a major consideration when tests are used for classification purposes, as contrasted with selection. In selection decisions, each individual is either accepted or rejected, as in admitting students to college or hiring job applicants. In classification decisions, no one is rejected or eliminated from the program. Rather, all are assigned to appropriate treatment, so as to maximize the effectiveness of outcomes. One example of classification decisions is the assignment of individuals from an available personnel pool to training programs for occupational specialties. Another example is the counseling of students regarding field of concentration and career choice.

Ideally, a classification battery should include tests that yield very different validity coefficients with different criteria. The object of such a battery is to predict the *differences* between each person's performance in two or more jobs or other criterion situations. In the use of batteries for occupational classification, we need to identify the major constructs covered by the tests, on the one hand, and those covered by the job functions, on the other. The procedures used for this purpose can be illustrated by factor analysis of the tests and by job analysis expressed in terms of critical behavioral requirements. Validity generalization can then be investigated within functional job families, that is, groups of jobs that share major behavioral constructs, regardless of superficial task differences.

Such dual analyses of tests and jobs have been applied with promising results in recent research on the validity of the General Aptitude Test Battery (GATB) for some 12,000 jobs described in the *Dictionary of Occupational Titles* of the U.S. Employment Service (U.S. Department of Labor, 1983a, 1983b, 1983c). For this analysis, the jobs were classified into five functional job families. Factor analyses of the test battery yielded three broad group factors, identified as cognitive, perceptual, and psychomotor abilities. A meta-analysis of data from over 500 U.S. Employment Service (USES) validation studies was then conducted with the newly developed validity generalization techniques. This procedure yielded estimated validities of the appropriate composites for all jobs within each job family.

A more narrowly focused demonstration of the dual identification of behavioral constructs in tests and criteria also utilized USES data (Gutenberg, Arvey, Osburn, & Jeanneret, 1983). In this study, the job analysis dimensions pertaining to decision making and information processing correlated positively with the validities of the cognitive GATB tests (general, verbal, and numerical aptitudes); and they correlated negatively with the validities of psychomotor tests (finger and manual dexterity). In other words, the more a job called for decision making and information processing, the higher was the correlation of job performance with the cognitive tests and the lower was its correlation with the psychomotor tests. There is evidence that these results, as well as those of the previously cited, more broadly oriented studies, reflect an underlying dimension of *job complexity*. This dimension seems to be a major determinant of the differential validity of tests for predicting job performance (U.S. Department of Labor, 1983c).

Test Bias

Differential validity with regard to populations (rather than criteria) is a major concept in discussions of test bias. One question asked in this connection is whether the test may be valid for the majority group and not valid for a minority group. This is sometimes called single-group validity. In accordance with this usage the term *differential validity* is reserved for situations where both groups yield statistically significant validity coefficients, but one is significantly higher than the other. Empirical research with ability tests administered to black and white samples in the United States has failed to support either of these hypotheses about group differences in test validity. A comprehensive meta-analysis covering 39 industrial studies demonstrated that the discrepancies in validity coefficients between blacks and whites did not exceed chance expectancy (Hunter, Schmidt, & Hunter, 1979). It could be argued that, because of inadequate sample sizes and other methodological limitations, these results are merely inconclusive. It is noteworthy, however, that no evidence of differential validity was found in well-designed, large-scale studies of industrial samples (Campbell, Crooks, Mahoney, & Rock, 1973) or of army personnel (Maier & Fuchs, 1973). In general, the methodologically sounder studies proved to be those less likely to find differential validity. Similar results have been obtained in numerous investigations of black and white college students (Breland, 1979). Validity coefficients of the SAT and other college admission tests for black students were generally as high as those obtained for white students, or higher. At a very different educational level, the same results were obtained with large samples of black and white first-grade schoolchildren (Mitchell, 1967). When two educational readiness tests were correlated with end-of-year grades, the validities of total scores and of subtests were closely similar for the two ethnic groups, although tending to run somewhat higher for the blacks.

Even when a test is equally valid for two groups, however, it is possible that criterion performance is underpredicted for one group and overpredicted for the other. This point can be more readily understood if we visualize the relation between test and criterion by means of the familiar scatter diagram or bivariate distribution.[7] If test scores are represented along the horizontal axis (X) and criterion measures along the vertical axis (Y), each individual can be plotted by a point showing his or her standing in both variables. The straight line fitted to these points is the regression line for the particular group. If both variables have been expressed as basic standard scores, the slope of the regression line is exactly equal to the Pearson r between test and criterion. Hence, any difference between the validity coefficients obtained for two groups is known as *slope bias*.

The regression lines for two groups may, however, have the same slope—they may be parallel lines—and yet they may intersect the Y-axis at different points. These points are the Y-intercepts of the two lines; hence such group differences are designated *intercept bias*. Parenthetically, the terms *test bias* and *test fairness* are often used to refer specifically to intercept bias. By whatever name, intercept bias means that the identical test score would correspond to different criterion scores if predicted from the separate regression lines of the two groups; or conversely, different test scores would predict the same criterion performance when obtained by a person in one or the other group. Suppose, for example, that the majority excels on the test, but majority and minority perform equally well on the criterion. Selecting all applicants in terms of a test cutoff established for the majority

---

[7]Technical discussions of this *regression model*, in relation to other models of test bias, can be found in Cleary (1968); Gross and Su (1975); Gulliksen and Wilks (1950); Humphreys (1952); Hunter, Schmidt, and Rauschenberger (1984); and Petersen and Novick (1976). See also Anastasi (1982, pp. 183–191).

group would thus discriminate unfairly against the minority. Under these conditions, use of the majority regression line for both groups *underpredicts* the criterion performance of minority group members. This situation is most likely to occur when a large proportion of test variance is irrelevant to criterion performance and measures functions in which the majority excels the minority. Systematic comparison of major behavioral constructs in both test and job performance provides a safeguard against choosing such a test.

If, however, the two groups differ in a third variable that correlates positively with both test and criterion, then the test will *overpredict* the performance of minority group members (Linn & Werts, 1971; Reilly, 1973). Under these conditions, the use of the same cut-off score for both groups favors the minority. The findings of empirical studies do in fact support this expectation. Well-controlled studies with tests in current use have found either no significant differences or, more often, a tendency to overpredict the criterion performance of minority groups and hence to favor the members of minority groups in selection decisions. Such results have been obtained in the prediction of college grades (Breland, 1979), law school grades (Linn, 1975), performance in military training programs (Maier & Fuchs, 1973; Shore & Marion, 1972), and a variety of industrial criteria (Campbell et al., 1973; Gael, Grant, & Ritchie, 1975a, 1975b; Grant & Bray, 1970; Hunter, Schmidt, & Rauschenberger, 1984).

Psychological Interpretation of Test Scores

It is apparent that the test user should be familiar with current developments in the statistical concepts and methodology employed in test construction. Such knowledge is essential in understanding the information provided in test manuals and related publications. And this information is the basis for both choosing an appropriate test and correctly interpreting the test scores. At the same time, the test user needs some knowledge of current developments in psychology. Common misuses and misinterpretations of tests often arise from misconceptions, not about the statistics of testing, but about the behavior the tests are designed to measure (Anastasi, 1967). I shall cite a few outstanding examples from ability testing, where current confusions and controversies are most conspicuous.

Aptitude and Achievement Tests

Let us consider the traditional distinction between aptitude and achievement tests (Anastasi, 1984). Aptitudes are typically defined more precisely than is intelligence, and they refer to more narrowly limited cognitive domains. Nevertheless, like intelligence, they have traditionally been contrasted with achievement in testing terminology. This contrast dates from the early days of testing, when it was widely assumed that achievement tests measured the effects of learning, whereas intelligence and aptitude tests measured so-called innate capacity, or potentiality, independently of learning. This approach to testing in turn reflected a simplistic conception of the operation of heredity and environment that prevailed in the 1920s and 1930s (Cravens, 1978; see also Anastasi, 1979).

These early beliefs led over the years to strange uses of tests, including attempts to compute some index, such as a ratio or a difference-score, that allegedly separated the influence of heredity from that of environment in the individual's performance. Thence arose such byproducts as the now defunct achievement quotient, as well as the still extant classification into underachievers and overachievers. Despite repeated efforts by testing specialists and psychological researchers to dispel the early misconceptions about aptitude and achievement tests, these misconceptions have proved highly viable among the general public and especially among some test users and test critics. One possible explanation for the survival of these beliefs is to be found in the popular desire for magic—the desire for easy answers, quick solutions, and shortcuts.

Actually, all cognitive tests, whatever they may be called, show what the individual is able to do at the time; they do not explain why the individual performs as he or she does. Both aptitude and achievement tests can be best described as tests of *developed abilities,* a term that is appearing increasingly often in current testing literature. Aptitude and achievement tests can be ordered along a continuum of developed abilities. Those near the center are so similar as to be nearly indistinguishable. As we approach the extreme positions, we can identify two major differences.

The first difference between aptitude and achievement tests pertains to *test use.* Traditional achievement tests are designed and used primarily to assess current status; traditional aptitude tests are designed and used to predict future performance. What can the individual learn—how far and how fast can he or she progress—when put through a particular course of study, educational program, industrial apprenticeship, or other systematic learning experience? At this point, the reader may be thinking that traditional achievement tests, too, can often serve as effective predictors of future learning. True! An achievement test in arithmetic is a good predictor of subsequent performance in an algebra class. And it must also be remembered that all tests show only what the individual can do at the time. How, then, can aptitude tests predict future progress? They can do so only by assessing the prerequisite skills and knowledge needed in order to advance toward the desired performance goal.

The second difference is to be found in the degree of *experiential specificity* underlying the construction of aptitude and achievement tests. Achievement tests are typically designed to reflect closely what the individual has learned within a clearly and narrowly defined knowledge domain; they are closely tied to a specified set of prior learning experiences. Obvious examples are a test in solid geometry, or medieval history, or motor vehicle operation. At the opposite extreme are tests like the Stanford-Binet, which specifies little about the experiential pool beyond growing up in the twentieth-century American culture.

Intelligence Tests

This brings me to the subject of intelligence tests, the most widely misunderstood of all aptitude tests. The scores from these tests, whether reported as IQs or by some more innocuous term, have been so commonly misinterpreted that group intelligence tests were banned from schools in several parts of the country. Individual tests like the Binet and Wechsler scales were usually retained, on the assumption that they were used by trained clinical psychologists and hence were less subject to misinterpretation—an assumption that may not always hold. Another attempted solution was the elimination of the terms *intelligence* and *IQ* from nearly all recently published or revised tests. These precautions may have helped, but they do not go very far in the face of persistent demands for shortcuts and quick answers.

If properly interpreted, however, such tests can serve important functions in many practical contexts. Let us consider what traditional intelligence tests actually measure (Anastasi, 1983c). First, like all cognitive tests, they can show only what the individual knows and can do at the time. Intelligence tests are descriptive, not explanatory. They do not reveal the causes of individual differences in performance. To investigate such causes, we need additional data from other sources such as the individual's experiential history. Second, the tests do not measure all of human intelligence. There are many kinds of intelligence. Each culture demands, fosters, and rewards a different set of abilities, which constitute intelligence within that culture. Research in cross-cultural psychology provides a rich store of examples to illustrate this fact (Berry, 1972; Goodnow, 1976; Neisser, 1976, 1979). A frequent cultural difference pertains to the emphasis placed on generalization and abstract thinking, and the extent to which behavior is linked to specific contexts.

It is apparent that the term *intelligence* is too broad to designate available intelligence tests. They can be more accurately described as measures of academic intelligence or scholastic aptitude. They measure a kind of intelligent behavior that is both developed by formal schooling and required for progress within the academic system. To help define the construct measured by these tests, there is a vast accumulation of data derived from both clinical observations and validation studies against academic and occupational criteria. The findings indicate that the particular combination of cognitive skills and knowledge sampled by these tests plays a significant part in much of what goes on in modern, technologically advanced societies. In the interpretation of intelligence test scores, the concept of a segment of intelligence, albeit a broadly applicable and widely demanded segment, is replacing that of a general, universal human intelligence.

Coaching and Test Validity

A question that has aroused considerable practical interest is that of coaching and test performance (Anastasi, 1981). Of particular concern is the possible effect of intensive coaching on such tests as the College Board SAT. On the one side, there are the rather extreme claims made by some commercial coaching schools. On the other, there is some well-designed research on this question, some of it conducted under the auspices of the College Board (Messick, 1980a; Messick & Jungeblut, 1981). In general, such research indicates that intensive drill on items similar to those on the SAT is unlikely to produce score gains appreciably larger than those found when students are retested with the SAT after a year of regular high school instruction. Any generalization about coaching as a whole, however, is likely to be misleading because of differences in the nature of the tests, the prior experiences of the samples examined, and the kind and duration of training provided in the coaching program. There are also methodological flaws that make the findings of several studies uninterpretable.

The basic question is not how far test scores can be improved by special training, but how such improvement relates to intellectual behavior in real-life contexts. To answer this question, we must differentiate among three approaches to improving test performance and consider how they affect the predictive validity of the test. The first is coaching, narrowly defined as intensive, short-term, massed drill, or "cramming," on items similar to those in the test. Insofar as such coaching raises test scores, it is likely to do so without corresponding improvement in criterion behavior. Hence, it thereby reduces test validity. It should be added that well-constructed tests employ item types shown to be least susceptible to such drill (Donlon, 1984; Evans & Pike, 1973).

A second approach, illustrated by the College Board (1983b) booklet, *Taking the SAT*, is designed to provide test-taking orientation and thereby minimize individual differences in prior test-taking experience. These differences represent conditions that affect test scores as such, without necessarily being reflected in the broader behavior domain to be assessed. Hence these test-orientation procedures should make the test a more valid instrument by reducing the influence of test-specific variance. Finally, training in broadly applicable cognitive skills, if effective, should improve the trainee's ability to cope with subsequent intellectual tasks. This improvement will and should be manifested in test performance. Insofar as both test scores and criterion performance are improved, this kind of training leaves test validity unchanged, while enhancing the individual's chances of attaining desired goals. Such broadly oriented training is receiving increasing attention today (Anastasi, 1983c). It reflects the growing recognition that the nature and extent of intellectual development depend on one's learning history.

References

American Psychological Association, American Educational Research Association, & National Council on Measurement in Education. (1954). *Technical recommendations for psychological tests and diagnostic techniques.* Washington, DC: American Psychological Association.

American Psychological Association, American Educational Research Association, & National Council on Measurement in Education. (1966). *Standards for educational and psychological tests and manuals.* Washington, DC: American Psychological Association.

American Psychological Association, American Educational Research Association, & National Council on Measurement in Education. (1974). *Standards for educational and psychological tests.* Washington, DC: American Psychological Association.

American Psychological Association, American Educational Research Association, & National Council on Measurement in Education. (in press). *Standards for educational and psychological testing.* Washington, DC: American Psychological Association.

Anastasi, A. (1967). Psychology, psychologists, and psychological testing. *American Psychologist, 22,* 297–306.

Anastasi, A. (1970). On the formation of psychological traits. *American Psychologist, 25,* 899–910.

Anastasi, A. (1979). A historian's view of the nature–nurture controversy [Review of *The triumph of evolution: American scientists and the heredity–environment controversy, 1900–1941*]. *Contemporary Psychology, 24,* 622–623.

Anastasi, A. (1981). Coaching, test sophistication, and developed abilities. *American Psychologist, 36,* 1086–1093.

Anastasi, A. (1982). *Psychological testing* (5th ed.). New York: Macmillan.

Anastasi, A. (1983a). Evolving trait concepts. *American Psychologist, 38,* 175–184.

Anastasi, A. (1983b). Traits, states, and situations: A comprehensive view. In H. Wainer & S. Messick (Eds.), *Principals of modern psychological measure-*

ment: A festschrift for Frederic M. Lord (pp. 345–356). Hillsdale. NJ: Erlbaum.

Anastasi, A. (1983c). What do intelligence tests measure? In S. B. Anderson & J. S. Helmick (Eds.), *On educational testing: Intelligence, performance standards, test anxiety, and latent traits* (pp. 5–28). San Francisco: Jossey-Bass.

Anastasi, A. (1984). Aptitude and achievement tests: The curious case of the indestructible strawperson. In B. S. Plake (Ed.), *Social and technical issues in testing: Implications for test construction and usage* (pp. 129–140). Hillsdale, NJ: Erlbaum.

Andersen, E. B. (1983). Analyzing data using the Rasch model. In S. B. Anderson & J. S. Helmick (Eds.), *On educational testing: Intelligence, performance standards, test anxiety, and latent traits* (pp. 193–223). San Francisco: Jossey-Bass.

Angoff, W. H. (1974). Criterion-referencing, norm-referencing, and the SAT. *College Board Review, 92,* 3–5,21.

Atkinson, J. W. (1981). Studying personality in the context of an advanced motivational psychology. *American Psychologist, 36,* 117–128.

Atkinson, J. W., & Birch, D. (1978). *An introduction to motivation* (2nd ed.). New York: Van Nostrand Reinhold.

Baker, F. B. (1977). Advances in item analysis. *Review of Educational Research, 47,* 151–178.

Bennett, G. K., Seashore, H. G., & Wesman, A. G. (1984). *Differential aptitude tests: Technical supplement.* Cleveland, OH: Psychological Corporation.

Berry, J. W. (1972). Radical cultural relativism and the concept of intelligence. In L. J. Cronbach & P. J. D. Drenth (Eds.), *Mental tests and cultural adaptations* (pp. 77–88). The Hague: Mouton.

Breland, H. M. (1979). *Population validity and college entrance measures* (College Board Research Monograph No. 8). New York: College Entrance Examination Board.

Campbell, J. T., Crooks, L. A., Mahoney, M. H., & Rock, D. A. (1973). *An investigation of sources of bias in the prediction of job performance.* Princeton, NJ: Educational Testing Service.

Cleary, T. A. (1968). Test bias: Prediction of grades of Negro and white students in integrated colleges. *Journal of Educational Measurement, 5,* 115–124.

College Entrance Examination Board (1983a). *The SAT: About taking the Scholastic Aptitude Test.* New York: Author. (Slide show to accompany 1983b)

College Entrance Examination Board (1983b). *Taking the SAT: A guide to the Scholastic Aptitude Test and the Test of Standard Written English.* New York: Author.

College Entrance Examination Board (1983c). *200–800: What does it all mean? How to interpret SAT and achievement test scores.* New York: Author. (Slide show to accompany 1984b)

College Entrance Examination Board (1984a). *ATP guide for high schools and colleges 1984–85.* New York: Author.

College Entrance Examination Board (1984b). *Your score report 1984–85.* New York: Author.

Cravens, H. (1978). *The triumph of evolution: American scientists and the heredity–environment controversy, 1900–1941.* Philadelphia: University of Pennsylvania Press.

Cronbach, L. J. (1951). Coefficient alpha and the internal structure of tests. *Psychometrika, 16,* 297–334.
Donlon, T. F. (Ed.) (1984). *The technical handbook for the College Board Scholastic Aptitude Test and achievement tests.* New York: College Entrance Examination Board.
Ebel, R. L. (1962). Content standard test scores. *Educational and Psychological Measurement, 22,* 15–25.
Ebel, R. L. (1965). *Measuring educational achievement.* Englewood Cliffs, NJ: Prentice-Hall.
Ebel, R. L. (1972). Some limitations of criterion-referenced measurement. In G. H. Bracht, K. D. Hopkins, & J. C. Stanley (Eds.), *Perspectives in educational and psychological measurement* (pp. 144–149). Englewood Cliffs, NJ: Prentice-Hall.
Evans, F. R., & Pike, L. W. (1973). The effects of instruction for three mathematics item formats. *Journal of Educational Measurement, 10,* 257–272.
Gael, S., Grant, D. L., & Ritchie, R. J. (1975a). Employment test validation for minority and nonminority clerks with work sample criteria. *Journal of Applied Psychology, 60,* 420–426.
Gael, S., Grant, D. L., & Ritchie, R. J. (1975b). Employment test validation for minority and nonminority telephone operators. *Journal of Applied Psychology, 60,* 411–419.
Ghiselli, E. E. (1959). The generalization of validity. *Personnel Psychology, 12,* 397–402.
Ghiselli, E. E. (1966). *The validity of occupational aptitude tests.* New York: Wiley.
Glaser, R. (1963). Instructional technology and the measurement of learning outcomes. *American Psychologist, 18,* 519–522.
Goodnow, J. J. (1976). The nature of intelligent behavior: Questions raised by cross-cultural studies. In L. B. Resnick (Ed.), *The nature of intelligence* (pp. 169–188). Hillsdale, NJ: Erlbaum.
Grant, D. L., & Bray, D. W. (1970). Validation of employment tests for telephone company installation and repair occupations. *Journal of Applied Psychology, 54,* 7–14.
Green, B. F. (1983a). Adaptive testing by computer. In R. B. Ekstrom (Ed.), *Measurement, technology, and individuality in education* (pp. 5–12). San Francisco: Jossey-Bass.
Green, B. F. (1983b). The promise of tailored tests. In H. Wainer & S. Messick (Eds.), *Principals of modern psychological measurement: A festschrift for Frederic M. Lord* (pp. 69–80). Hillsdale, NJ: Erlbaum.
Gronlund, N. E. (1974). *Determining accountability for classroom instruction.* New York: Macmillan.
Gronlund, N. E. (1977). *Constructing achievement tests* (2nd ed.). Englewood Cliffs, NJ: Prentice-Hall.
Gronlund, N. E. (1981). *Measurement and evaluation in teaching* (4th ed.). New York: Macmillan.
Gross, A. L., & Su, W. H. (1975). Defining a "fair" or "unbiased" selection model: A question of utilities. *Journal of Applied Psychology, 60,* 345–351.
Guilford, J. P., & Fruchter, B. (1978). *Fundamental statistics in psychology and education* (5th ed.). New York: McGraw-Hill.
Guion, R. M. (1976). Recruiting, selection, and job placement. In M. D. Dunnette (Ed.), *Handbook of industrial and organizational psychology* (pp. 777–828). Chicago: Rand McNally.

Guion, R. M. (1983, April). Disunity in the trinitarian concept of validity. In P. Sandifer (Chair), *Clearing away the cobwebs: A closer look at content validity.* Symposium conducted at the meeting of the American Educational Research Association, Montreal.

Gulliksen, H. (1950). *Theory of mental tests.* New York: Wiley.

Gulliksen, H., & Wilks, S. S. (1950). Regression tests for several samples. *Psychometrika, 15,* 91–114.

Gutenberg, R. L., Arvey, R. D., Osburn, H. G., & Jeanneret, R. R. (1983). Moderating effects of decision-making/information-processing job dimensions on test validities. *Journal of Applied Psychology, 68,* 602–608.

Hambleton, R. K., & Cook, L. L. (1977). Latent trait models and their use in the analysis of educational test data. *Journal of Educational Measurement, 14,* 75–96.

Harman, H. H. (1976). *Modern factor analysis* (3rd ed.). Chicago: University of Chicago Press.

Hopkins, K. D., & Stanley, J. C. (1981). *Educational and psychological measurement and evaluation* (6th ed.). Englewood Cliffs, NJ: Prentice-Hall.

Humphreys, L. G. (1952). Individual differences. *Annual Review of Psychology, 3,* 131–150.

Hunter, J. E., Schmidt, F. L., & Hunter, R. (1979). Differential validity of employment tests by race: A comprehensive review and analysis. *Psychological Bulletin, 86,* 721–735.

Hunter, J. E., Schmidt, F. L., & Rauschenberger, J. (1984). Methodological, statistical, and ethical issues in the study of bias in psychological tests. In C. E. Reynolds (Ed.), *Perspectives on bias in mental testing* (pp. 41–99). New York: Plenum.

Jackson, D. N. (1970). A sequential system for personality scale development. In C. D. Spielberger (Ed.), *Current topics in clinical and community psychology* (vol. 2, pp. 61–96). New York: Academic Press.

Jackson, D. N. (1973). Structured personality assessment. In B. B. Wolman (Ed.), *Handbook of general psychology* (pp. 775–792). Englewood Cliffs, NJ: Prentice-Hall.

Kuder, G. F., & Richardson, M. W. (1937). The theory of estimation of test reliability. *Psychometrika, 2,* 151–160.

Linn, R. L. (1975). Test bias and the prediction of grades in law school. *Journal of Legal Education, 27,* 293–323.

Linn, R. L., & Werts, C. E. (1971). Considerations for studies of test bias. *Journal of Educational Measurement, 8,* 1–4.

Lord, F. M. (1977). A broad-range tailored test of verbal ability. *Applied Psychological Measurement, 1,* 95–100.

Lord, F. M. (1980). *Applications of item response theory to practical testing problems.* Hillsdale, NJ: Erlbaum.

Maier, M. H., & Fuchs, E. F. (1973). *Effectiveness of selection and classification testing* (Res. Rep. 1179). Arlington, VA: U.S. Army Research Institute for the Behavioral and Social Sciences.

Maier, M. H., & Hirshfeld, S. F. (1978). *Criterion-referenced job proficiency testing: A large scale application* (Res. Rep. 1193). Arlington, VA: U.S. Army Research Institute for the Behavioral and Social Sciences.

Messick, S. (1980a). *The effectiveness of coaching for the SAT: Review and reanalysis of research from the fifties to the FTC.* Princeton, NJ: Educational Testing Service.

Messick, S. (1980b). Test validity and the ethics of assessment. *American Psychologist, 35,* 1012–1027.

Messick, S., & Jungeblut, A. (1981). Time and method in coaching for the SAT. *Psychological Bulletin, 89,* 191–216.

Mischel, W. (1977). On the future of personality measurement. *American Psychologist, 32,* 246–254.

Mischel, W. (1979). On the interface of cognition and personality: Beyond the person–situation debate. *American Psychologist, 34,* 740–754.

Mischel, W., & Peake, P. K. (1982). Beyond déjà vu in the search for cross-situational consistency. *Psychological Review, 89,* 730–755.

Mitchell, B. C. (1967). Predictive validity of the Metropolitan Readiness Tests and the Murphy-Durrell Reading Readiness Analysis for white and Negro pupils. *Educational and Psychological Measurement, 27,* 1047–1054.

Neisser, U. (1976). General, academic, and artificial intelligence. In L. B. Resnick (Ed.), *The nature of intelligence* (pp. 135–144). Hillsdale, NJ: Erlbaum.

Neisser, U. (1979). The concept of intelligence. *Intelligence, 3,* 217–227.

Novick, M. R., & Lewis, C. (1967). Coefficient alpha and the reliability of composite measurements. *Psychometrika, 32,* 1–13.

Pearlman, K., Schmidt, F. L., & Hunter, J. E. (1980). Validity generalization results for tests used to predict job proficiency and training success in clerical occupations. *Journal of Applied Psychology, 65,* 373–406.

Petersen, N. S., & Novick, M. R. (1976). An evaluation of some models for culture-fair selection. *Journal of Educational Measurement, 13,* 3–29.

Reilly, R. R. (1973). A note on minority group test bias studies. *Psychological Bulletin, 80,* 130–132.

Schmidt, F. L., Gast-Rosenberg, L., & Hunter, J. E. (1980). Validity generalization results for computer programmers. *Journal of Applied Psychology, 65,* 643–661.

Schmidt, F. L., & Hunter, J. E. (1977). Development of a general solution to the problem of validity generalization. *Journal of Applied Psychology, 62,* 529–540.

Schmidt, F. L., Hunter, J. E., & Pearlman, K. (1981). Task differences as moderators of aptitude test validity in selection: A red herring. *Journal of Applied Psychology, 66,* 166–185.

Schmidt, F. L., Hunter, J. E., Pearlman, K., & Shane, G. S. (1979). Further tests of the Schmidt-Hunter Bayesian validity generalization model. *Personnel Psychology, 32,* 257–281.

Schmidt, F. L., Hunter, J. E., & Urry, V. W. (1976). Statistical power in criterion-related validation studies. *Journal of Applied Psychology, 61,* 473–485.

Shore, C. W., & Marion, R. (1972). *Suitability of using common selection test standards for Negro and white airmen* (AFHRL-TR-72-53). Lackland Air Force Base, TX: Personnel Research Division, Air Force Human Resources Laboratory.

Spielberger, C. D., Gorsuch, R. L., & Lushene, R. E. (1970). *STAI manual for the State–Trait Anxiety Inventory.* Palo Alto, CA: Consulting Psychologists Press.

Swezey, R. W., & Pearlstein, R. B. (1975). *Guidebook for developing criterion-referenced tests.* Arlington, VA: U.S. Army Research Institute for the Behavioral and Social Sciences.

Thorndike, R. L., & Hagen, E. (1977). *Measurement and evaluation in psychology and education* (4th ed.). New York: Wiley.
Thurstone, L. L. (1925). A method of scaling psychological and educational tests. *Journal of Educational Psychology, 16,* 433–451.
Thurstone, L. L. (1947). The calibration of test items. *American Psychologist, 2,* 103–104.
Urry, V. W. (1977). Tailored testing: A successful application of latent trait theory. *Journal of Educational Measurement, 14,* 181–196.
U.S. Department of Labor, Employment and Training Administration (1983a). *The dimensionality of the General Aptitude Test Battery (GATB) and the dominance of general factors over specific factors in the prediction of job performance* (USES Test Res. Rep. No. 44). Washington, DC: U.S. Government Printing Office.
U.S. Department of Labor, Employment and Training Administration (1983b). *Overview of validity generalization* (USES Test Res. Rep. No. 43). Washington, DC: U.S. Government Printing Office.
U.S. Department of Labor, Employment and Training Administration (1983c). *Test validation for 12,000 jobs: An application of job classification and validity generalization analysis to the General Aptitude Test Battery* (USES Test Res. Rep. No. 45). Washington, DC: U.S. Government Printing Office.
Weiss, D. J. (1976). *Computerized ability testing, 1972–1975* (Final Report of Project NR 150-343). Minneapolis: Psychometric Methods Program, Department of Psychology, University of Minnesota.
Weiss, D. J., & Davison, M. L. (1981). Test theory and methods. *Annual Review of Psychology, 32,* 629–658.
Womer, F. B. (1970). *What is National Assessment?* Ann Arbor, MI: National Assessment of Educational Progress.
Wright, B. D. (1977). Solving measurement problems with the Rasch model. *Journal of Educational Measurement, 14,* 97–116.

N. DICKON REPPUCCI
PSYCHOLOGY IN THE PUBLIC INTEREST

N. DICKON REPPUCCI

N. Dickon Reppucci earned his doctorate in clinical psychology in 1968 at Harvard University. He was a faculty member in the Department of Psychology at Yale University until 1976, when he accepted his current position as a professor of psychology and the director of the community psychology program at the University of Virginia in Charlottesville. He holds a joint appointment in the university's Institute of Clinical Psychology and is a consultant to the university's Institute for Law, Psychiatry and Public Policy. He is a fellow of APA's divisions 12, 27, 37, and 41 and is president-elect of Division 27 (Community Psychology).

Reppucci has served on several editorial boards of professional journals, on NIMH's internal review committee on Crime and Delinquency, and as chair of BSERP's Task Force on Psychology and Public Policy. He is author or co-author of more than 50 articles and book chapters, as well as the 1984 volume *Children, Mental Health and the Law*. His research and teaching interests include mental health, law and children, organized youth sports, institutional change, and preventive interventions.

N. DICKON REPPUCCI

PSYCHOLOGY IN THE PUBLIC INTEREST

I began writing this lecture with trepidation. I felt this way for several reasons. First, the goal of the G. Stanley Hall lectures is to provide coverage of a topic that would be suitable for an undergraduate introductory psychology course. But because this topic is not usually covered in introductory courses, I had no models. Thus one of my tasks was to decide what should constitute this coverage, and this has been by no means easy. Second, the criteria for these lectures suggest that the literature of the previous five years should be emphasized. This has proven to be impossible. Although the *American Psychologist* has published a public policy section since mid-1982, there are no journals devoted to a public interest psychology per se. As a result there is no place that one can readily find the most current and rigorously reviewed research; therefore a ready-made framework in which to develop and deal with accepted topics in public interest psychology does not exist.

I thank my colleagues on the Task Force on Psychology and Public Policy— Arnold Kahn, Paul Kimmel, Sheldon Korchin, Michael Saks, Irma Serrano-Garcia, Edward Seidman, and Sandra Tangri—for their stimulating ideas, discussion, and criticism. I also thank Christine Reppucci for her constructive criticism and Debbie Mundie for typing the manuscript under time pressure. Finally, I dedicate this chapter to Sheldon Korchin and Seymour B. Sarason for their wisdom, humanitarianism, and friendship. They exemplify psychologists who have contributed to the public interest.

Public interest psychology sounds like a unified entity. But just as there is an immense range to psychology itself, as is clearly suggested by the range of topics in these lectures and by the contents of any introductory psychology textbook, there is likewise an immense range of areas that can provide knowledge for application in the public interest. This presented a third difficulty. Finally, and perhaps most importantly, what made my task most difficult is the continuing controversy about the roles of psychology and psychologists in the formation and implementation of public policy. This controversy is a modern-day version of the dichotomy between pure and applied psychology that was first crystallized by Titchener, who, as quoted by O'Donnell (1979), argued that "psychology's rush toward technology threatened scientific overreach" (p. 290). The controversy was reinforced by Boring's enormously influential *History of Experimental Psychology* (1929).

Today this controversy has moved from the applied versus basic distinction to the arena of public policy. As Bandura (1974) attests: "As a science concerned about the social consequence of its applications, psychology must also fulfill a broader obligation to society by bringing influence to bear on public policies to ensure that its findings are used in the service of human betterment" (p. 859). And, according to Atkinson:

> The psychologist's job as a scientist is to search for data, principles and laws that enlarge our understanding of psychological phenomena ... there is no reason why psychologists should not advocate political viewpoints, but they should advocate them only as individual citizens. The psychologist's role as a scientist is to set forth the facts, and to set forth these facts in as value free a fashion as possible. (1977, p. 207)

Both of these statements imply that psychological knowledge that is relevant for policy exists, but Bandura clearly suggests a more activist role than does Atkinson. In this chapter, I assume the validity of the claim that psychological knowledge exists; it should be noted, however, that there are critics who suggest that the knowledge itself does not exist (e.g., Koch, 1980; Scriven, 1980).

Although the most expansive psychologists among us have called for a public affairs psychology (e.g., Brayfield & Lipsey, 1976) that would have psychologists involved in public policy, "especially as it may be proposed or expressed in the form of legislation, defined or clarified through administrative regulations, implemented through government agency actions or operations, or assessed or interpreted by judicial review" (Brayfield & Lipsey, quoted in Zilbergeld, 1983, p. 93). This expansive view has been criticized as psychologists wanting to help run the government (Zilbergeld, 1983). Others have called for limits for psychologists as advocates (e.g., Kimble, 1982), limits based on some system that will recognize where psychological expertise ends and personal values begin.[1]

Although I will return to this debate later in this chapter, my first goal is to provide a framework for a psychology in the public interest. To that end, I delineate some focal issues and some of the roles of psychologists engaged in a public interest psychology. This entails discussing the public policy process itself and providing examples both of psychologists' activities and of research that has been used in the public interest. I conclude with a discussion of what I call "a dilemma of values."

I wish to acknowledge that much of this material is based directly on my work and the work of my colleagues on the Task Force on Psychology and Public Policy, which is sponsored by the American Psychological Association's (APA) Board of Social and Ethical Responsibility in Psychology (BSERP). The Task Force submitted its final report in May 1984 (available from the Office of Social and Ethical Responsibility, APA). As Chair of that Task Force for its four-year life span, I had the opportunity to read widely; to participate in several animated discussions; to compose an overview on the topic of psychology and public policy (Reppucci & Kirk, 1983, 1984), upon which parts of this chapter are based; and to become aware of how rapidly organized psychology has increased its involvement in public policy.[2]

Definition and Focal Issues

What is a psychology in the public interest? A public interest psychology is one that views research as acquiring value when its findings are used to promote human welfare. It does not view psychological research as an end in itself. The consumers may be scientists, science administrators, social service managers, practitioners, or the general public. The public interest psychologist has the responsibility to support programs to disseminate and promote the use of the findings of psychological research. In other words, the traditional value of seeking knowledge for the sake of understanding is combined with the co-equal value of utilizing that knowledge for the sake of action.

---

[1] For a critique of APA's involvement in advocacy issues in the public arena, see Robinson, 1984.

[2] During the past decade, APA has initiated many activities in the realm of public policy, not the least of which is the establishment of an Office of National Policy Studies. I do not deal with any of these developments in the present chapter. The interested reader should refer to the final report of the Task Force on Psychology and Public Policy.

In a 1981 survey of the public interest activities of a random sample of 990 APA members, the median person reported spending nearly 300 hours a year on these activities (Good, Simon, & Coursey, 1981). Only 4 percent of the sample reported doing no public interest work at all during the past year. Unfortunately, the definition of public interest that was used was so broad that it ranged from providing professional services without compensation to arranging work hours so that underserved populations could take advantage of services, from whistle blowing to testifying before a governmental body on a subject in which the individual has knowledge and expertise as a psychologist.

In this chapter, I limit the discussion of psychology in the public interest to activities that are related to the use of psychology in relation to public policy. First, I wish to state two facts. Fact 1: Although many psychologists have been involved over the decades with both research and action on problems that affect the welfare of society and which they view as having both direct and indirect implications for public policy (Korten, Cook, & Lacey, 1970), it is also true that psychology has been much less involved in public policy than have other social sciences, such as economics, political science, and law. As Saks (1978) points out: "Except in the dreams of some psychologists and the delusions of others, the makers of social policy make little use of behavioral science knowledge or of behavioral scientists" (p. 680). As a result, a psychological perspective is frequently lacking in the public policy process.

Fact 2: Psychologists, in their work and in their training, have spent little time understanding, researching, or participating in the process of policy formation, implementation, and evaluation. Although there have been several calls for psychologists to do this (e.g., Bevan, 1976, 1980a, 1980b; Jackson, 1980), few have accepted the challenge. Only recently have psychologists (e.g., Kiesler, 1980a, 1980b, 1982; Zigler, Kagan, & Klugman, 1983) even begun to integrate psychological findings in a fashion that is directly related to their use in the formulation of public policy.

These two facts do not mean that psychology has had no impact on public policy. Anton (1984), a noted political scientist and former editor of the journal *Policy Sciences,* recently suggested that the development and refinement of mass public opinion surveys, which he considers to be psychology's major contribution to public policy, "may be the single most significant social science contribution to public policy in this century" (p. 207). Depending on one's viewpoint, of course, this may be a damning tribute. Moreover, depending upon one's values, it can be argued that when psychology has been involved in policy formation, it has contributed both to ill-advised policies such as the widespread misuse of standardized IQ and achievement testing that has resulted in bias to minority groups (Albee, 1981; Kamin, 1974; Levine, 1976; Olmedo, 1981; Reschley, 1981) and to more enlightened policies such as the U.S. Supreme Court's use of Clark's research on the psychological impact of prejudice and discrimination on black children in the 1954 decision that racial segregation in public schools is unconstitutional (*Brown v. Board of Education,* 1954; Clark & Clark, 1958; see also Cook, 1984). Thus at times, the impact of psychology has had the unintended consequence of appearing to be exactly opposite to its stated emphasis on individual well-being (Miller, 1969); whereas at other times, psychology's perspective has had a positive tempering effect on policies that may well have neglected individual differences.

In his 1969 APA presidential address, George Miller focused on the issue of how psychology can promote human welfare. He concluded that psychology's "real strength in promoting human welfare will come from our scientific knowledge" (p. 1065), but that "nothing would be more relevant to human welfare . . . than to discover how best to give psychology away" (p. 1074). In other words, psychologists need to develop a psychology in the public interest. The following year APA published a nontechnical volume entitled *Psychology and the Problems of Society* (Korten et al., 1970) as "a small step toward 'giving psychology away' " (p. iv). Yet six years later in 1976 and again as APA president in 1982, William Bevan found it necessary to reiterate the theme that psychology must find a way to give its knowledge to the public for both the sake of human welfare and the continued viability of the discipline.

Of course, the issue of which psychologist should give what psychology to whom has many different answers. An organization such as APA that has 40 nonexclusive divisions to express the dominant interests of its membership is bound to have a large diversity of perspectives and opinions. Moreover, this fragmentation of psychology is not a new development. Toulmin (1981) has pointed out that psychology has provided scope for several distinct models of scientific investigation and theoretical analysis. Among these models are sensory, cognitive, developmental, social, educational, clinical, and community psychologies as well as neurophysiology, psycholinguistics, and behaviorism. Koch (1980) has argued that this diversity and noncohesiveness of psychology should be recognized by relabeling the discipline "the psychological studies."

The policy implication of the existence of psychological studies rather than a unified psychology is simple: Which kind of psychologist is called upon to interact in a policy situation will significantly affect results. Each subfield of psychology has its own slant on what the relevant variables are in any given situation. As an example, consider White's (1980) list of variables that have been of interest to

psychologists in explaining how children learn to read:
1. visual field configuration translated into patterned retinal firings
2. organized oculomotor activities
3. motivation to read
4. teacher influence
5. parental role in expectation and school attendance
6. legal mandate for schooling and the teaching of reading
7. high-technology society that demands literacy of its citizens
8. taxpayers' appropriation of funds for a school and teacher.

None of these explanations can be reduced to any other without changing the essential nature of the explanation. Psychologists working at the biological end of psychological explanation (items 1 and 2) are apt to have quite different perceptions of reading than are those working in the social range of psychological explanation (items 3, 4, and 5). Both will differ from the perceptions of psychologists working at the societal-cultural level of psychological explanation (items 6, 7, and 8).

The types of explanatory variables sought out by these differing perspectives significantly affect the kinds of policy-related studies undertaken and the policy recommendations generated. As an example, psychologists interested in variable levels 1 and 2 are far more likely to recommend early screening of visual acuity and oculomotor control than they are to recommend media campaigns or alternative funding plans (levels 7 and 8). Policymakers may be in a position to consider intervention at any of these levels and need to be aware that psychologists have biases that generally prevent them from giving equal consideration to all the various levels of intervention.

This state of affairs is often perplexing to policymakers who hope for answers rather than perspectives. As they become aware of this fragmentation of psychological science, they often learn to lower any expectations they may have for receipt of crystallized advice from psychology. Although this awareness may lead to lessened reliance on psychological knowledge than many psychologists might wish, it is nevertheless something that policymakers need to know.

The reverse is equally true: Psychologists need to be more aware of the structure and process of public policymaking. Bevan (1980b) feels that the integrity of the basic research undertaking is threatened unless scientists of all ilk "acquire a better understanding of the mechanisms and strategies by which policy is established" (p. 787). He continues:

> Many . . . would probably be surprised if not disturbed to realize that policy hardly ever exists as a totally explicit, completely rational, clearly formulated, and fully comprehensive set of statements. . . . policy is more often than not nothing more than what

> a particular bureaucrat elects to do about a particular matter at a particular time. (p. 787)

Furthermore, he strongly suggests that scientists at university departments need both to understand the policy process themselves and to teach their students how science, politics, and government interact as social consensual systems.

Bevan is arguing for a conception of science that takes into account the social, political, and economic reality of a society with limits. In particular, he is arguing for a psychology that not only talks about promoting human welfare based on scientific findings that will somehow be put into the public domain, but one that consciously contributes to the policy process from a position of understanding and strength.

Academic psychology has experienced considerable turmoil over the substantive nature of its contribution to public policy. All through the 1960s and 1970s various spokespersons in psychology have called for increased public policy awareness and contribution from psychologists (e.g., Miller, 1969; Bevan, 1976, 1980a, 1980b; Monahan, 1977; Kiesler, 1980b; Segall, 1976) as part of a perceived cultural demand for relevance. Various reactions to Miller's 1969 call for "giving away psychology" were compiled at the First Houston Symposium on Psychology and Society (Kasschau & Kessel, 1980), but essentially the internal demand for relevance and vigor in policy matters has not yet been met (Bevan, 1980b).

In 1966, Bauer stated that "it has been mainly the representatives of other disciplines, particularly political scientists and students of public and business administration, who have done the work and shaped the field of public policy as it now stands. There is a handful of psychologists who are an exception to this generalization" (p. 933). Fifteen years later, Kiesler said:

> Over the course of their history, psychologists have emphasized theoretically oriented laboratory research. Such an approach has been very effective in the development of psychology as a scientific enterprise ... however, it has also led to a lack of involvement with problem-oriented research, and our contacts with broad problems often seem to be superficial compared with, say, economists. (1980b, p. 63)

These two quotations suggest that relatively little of substance has changed over the past fifteen years in terms of psychology's involvement in public policy issues. As Bauer points out, there have been a few psychologists all along who have been involved in public policy, but, as Kiesler emphasizes, there is still a generalized lack of involvement. This is not to say that much of relevance to the relation between psychology and public policy has not occurred during this time period, but rather to note that as a scientific discipline, research is still concentrated in the psychological laboratory and not with problem-oriented research in the field.

The basis for this concentration is probably related to the previously mentioned controversy about basic and applied research that has characterized psychology from its beginnings. An underlying assumption has been that "truth" resides in "hard" science, such as basic laboratory experimentation, whereas myth resides in "soft" science, such as applied problem-focused research in the field. Although such eminent psychologists as Garner (1972) and Sarason (1975) have eloquently argued this point, the split has adversely affected the involvement of psychology in policy issues.

Nevertheless, much has changed or is in the process of changing both worldwide and in psychology specifically. The golden age of public support for science has ended (the peak year for support was fiscal year 1967 according to Bevan, 1980a) and an era of limited resources and public accountability has begun. For psychology itself, there has been a proliferation of research areas that have a major applied focus, for example, community, health, environment, prevention, ecology, and law, as well as increasing applied emphases in more traditional areas such as applied developmental, applied social, and applied experimental. In addition, advances in research methodology and statistical techniques (Campbell & Stanley, 1966; Cook & Campbell, 1979; Joreskog, 1970) have made investigations possible that were not feasible in earlier eras. Finally, the increasing acceptance of applied social research as a legitimate academic venture (Bickman, 1980–1983; Kidd & Saks, 1980, 1983; Stephenson & Davis, 1981) has encouraged investigation in policy-relevant areas.

Several psychologists (e.g., Fairweather & Tornatzky, 1977; Goodwin, 1971; Goodwin & Tu, 1975; Greenberger, 1983; Kiesler, 1980a, 1982; Masters, 1984; Stern & Gardner, 1981) have argued that social research should be made more directly relevant to public policy issues. One key method for doing this is to be where the action is on some kind of continuing basis and to involve appropriate people in both the design of the research and the discussion of its results. The focus of attention should be on major policy issues that affect large numbers of people but that have traditionally been ignored by psychologists, for example, the social security system (Goodwin & Tu, 1975), welfare-poverty programs (Goodwin, 1971), and energy use (Stern & Gardner, 1981).

In essence, these researchers and others are pleading for the adoption of an action research focus similar to that advocated by Lewin (1946, 1947, 1951) but largely neglected by most psychologists. Central features of Lewin's model include problem focus, feedback, and collaboration among researchers, service providers (e.g., teachers, mental health practitioners, and welfare workers), and recipients of the services (e.g., students or clients). Lewin would have supported Atkinson's (1977) emphasis on searching for knowledge for the sake of understanding but also Bandura's (1974) emphasis on using that knowledge for the sake of action. One of Lewin's most famous comments is "nothing is so practical as a good theory," but the context in which this was stated is usually forgotten: "[Close cooperation between theoretical and applied psychology] can be accomplished . . . if the theorist does not look toward applied problems with highbrow aversion or with a fear of social problems, and if the applied psychologist realizes that there is nothing so practical as a good theory" (1951, p. 169).

The major point is that research that is formulated and undertaken in natural environments within a theoretical framework may be more directly relevant to public policy issues than is theoretical research that is conducted in the artificial environment of the psychological laboratory. This is not to suggest that the experimental rigor of the laboratory should be abandoned. On the contrary, as much experimental rigor as possible should be used in applied research designs (e.g., Campbell, 1969; Fairweather & Tornatzky, 1977; Ketterer, Price, & Polister, 1980), while recognizing that the nature of natural contexts is such that multiple uncontrolled factors will be operating. The advantage gained, however, may be increased generalizability of findings, especially if both individual- and system-level variables are taken into account (Seidman, 1981). Such results may be viewed by policymakers as more meaningful and less as "statistical numerology" as suggested by Justice Powell in *Ballew v. Georgia* (1978). If so, the potential contribution of psychology may become more valued by policymakers in general.

I now move to a discussion of roles for psychologists in public policy. It should be noted that these roles have been differentiated for the sake of clarity but that in reality they are often overlapping and in many cases a psychologist may be performing more than one role at any given time. This discussion is followed by a brief examination of the policy process itself, and then by a few examples of psychological research that have informed public policy.

Roles for Psychologists in Public Policy

Expert Witness

The role of expert witness (Segall, 1976) occurs when the psychologist offers what he or she knows to those who can apply it. The judgment as to the relevance of the information and its implications for a particular policy dilemma is left to the policymakers. Psychologists have been practicing this model for years, although it has been relatively rare until recently that psychologists have testified before legislative committees and in courts as other than clinical experts on a particular individual.

Perhaps the best example as to how this role may work operationally is provided by Loftus and Monahan's (1980) documentation of the use of psychological research as legal evidence. These investigators have served as expert witnesses regarding eyewitness testimony and prediction of dangerousness. In this role, they provided information based on psychological research relating to these topics in general, not in regard to any specific case. For example, in a case concerning whether person X is likely to commit a violent act at a future time, data are presented from studies that have attempted to validate clinical and actuarial predictions of violent behavior with respect to persons released from mental hospitals or prisons. These data demonstrate that, with follow-up periods of from 1 to 5 years after release, at least two out of three, and at times over nine out of ten, positive predictions were false. Thus, most persons predicted to be violent were not. This information can be used by judge and jury in weighing the evidence in the particular case. Such testimony has clearly had influence; for example, the death penalty has not yet been imposed in any case in which it has been introduced.

Translator and Consultant

Closely related to the expert witness role are the roles of translator and consultant (Kiesler, 1983). A psychologist translator's role is to communicate the findings of psychology and the behavioral sciences in a language and form that is easily comprehended by the educated public, including policymakers. A psychologist who is a science writer for *Psychology Today* represents the more general role, whereas a psychologist staff person for a legislative committee or governmental task force represents the more specific direct link to public policy.

The psychologist consultant is expected to provide expertise on relevant psychological information to governmental, grass roots, and other interest groups. The consultant is usually hired or recognized (e.g., as a witness before a legislative hearing) because of his or her expertise in the area of concern to the group. For example, the Children's Defense Fund (a private advocacy organization for children) or a governmental select committee on children and families may each seek the advice of a developmental, community, or clinical psychologist whose expertise is children and families to advise it on policy stances that can be supported by psychological theory or empirical data.

Researcher or Policy Evaluator

Probably the most common role for a psychologist in public policy is that of researcher (Kiesler, 1983) or policy evaluator (Segall, 1976). It is in this role that psychologists can most readily bring their methodological sophistication to bear. The results of evaluation and analysis can help policymakers determine whether a program, intervention, or treatment was carried out as planned (process evaluation) or was effective in terms of intended outcomes (impact or outcome evaluation). Comprehensive evaluation encompasses both of these assessments. The results may contribute to (a) the destruction of popular myth, for example, that psychotherapy is always an effective cure or that sex education yields increased sexual activity; (b) the provision of measures of public accountability, for example, measuring the quality and quantity of services actually obtained in public health clinics; (c) the development of a rational effort to plan and to implement new social resource programs such as Head Start; and (d) the modification and refinement of social policies by evaluating alternatives, such as the impact of different outpatient placements on mental patients. Psychologists may be hired directly as policy evaluators, or they may engage in research of direct or indirect relevance to public policy as faculty members at universities or private research institutes.

It is important to emphasize that the policy evaluator role is mainly concerned only with the psychologist's methodological expertise. His or her job "is not to say *what is to be done*, but rather to say *what has been done*" (Campbell, 1975, p. 27). However, with few exceptions, none of our major social ameliorative programs have had adequate evaluations (Campbell, 1969, 1975). Even under the best of conditions, the difficulties entailed in arriving at valid assessment of actual social programs are legion (Cook & Campbell, 1979). For example, comparison programs are seldom possible. Yet comparison is the sine qua non of evaluation. It is only in the last two decades that research designs and statistical methodology have become available (Campbell & Stanley, 1966; Cook & Campbell, 1979; Linney & Reppucci, 1982), partially to counter the various internal and external validity threats. In addition, it is reasonable to examine patterns of results from several evaluations and arrive at statements that can inform public policy even though each of the individual studies may be flawed (Bronfenbrenner, 1975; Kiesler, 1982).

Although there has been much discussion of the need for evaluation research in public policymaking (e.g., Nagel, 1975; Weiss, 1975, 1977), there has been a general concern about the quality of existing research. In a sociological study (Bernstein & Freeman, 1975) of such evaluations, only 152 of 236 were of the comprehensive variety, and of these, less than 20 percent consistently followed generally accepted procedures with respect to design and data analysis. Quality of research was related to characteristics of the researchers themselves, including discipline and level of education. Psychologists predominated as directors of projects that were rated high in quality, and more people with doctorates were represented in high quality projects than were people with lesser degrees. In addition, research carried out by investigators in academic versus entrepreneurial settings tended to be of higher quality. What this suggests is that psychologists with sound methodological backgrounds have a solid contribution to make as policy evaluators.

Administrator

A fourth role is that of agency or program administrator in education, health, mental health, welfare, corrections, and science policy (Kiesler, 1983). Psychologists have increasingly taken administrative positions in human service organizations (e.g., as superintendent of a correctional facility, as director of a community mental health center, or as head of an NIMH center) and as a result have become directly responsible for the formation and implementation of social policy (see Reppucci & Sarason, 1979). In such positions, the psychologist may often be expected to act in the role of expert, translator, consultant, or researcher.

Activist-Collaborator

Recently, Jackson (1980) has suggested that a key role for psychologists is the activist-collaborator. This role incorporates many of the previous ones but, in addition, it suggests that the guise of neutrality may be abandoned. Jackson feels that psychologists should be willing to advocate solutions to social problems and "to utilize legal methods and procedures for influencing legislation affecting psychology and human welfare" (p. 159). Although Jackson believes that policy decisions should be left to policymakers and not to psychologists, the activist-collaborator role clearly suggests that psychologists should bring as much influence to bear as possible in order to ensure that social policy is informed by psychological knowledge. Clearly this role is controversial and goes beyond the limits of advocacy that would be endorsed as legitimate by many psychologists.

Social Engineer

Another role that deserves mention is that of social engineer, which implies "the intentional use of techniques of behavioral control" (Segall, 1976, p. 27). This model has been applied in various small-scale projects in educational and clinical settings, but not in a massive public program of manipulation. Yet understandably, it is this model that has caused the most controversy and concern in the public and political mind. Probably the best example of this model is B. F. Skinner's book, *Beyond Freedom and Dignity* (1971), in which Skinner summarizes some basic principles that reveal how human behavior can be shaped and controlled by environmental forces and argues that this knowledge should be used to produce planned social change. The fact is that such widespread environmental controls as would be necessary to accomplish Skinner's goals do not exist (Reppucci & Saunders, 1974), at least not yet. Nevertheless, this fact has done nothing to alleviate the nightmarish visions that Skinner's views and the term "behavioral modification" have generated for a large proportion of the public (Saunders & Reppucci, 1978). I will not discuss this role further because it is essentially nonexistent. I mention it, however, because to many this could be the end product if psychology is allowed to relate to the policy process.

In all of the roles I have mentioned, what distinguishes psychologists from other specialists is their expertise in understanding human behavior. Psychologists possess a unique commitment to individuals and their well-being and place emphasis on scientific rigor, verifiable knowledge, and an awareness of social and cultural relativism. As a result, psychologists can synthesize information about human behavior to provide a more complete knowledge base for the consideration of alternate policies (Kiesler, 1983). Regardless of which role, or combination of roles, is adopted, psychologists must develop an understanding of the policy process.

The Public Policy Process

In order to help the reader conceptualize the public policy process, I divide the process into five interrelated stages. In practice, these stages are complex, do not always occur in an orderly or sequential fashion, and are characterized by numerous feedback loops. Moreover, these stages remain similar whether public policy is conceptualized from a "top-down" or a "bottom-up" strategy perspective. The five stages and several skills that psychologists can bring to each stage are as follows.

Stage 1. Problem Identification and Definition

In this stage, the goal is to identify and define the set of conditions that constitute a social problem worthy of recognition and action. Although policy analysis, that is, the application of evidence, reason, and a valuative framework to public decisions, may be brought to bear at all stages of the policy process, it is crucial in this first stage. The identification and definition of a problem and its implicit and unexamined premises are critical for each subsequent stage of the policy process (Henley, 1982; Mitroff & Turoff, 1973; Sarason, 1978; Seidman, 1983).

Problem definitions are based on assumptions about the causes of the problem and where they lie, and these assumptions are often about human behavior. Different social and cultural definitions may be appropriate (Maruyama, 1983). Moreover, problem definitions clearly yield proposed problem solutions (Caplan & Nelson, 1973; Seidman, 1983). For example, if juvenile delinquency is defined as an individual problem, it will suggest interventions focused on the individual, such as individual counseling or psychotherapy; if defined as a family problem, it will suggest interventions with families; and if defined as a community problem, it will suggest community solutions such as the development of a teen center.

There are several ways that psychologists can be helpful in working with policymakers (top-down) and program recipients (bottom-up) to select and define issues. In addition to questioning assumptions and presenting alternate definitions and consequent approaches, psychologists can gather data through attitude and epidemiological surveys and questionnaires that will expand, validate, or invalidate current thinking. They can also assist in bringing together information from different groups involved in the issue or the group members themselves. Group dynamics and conflict resolution skills may contribute to better definitions of the issues involved.

Stage 2. Policy Formation

Stage 2 involves the development of a plan, method, and prescription for acting on a problem. Psychologists can assist the formation of plans of action in several different ways. They can
- critically review and analyze the extant social science literature (e.g., meta-analysis or secondary analysis)
- survey and interview knowledgeable parties (i.e., experts or potential recipients)
- bring actors with divergent perspectives together to decide on an optimal plan of action (e.g., the Delphi technique)
- implement, evaluate, and compare, on a reduced scale, what appear to be the best possible policies (see, e.g., Campbell, 1969; Fairweather & Tornatzky, 1977)

Stage 3. Policy Adoption

The focal goal of this stage is gaining sanction from the relevant official body for a plan of action. Adoption can be achieved by making use of organizational, networking, group dynamic, and other types of interpersonal influence and communication skills. Psychologists familiar with the skills, training, and problems inherent in these processes can offer their services to the parties involved or become involved themselves in these activities. Data can also be collected on optimal strategies for securing policy adoption (see Fairweather, Sanders, & Tornatzky, 1974; Saunders & Reppucci, 1977). In addition, expert testimony can play a critical role in policy adoption. Psychologists can help others prepare testimony or testify themselves as expert witnesses (e.g., Loftus & Monahan, 1980).

Stage 4. Policy Implementation

This stage is concerned with ensuring that the designated plan of action is delivered in the intended manner to the targeted constituents. Although implementation may involve different actors than does adoption, a similar set of interpersonal influence and communication skills is needed. In addition, a thorough understanding of the issues relating to creating new settings (Sarason, 1972) or to changing established settings (Reppucci & Saunders, 1983) may be necessary. The activities available to psychologists may be more direct in policy implementation as they are more likely to be part of the programs themselves. Clinical supervision and organizational consultation are examples of these more direct involvements. Finally, process evaluation to determine the strength and integrity of the implemented policy may be a beneficial service (Sechrest, West, Phillips, Redner, & Yeaton, 1979).

Stage 5. Policy Impact

How effective is the program in meeting its goals? Are there any unintended consequences? In this final stage, psychologists can bring many of their skills in research design and methodology to bear on evaluating the efficacy of program procedures and outcomes. They can take the perspective of the recipients as well as the official goals of the policymakers into consideration. They can examine both target outcomes and side effects. Evaluations can be made of already established social programs as well as new ones. Translation skills are especially important in transmitting findings to program managers and suggesting changes in the policies and/or their implementation to increase their effectiveness (for an extended discussion, see Campbell, 1969; Fairweather & Tornatzky, 1977).

Throughout all of these stages, the psychologist, in his or her role as expert witness, administrator, translator, consultant, activist-collaborator, or researcher-evaluator, must not ignore the fact that power and social values play major roles. To do so is folly. What Lewin said in regard to action research is equally cogent for public policy involvement: "The social scientist... has to see realistically the problems he is to study, without... becoming a servant of vested interests.... The problem of values, objectives, and of objectivity are nowhere more interwoven and more important than in action research" (1947, p. 153).

Although this delineation of the policy process into five stages is a helpful cognitive framework for understanding, there are many subtleties to the process that are not obvious from it, and yet, must be comprehended both on a cognitive and on an emotional level. Bauer (1966) wrote a most lucid, if unheeded, article on several of these issues. First, there is the lack of understanding among many psychologists that the distinctive mission of the policymaker is that he or she must mediate among conflicting sets of values and interests. The policymaker must judge what is possible as well as what may be preferable and must form judgments that are specific to a given situation at a given time rather than what might be correct for a class of situations. In addition, a policymaker must balance any specific issue with a wide range of other issues. Once this phenomenology is understood, it becomes clear that policy formation is a social process with intellectual elements rather than a purely rational intellectual process.

A second issue that Bauer addresses is the lack of unity with respect to any given problem. He states:

> This lack of unity of the problem, especially the diversity of interests and values, precludes the sort of determinate identification of a single "best" policy that is implied in the usual conception of decision making. The more appropriate model for this aspect of the policy process is that of bargaining or negotiation among parties whose interests are not identical.... However... psychologists have given relatively little attention to situations in which persisting conflict of interests is involved. When we talk about "conflict resolution," it seems... we are concerned with methods of making conflict disappear. (1966, pp. 935–936)

As a result, much of the laboratory research of experimental social psychologists on decision making and other topics that has sought main effects tends to be irrelevant to the actual policy formation process in which an infinite number of higher order interactions are involved. Campbell (1969, 1975) and other community, social, and ecological psychologists have frequently alerted us to this issue, especially during the past two decades; yet, the search for main effects in the experimental laboratory has persisted as a major activity of many research psychologists.

Related to this issue is the third and perhaps most important proposition: Any policy occurs within a political context, and serious policymaking does not involve decisive resolutions of a problem. As Bauer says:

> One of the fallacies of treating the policy process as decision making is that it assumes that someone is aware of the problem, that he can devote full time and attention to it, and that the issue has a clear-cut beginning and end. In practice, other events compete for his resources, including time, attention, and energy.
>
> ... In any ongoing institution, the ability to get important things done is dependent upon maintaining a reservoir of goodwill. ... it should be considered neither surprising nor immoral that, when an issue is of low salience, the sensible individual may use it to build goodwill for the future, or pay off past obligations, by going along with some individual for whom the issue is of high salience. (pp. 937–938)

Once this vital factor of political context is comprehended, the process of policy formation as it actually occurs becomes more understandable. It suggests "points of leverage" (people, institutions, or lobby groups for whom a given issue is of high salience) that could influence the outcome of the process.

Moreover, it gives meaning to Weiss's (1976) concept of "politically useful" research. Such research has the following qualities. (a) it is available when needed (i.e., the timing is right); (b) it is communicated in language so that policymakers can understand what was done, what was found, and what it means; and (c) the findings suggest politically and economically feasible action alternatives, not sweeping societal changes that are impossible to implement. Another quality that enhances the perceived political usefulness of such research is when the results reinforce the policymaker's own views (Weiss & Bucuvalas, 1977).

Contributions of Psychological Knowledge to Public Policy

Once aware of the complexity of this "culture of policy" (Saks, 1978), psychologists can turn to the crucial question, "What knowledge does psychology have to give away?" Clearly there is no single answer to this question and as I emphasized earlier, any answer would be dependent upon the psychologist asked. Therefore, what follows is a mere sample of a large universe of possible examples from several areas of psychological knowledge that either have been or could be

Increasing Juror Comprehension

Psycholinguistic research suggests several variables that may influence a policymaker's understanding and use of scientific information. Among these are grammatical constructions (e.g., verb structure, sentence complexity, and length); vocabulary (e.g., use of concrete versus abstract words or of high versus low frequency words); and length and organization of the information (Massad, Sales, & Sabatier, 1983). Elwork, Sales, and Alfini (1982) focused on grammatical construction in order to improve the comprehension of jury instructions. They noted that self-embedded sentences frequently occur in jury instructions and create comprehension problems for the jurors. As an example they cited the following instruction: "It will be your duty, when the case is submitted to you, to determine from the evidence admitted for your consideration, applying thereto the rules of law contained in the instructions given by the court, whether or not the Defendant is guilty of the offense charged." Based on principles derived from psycholinguistic, educational, and cognitive psychology, Elwork et al. rewrote this instruction to read: "Your duty is to determine whether the Defendant is guilty of the offense charged. You must do this by applying the laws that are contained in these instructions, to the evidence that has been admitted for your consideration" (p. 170). The investigators reported an increase in juror comprehension of 30 percent or more with the revised instructions. It seems to be only a slight extrapolation to suggest that a psychologist-translator could use these same principles to report research findings so that they are maximally comprehensible for policymakers (Massad et al., 1983).

Decreasing Television Violence

Hennigan, Flay, and Cook (1980) reported the following example of social science knowledge being used to affect public policy concerning television violence. In the early 1970s, at the bequest of U.S. Senator John Pastore, the Surgeon General commissioned several social scientists to conduct a series of studies addressing the relation between television violence and viewers' behavior. Their results, which suggested a strong relationship, were presented before a special Senate committee. Subsequently, the three major broadcasting networks reduced the level of television violence and instituted a family viewing period during the early evening hours.

Protecting the Rights of Donors

In a marvelously candid article, Saks (1978) argued for training psychologists to apply basic research knowledge to social problems and to assume more active policymaking roles. His vehicle for doing this was a description of his appointment and his contributions to a legislative subcommittee on organ and tissue transplants. He was appointed because of his expertise as a methodologist, not as a social psychologist. This was most satisfactory to him since he had many doubts as to any substantive knowledge that he might possess. To his surprise, however, he found that he possessed a great deal of relevant social psychological knowledge that was quite independent of his methodological sophistication. I quote but one of his examples in which he demonstrates how psychological constructs related to attribution processes were informative to the policy debate.

> A person asked to donate an organ or tissue to a dying relative is often in a terrible double bind. If inclined to donate, one's spouse and children often argue against it: their welfare will be jeopardized by the risks attending the donation; to donate is to neglect one's responsibilities to them. Those closer to the recipient place countervailing pressure on the prospective donor: not to donate is to condemn their loved one to death. Disruption of family relations may accompany a donation decision regardless of which choice is made (Bennett & Harrison, 1974; Eisendrath, Guttman, & Murray, 1969; Kemph, Bermann, & Coppolillo, 1969).
> ... To reduce such conflicts, some physicians devised a clever and humane deception. If a prospective donor elects not to donate, the physicians tell the family that the person was found biologically incompatible. Prospective donors are informed in advance that this use is available to them. In attribution-process terms, they are turning personal causation into impersonality. . . . That is, if a person is perceived as *choosing* not to help (a dispositional attribution), the family can become hostile over the decision. But people cannot be blamed for having incompatible organs or blood (a situational attribution). (pp. 685–686)

Unfortunately, the physicians' scheme, aside from being ethically questionable, has a serious pragmatic flaw. Because many donors and their families know about this ruse, relatives do not know whether the prospective donor is really biologically incompatible or if he or she refused to donate and the physicians' policy of deception has been invoked. Thus, unambiguous situational attributes are now impossible within those families where donations did not occur (Jones &

Davis, 1965). The result is a residue of suspicion and hostility. Saks concluded that psychological knowledge clearly exists that is relevant to social problems and public policy but that the application of this knowledge is not automatic. Reconceptualizing the facts of a problem within a psychologically informed framework may allow new insight into a problem that otherwise would not be obvious.

Administering Project Head Start

The work of Zigler and his colleagues (Stipek, Valentine, & Zigler, 1979; Valentine & Zigler, 1983; Zigler & Valentine, 1979) provides a fascinating example of the use of psychological theory and data to affect social policy by viewing the development, implementation, and maintenance of the Head Start program. Although it is beyond the scope of this chapter to do more than provide the most cursory of summaries, the work of Zigler and his colleagues should be examined in detail for a comprehensive view of the policy context as well as the content of this program.

Project Head Start is composed of several programs, the basic one being a center-based preschool educational program, which served 376,000 predominantly poor children between the ages of three and five in 1980. When Head Start began in 1965 it was informed by theories of child development, especially those of Bloom (1964) and Hunt (1961), who posited that environmental enrichment has the potential to improve a person's intellectual abilities and who suggested that the "critical period" for intervention was in the first 5 years of life (Bloom, 1964). These theories signaled a rejection of strict hereditarian views of development. In conjunction with an adaptation of Lewis's (1961) "culture of poverty" theory, which suggested that through patterns of socialization and a lack of appropriate environmental stimulation the poor develop a world view and intellectual capabilities that do not equip them for success in American society, these developmental theories provided the intellectual framework for the design of Head Start.

As these theories changed over the ensuing years, for example, when developmental psychologists suggested that there were innate developmental stages unique to every person that reflected underlying competencies that may or may not be expressed in performance (a rejection of the critical periods theory), so did Head Start demonstrate its flexibility and adaptability by changing goals and problem definitions. For example, Head Start has now evolved into a program that stresses the central importance of the family, considers all periods of a child's life as important, and recognizes that children and families have needs for several types of services (Valentine & Zigler, 1983).

Over the years, Head Start programs have been subjected to numerous evaluations. Perhaps the best known of these is the evaluation by the Westinghouse Learning Corporation (Cicirelli, 1969), because the results were used as the basis for policy recommendations for program cutbacks in 1969. In essence, the study suggested that although Head Start children demonstrated improved performance in cognitive functioning, the gains had faded by the time the children reached primary grades. What this study failed to do was either to use a broad range of outcome measures or to account for the differences in the quality of program implementation, such as differences in staff/child ratios, in program content, or in staff quality.

In subsequent studies (Emmerich, 1973), which measured program quality and broadened the scope of outcome measures to include socioemotional development, parental involvement, and consumer satisfaction, Head Start children demonstrated significantly better school performance in later years, as well as gains in school readiness, cognitive functioning, and social behavior in the short run. In addition, more recent studies (Valentine & Zigler, 1983) of the impact of early intervention programs on disadvantaged children have demonstrated long term gains, such as better reading and math performance than had children who did not have preschool experience. Moreover, parental involvement was found to be an important mediating factor. This research has resulted in budgetary increases for the Head Start program.

The program evaluations of Head Start suggest several general themes: (a) the availability of comprehensive data on program effectiveness is critical to making informed public policy decisions; (b) an understanding of the limitations of the methodologies used to evaluate social programs is important especially when there are multiple goals that require multiple measures; and (c) evaluations of a social program should be used to enhance the quality of the program being evaluated, not just to justify its existence. For example, Head Start has become a means of testing out different approaches to the delivery of services to young children and their families (Valentine & Zigler, 1983).

Before I conclude the discussion of Head Start, it is important to note that "to explain why a particular policy emerges at a given point of time requires an appreciation of how the social and political climate 'set the stage' for the acceptance of the theories and problem definitions that lead to policy formation" (Valentine & Zigler, 1983, p. 267). In the case of Head Start, the program that emerged and the form that it took reflected a convergence of political, social, and economic factors with social science theories. However, whereas scientific evidence played a key role in the construction of social policy in this case, the existence of a broad-based political constituency has been a key reason for its survival through major political upheavals.

In other words, as I have stressed throughout this chapter, for psychology to be effective in the realm of public policy it must be attuned to the culture of policy as well as to its own theories and data.

Disseminating Research Results to Policymakers

Although psychological knowledge may exist, if it is not disseminated in a form that is usable, it is useless to policymakers. During the past decade, increasing attention has been paid to factors that influence the utilization of social science information in the policy process (e.g., Massad, Sales, & Acosta, 1983). The importance of determining what these factors are is nowhere better illustrated than in the area of the provision of services.

At the research level, millions of dollars are spent annually to develop new information and techniques to improve the quality of human services. Unfortunately most federally funded program research never gets communicated to those who could put it into operation, that is, to human service administrators (Fairweather et al., 1974). The basic assumptions among researchers seem to be that (a) publication of information is a universally viable method of disseminating information to these administrators, and (b) channels of communication are the same for administrators of different human service institutions.

In an effort to examine these assumptions my colleague and I (Saunders & Reppucci, 1977) collected data from three groups of administrators: superintendents of juvenile correctional facilities, directors of institutions for the mentally retarded, and principals of elementary schools. The results did not support the assumptions. To learn about innovation and research, superintendents of juvenile correctional facilities relied most heavily upon resources extrinsic to the institutions in which the administrators work, such as special conferences and outside consultants. In contrast, directors of institutions for the retarded relied principally upon systemic resources, for example, staff resources and departmental meetings intrinsic to the settings in which the administrators work. Finally, principals of elementary schools relied primarily upon reading professional literature. It is worth noting that reading professional books and journals was not a robust method of communication for either superintendents or directors.

These results have clear implications for public policy. If a goal of research is to bring about change in human service institutions, it is necessary to have differential communications tailored to tap into the varying communication channels of the policymakers in these institutions. For example, if the research is relevant to juvenile correctional institutions, the researcher should arrange to disseminate his or her findings by attending and making presentations at conferences that the administrators of these facilities attend. Likewise, if the research is relevant to elementary education, it should be published in journals that principals read, such as *Phi Delta Kappa,* not the *Journal of Educational Psychology.* This is not to suggest that publication in professional journals that a psychological colleague would be likely to read is unimportant, but rather to emphasize that deciding to publish only there means reaching a selective audience and, therefore, in many cases to have no public policy impact at all. This may be acceptable to some but it should not be acceptable to researchers who want their findings to be used in the public interest. Research regarding various aspects of utilization, such as channels of dissemination, can provide information on how psychological knowledge can have an impact on the policy process.

The Dilemma of Values

What these examples all convey is that psychology does have knowledge, both substantive and methodological, to give away in the public interest. However, once this proposition is accepted, another equally important issue arises. "Is the relevant scientific knowledge or professional opinion clearly differentiated from a *social* judgment?" (Brayfield, 1967, p. 186). In a sense, this question presages Miller's (1969) emphatic statement that psychology's strength lies in its scientific base and that it should not endorse social actions or positions based on social values rather than scientific fact, even though its major challenge is to give itself away in order to promote human welfare.

The statement also reflects the controversy regarding the role of psychology and public policy. A major problem, of course, is separating fact from values. Even following the basic canons of science, what is fact in one era may be fiction in another. For example, in the case of Head Start, what was accepted as knowledge in the early 1960s regarding child development was modified in the 1970s. Clearly, as new knowledge is developed as the result of scientific inquiry or of the integration of existing theory and data into new frameworks, what was thought at one time to be a valuable ore may turn into fool's gold at another.

Furthermore, unless the historical, cultural, and social context is taken into account, the application of the scientific-rational model of problem definition and solution is inappropriate as a guide to social action and policy formation. Even when the context is accounted for, Sarason (1978) has suggested that social problems are not like "once-and-for-all-you-don't-have-to-solve-it-again" problems of nature. A more appropriate goal may be to contribute information that may ameliorate a problem for a particular moment in history (Fairweather & Tornatzky, 1977).

To illustrate this dilemma, I turn to the 1908 landmark legal case *Muller v. Oregon*, which set the precedent for using social science data in the courts. In 1905 Curt Muller, the owner of a laundry in Portland, Oregon, was convicted of violating a state statute specifying that "no female can be employed in a mechanical establishment, factory or laundry more than ten hours during any one day" (Rosen, 1972, p. 77). Muller brought the case to the Supreme Court. Louis D. Brandeis represented the state of Oregon and prepared what has become known as the Brandeis Brief.

Brandeis decided on a radical type of defense. He had a staff of researchers gather facts published by experts in the field with respect to women and labor. These facts comprised the bulk of the brief that he presented to the Court to substantiate four specific hypotheses: (a) that men and women were physiologically different and that women were more likely to sustain injury resulting from unregulated industrial conditions; (b) that the health, safety, and morals of women were generally endangered by excessive hours of labor; (c) that economic benefits for the employer would result from shorter workdays for women; and (d) that individual health and improved home life would be fostered by shorter workdays. Based on these findings, Brandeis persuaded the Court that it should uphold Oregon's limitation of working hours for women.

Although the Brandeis Brief set judicial precedent, it also raised several problems and fears associated with the use of social science in the courts. Brandeis disavowed any need for the Court to ponder methodological issues of validity and reliability of the research it was being asked to consider, thereby claiming that "social science could be of invaluable assistance to the Court regardless of whether or not such research met conventional standards of scientific credibility" (Rosen, 1980, p. 10).

Another major concern is whether interpretation of the Constitution can or should rest on "the shifting sands of social science" (Tangri & Strasburg, 1979). In the last few decades, as the use of social science in the courts has increased, even more concern has been expressed. Consider, for example, Edmund Cahn's reaction to the use of social science data in *Brown v. Board of Education* in 1954: "Should fundamental rights . . . be tied to the tenuous and changing findings of social science?" (cited by Rosen, 1980, p. 4). Moreover, there is always the temptation to stray from the principle of objectivity whenever a social scientist puts his or her learning, knowledge, and interpretations of theory and data at the service of a worthwhile but nonetheless partisan cause. As Wolfgang (1974) said, "The social science researcher has a fear of his being captured subtly, and, perhaps even unconsciously, by the desire to prove his case, to show the kinds of evidence he believes and wants to believe exist" (p. 241). Nevertheless, even with these qualms, the strength of psychology and the other social sciences is to offer findings and insights in as objective a fashion as possible. Those that challenge common definitions of social reality may be especially informative, but it should be remembered that the court, like other policymaking entities, can accept or reject whatever information is brought before it.

The Brandeis Brief also demonstrates the critical influence of cultural, social, and political contexts. Note the following critique by Tangri and Strasburg (1979):

> The studies cited in the brief were used to argue for a policy which, though liberal for its time because it protected women from some harsh aspects of industrial employment, is considered by most feminists today to be conservative, discriminatory, and undesirable. Thus, because the value context has sufficiently changed, the studies might be interpreted today so as to support a quite different judicial decision, e.g., that if those hours of work are harmful to women they are probably also harmful to men, and everybody's hours should be shorter. (p. 338)

What this suggests is that scientific knowledge and professional opinion should be differentiated from social judgment. However, total differentiation is not always possible since both scientific facts and social contexts change. In addition, psychologists and other social scientists are not neutral about values, if for no other reason than that nobody is (Sarason, 1976). Like others, they are influenced by the economic, political, cultural, and social forces extant during the times in which they live (Levine & Levine, 1970; Rappaport, 1977; Reppucci & Saunders, 1977). They cannot always be aware of how these forces operate on their behavior, attitudes, and beliefs because these forces are usually diffuse and intertwined with common sense beliefs. Given the fact then, that total differentiation is impossible, should psychologists avoid the arena of public policy?

My answer is "No." Psychology has much knowledge to contribute to the public interest, and therefore involvement in public policy is essential. As psychology has moved from theory and the experimental laboratory to application in natural settings, the questions dealt with and the answers or recommendations given have increasingly become an indissolvable mixture of science and values. Every effort should be made to differentiate the two, but recognizing that total differentiation is impossible does not result in the conclusion that involvement should cease. However, it does present a dilemma of values to psychologists for which there are no easy answers. Although psychologists are ethically bound to guard against intentional misinterpretation of factual data (Massad, Sales, & Sabatier, 1983), they are being ethically and professionally appropriate not only to present theory and data for consumption by policymakers and the general public but also to advocate what they view to be in the public interest, that is, in the role of an activist-collaborator.

Although advocacy is not synonymous with involvement in public policy, it may well be a legitimate part of that involvement. Even though the dilemma of values that incorporates the twin problems of the changing facts of science and changing definitions of social problems depending upon time, place, and context is a real one, the promotion of the public interest is paramount. Perhaps the primary lesson is best captured in the words of the judicial scholar and Supreme Court Justice Learned Hand: "Of those qualities on which civilization depends, next after courage, it seems to me, comes an open mind, and, indeed, the highest courage is, as Holmes used to say, to stake your all upon a conclusion which you are aware tomorrow may prove false" (cited in Rosen, 1980, p. 15).

Conclusion

In a paper entitled *Veils, Values, and Social Responsibility*, which should be required reading for all psychologists, Judge David Bazelon (1982) takes to task psychologists who become involved with public policy for what he calls their "sins of nondisclosure." He makes several observations about psychologists in the policy arena. For one, they focus on making conclusory statements rather than providing intermediate observations and conceptual insights. Bazelon considers such statements as "next to useless to the ultimate decisions that can only be left to the public arena [because] they do not let [policymakers] isolate the facts to mix in with [their own] moral and social judgements" (p. 116). Also, they too frequently do not disclose the host of values that underlie their choice of facts. Finally, they obscure the uncertainties and divisions of opinion that may exist about their findings—too often the tentativeness and limitations of research findings are not explained.

Although one might expect Bazelon to conclude that psychologists should stay out of the public arena, he does not. He urges exactly the opposite, as do I. We psychologists should become more involved, but we should follow our own ethical guidelines that require us to "provide thorough discussion of the limitations" of our knowledge and to "acknowledge the existence of alternative hypotheses and explanations" (American Psychological Association, 1981, p. 633).

Let me close with this exhortation to psychologists in the public arena from Judge Bazelon:

You must find it in your nature to fully expose and disclose all of your methods, observations, uncertainties, opposing views, and underlying value choices. You must be able to put both your own work and the field in which you work into proper perspective. The public arena is not a client in therapy who needs to be reassured. It is also not a fellow scientist, who shares a common language and purpose with you. Rather, it is a place where awesome decisions must be made on the basis of limited knowledge and groping understanding.

The mind-set [of disclosure] I urge you to bring to the public arena should therefore combine the scientist's ease in admitting uncertainty and the clinician's tolerance of pragmatic decision making. It should combine the scientist's rigor with the clinician's appreciation of the broader human context. I know this is a tall order, but I also know that nothing else is acceptable. (pp. 119–120)

References

Albee, G. (1981). Psychology, politics, and social change. In R. Kasschau & C. Cofer (Eds.), *Psychology's second century: Enduring issues* (pp. 11–40). New York: Praeger.

American Psychological Association. (1981). Ethical principles of psychologists. *American Psychologist, 36*(6), 633–638.

Anton, T. J. (1984). Policy sciences and social sciences: Reflections from an editor's chair. In G. McCall & G. Weber (Eds.), *Social science and public policy: The roles of academic disciplines in policy analysis* (pp. 201–214). Port Washington, NY: Associated Faculty Press.

Atkinson, R. (1977). Reflections on psychology's past and concerns about its future. *American Psychologist 32*(3), 205–210.

Ballew v. Georgia, 435 U.S. 223, 246 (1978) (Powell, J., concurring).

Bandura, A. (1974). Behavior theory and the models of man. *American Psychologist, 29*(12), 859–869.

Bauer, R. A. (1966). Social psychology and the study of policy formation. *American Psychologist 21*(10), 933–942.

Bazelon, D. L. (1982). Veils, values, and social responsibility. *American Psychologist 37*(2), 115–121.

Bennett, A., & Harrison, J. (1974). Experience with living familial renal donors. *Surgery, Gynecology, and Obstetrics, 139*, 894–898.

Bernstein, I., & Freeman, H. (1975). *Academic and entrepreneurial research.* New York: Russell Sage Foundation.

Bevan, W. (1976). The sound of the wind that's blowing. *American Psychologist, 31*(7), 481–491.

Bevan, W. (1980a). Academic science and the federal government: Less wed, more locked. In R. Kasschau & F. Kessel (Eds.), *Psychology and society: In search of symbiosis* (pp. 187–217). New York: Holt, Rinehart & Winston.

Bevan, W. (1980b). On getting in bed with a lion. *American Psychologist, 35*(9), 779–789.

Bevan, W. (1982). A sermon of sorts in three plus parts. *American Psychologist, 37*(11), 1303–1322.
Bickman, L. (Ed.). (1980–1983). *Applied social psychology annual*. (Vols. 1–4). Beverly Hills, CA: Sage.
Bloom, B. (1964). *Stability and change in human characteristics*. New York: Wiley.
Boring, E. G. (1929). *A history of experimental psychology*. New York: Century.
Brayfield, A. H. (1967). Psychology and public affairs. *American Psychologist, 22*(3), 182–186.
Brayfield, A. H., & Lipsey, M. W. (1976). Public affairs psychology. In P. J. Woods (Ed.), *Career opportunities for psychologists* (pp. 259–267). Washington, DC: American Psychological Association.
Bronfenbrenner, U. (1975). Is early intervention effective? In M. Guttentag & E. L. Struening (Eds.), *Handbook of evaluation research* (Vol. 2, pp. 519–604). Beverly Hills, CA: Sage.
Brown v. Board of Education, 347 U.S. 483 (1954).
Campbell, D. T. (1969). Reforms as experiments. *American Psychologist, 24*(4), 409–429.
Campbell, D. T. (1975). The social scientist as methodological servant of the experimenting society. In S. Nagel (Ed.), *Policy studies and the social sciences*. Lexington, MA: Lexington Books.
Campbell, D. T., & Stanley, J. (1966). *Experimental and quasi-experimental design for research*. Chicago: Rand McNally.
Caplan, N., & Nelson, S. (1973). On being useful: The nature and consequences of psychological research on social problems. *American Psychologist, 28*(3), 199–211.
Cicirelli, V. G. (1969). *The impact of Head Start: An evaluation of the effects of Head Start on children's cognitive and affective development*. Washington, DC: National Bureau of Standards Institute of Applied Technology.
Clark, K. B., & Clark, M. P. (1958). Racial identification and preference in Negro children. In E. Maccoby, T. M. Newcomb, & E. L. Hartley (Eds.), *Readings in Social Psychology* (3rd ed., pp. 602–611). New York: Holt, Rinehart & Winston.
Cook, S. W. (1984). The 1954 social science statement and school desegregation: A reply to Gerard. *American Psychologist, 39*(8), 819–832.
Cook, T., & Campbell, D. T. (1979). *Quasi-experimentation: Design and analysis issues in field settings*. Chicago: Rand McNally.
Eisendrath, R., Guttman, R., & Murray, J. (1969). Psychological considerations in the selection of kidney transplant donors. *Surgery, Gynecology, and Obstetrics, 129*, 243–248.
Elwork, A., Sales, B., & Alfini, J. (1982). *Making jury instructions understandable*. Charlottesville, VA: Michie/Bobbs-Merrill.
Emmerich, W. (1973). *Disadvantaged children and their first school experiences: ETS—Head Start Longitudinal Study*. Princeton, NJ: Educational Testing Service.
Fairweather, G. W., Sanders, D. H., & Tornatzky, L. G. (1974). *Creating change in mental health organizations*. New York: Pergamon Press.
Fairweather, G. W., & Tornatzky, L. G. (1977). *Experimental methods for social policy research*. New York: Pergamon Press.
Garner, W. R. (1972). The acquisition and application of knowledge: A symbiotic relation. *American Psychologist, 27*(10), 941–946.

Good, P., Simon, G. C., & Coursey, R. D. (1981). Public interest activities of APA members. *American Psychologist, 36*(9), 963–971.

Goodwin, L. (1971). On making social research relevant to public policy and national problem-solving. *American Psychologist, 26*(5), 431–442.

Goodwin, L., & Tu, J. (1975). The social psychological basis for public acceptance of the social security system: The role for social research in public policy formation. *American Psychologist, 30*(9), 875–883.

Greenberger, E. (1983). A researcher in the policy area: The case of child labor. *American Psychologist, 38*(1), 104–111.

Henley, N. (1982, August). *Women as a social problem: Conceptual and practical issues in defining social problems.* Invited address presented at the annual convention of the American Psychological Association, Washington, DC.

Hennigan, K., Flay, B., & Cook, T. (1980). Give me the facts: Some suggestions for using social science knowledge in national policy making. In R. Kidd & M. Saks (Eds.), *Advances in applied social psychology* (Vol. 1). Hillsdale, NJ: Erlbaum.

Hunt, J. M. (1961). *Intelligence and experience.* New York: Ronald Press.

Jackson, J. (1980). Promoting human welfare through legislative advocacy: A proper role for the science of psychology. In R. Kasschau & F. Kessel (Eds.), *Psychology and society: In search of symbiosis* (pp. 147–162). New York: Holt, Rinehart & Winston.

Jones, E., & Davis, K. (1965). From acts to dispositions: The attribution process in person perception. In L. Berkowitz (Ed.), *Advances in experimental social psychology* (Vol. 2). New York: Academic Press.

Joreskog, K. (1970). A general model for analysis of covariance structures. *Biometrica, 57,* 239–251.

Kamin, L. (1974). *The science and politics of IQ.* New York: Wiley.

Kasschau, R., & Kessel, F. (Eds.). (1980). *Psychology and society: In search of symbiosis.* New York: Holt, Rinehart & Winston.

Kemph, J., Bermann, E., & Coppolillo, H. (1969). Kidney transplant and shifts in family dynamics. *American Journal of Psychiatry, 125,* 1485–1490.

Ketterer, R., Price, R., & Politser, P. (1980). The action research paradigm. In R. Price & P. Politser (Eds.), *Evaluation and action in the social environment* (pp. 1–15). New York: Academic Press.

Kidd, R., & Saks, M. (Eds.). (1980). *Advances in applied social psychology* (Vol. 1). Hillsdale, NJ: Erlbaum.

Kidd, R., & Saks, M. (Eds.). (1983). *Advances in applied social psychology* (Vol. 2). Hillsdale, NJ: Erlbaum.

Kiesler, C. A. (1980a). Mental health policy as a field of inquiry for psychology. *American Psychologist, 35*(12), 1066–1080.

Kiesler, C. A. (1980b). Psychology and public policy. In L. Bickman (Ed.), *Applied social psychology annual* (Vol. 1). Beverly Hills, CA: Sage.

Kiesler, C. A. (1982). Mental hospitals and alternative care: Noninstitutionalization as potential public policy for mental patients. *American Psychologist, 37*(4), 349–360.

Kiesler, C. A. (1983). Psychology and public policy. In E. M. Altmaier & M. E. Meyer (Eds.), *Applied specialties in psychology.* Reading, MA: Addison-Wesley.

Kimble, G. A. (1982). *The limits of advocacy.* Unpublished manuscript.

Koch, S. (1980). Psychology and its human clientele: Beneficiaries or victims?

In R. Kasschau & F. Kessel (Eds.), *Psychology and society: In search of symbiosis* (pp. 30–52). New York: Holt, Rinehart & Winston.
Korten, F. F., Cook, S. W., & Lacey, J. I. (1970). *Psychology and the problems of society*. Washington, DC: American Psychological Association.
Levine, M. (1976). The academic achievement test: Its historical context and social functions. *American Psychologist, 31*(3), 228–238.
Levine, M., & Levine, A. (1970). *A social history of the helping services: Clinic, court, school and community*. New York: Appleton-Century-Crofts.
Lewin, K. (1946). Action research and minority problems. *Journal of Social Issues, 2*, 34–46.
Lewin, K. (1947). Frontiers in group dynamics: Part II, Social planning and action research. *Human Relations, 1*, 143–153.
Lewin, K. (1951). *Field theory in social science*. New York: Harper.
Lewis, O. (1961). *Children of Sanchez*. New York: Basic Books.
Linney, J. A., & Reppucci, N. D. (1982). Research design and methods in community psychology. In P. Kendall & J. Butcher (Eds.), *Handbook of research methods in clinical psychology* (pp. 535–566). New York: Wiley.
Loftus, E., & Monahan, J. (1980). Trial by data: Psychological research as legal evidence. *American Psychologist, 35*(3), 270–283.
Maruyama, M. (1983). Cross-cultural perspectives on social and community change. In E. Seidman (Ed.), *Handbook of social intervention* (pp. 33–47). Beverly Hills, CA: Sage.
Massad, P., Sales, B., & Acosta, E. (1983). Utilizing social science information in the policy process: Can psychologists help? In R. Kidd & M. Saks (Eds.), *Advances in applied social psychology* (Vol. 2, pp. 213–229). Hillsdale, NJ: Erlbaum.
Massad, P., Sales, B., & Sabatier, P. (1983). Influencing state legislature decisions. In L. Bickman (Ed.), *Applied social psychology annual* (Vol. 4). Beverly Hills, CA: Sage.
Masters, J. C. (1984). Psychology, research, and social policy. *American Psychologist, 39*(8), 851–862.
Miller, G. A. (1969). Psychology as a means of promoting human welfare. *American Psychologist, 24*(12), 1063–1075.
Mitroff, I. I., & Turoff, M. (1973). Technological forecasting and assessment: Science and/or mythology. *Technological Forecasting and Social Change, 5*, 113–134.
Monahan, J. (1977). Community psychology and public policy: The promise and the pitfalls. In B. Sales (Ed.), *Psychology in the legal process* (pp. 197–214). New York: Spectrum Books.
Muller v. Oregon, 208 U.S. 412 (1908).
Nagel, S. (Ed.). (1975). *Policy studies and the social sciences*. Lexington, MA: Lexington Books.
O'Donnell, J. M. (1979). The crisis of experimentalism in the 1920s: E. G. Boring and his uses of history. *American Psychologist, 34*(4), 289–295.
Olmedo, E. L. (1981). Testing linguistic minorities. *American Psychologist, 36*(10), 1078–1085.
Rappaport, J. (1977). *Community psychology: Values, research and action*. New York: Holt, Rinehart & Winston.
Reppucci, N. D., & Kirk, R. (1983). Psychology and public policy. In R. Kidd & M. Saks (Eds.), *Advances in applied social psychology* (Vol. 2, pp. 163–187). New York: Erlbaum.

Reppucci, N. D., & Kirk, R. (1984). Psychology and public policy. In G. McCall & G. Weber (Eds.), *Social science and public policy: The roles of academic disciplines in policy analysis* (pp. 129–158). Port Washington, NY: Associated Faculty Press.

Reppucci, N. D., & Sarason, S. B. (1979). Public policy and human service institutions. *American Journal of Community Psychology, 7,* 521–542.

Reppucci, N. D., & Saunders, J. T. (1974). Social psychology of behavior modification: Problems of implementation in natural settings. *American Psychologist, 29*(9), 649–660.

Reppucci, N. D., & Saunders, J. T. (1977). History, action, and change. *American Journal of Community Psychology, 5,* 399–412.

Reppucci, N. D., & Saunders, J. T. (1983). Focal issues for institutional change. *Professional Psychology: Research and Practice, 14,* 514–528.

Reschly, D. J. (1981). Psychological testing in educational classification and placement. *American Psychologist, 36*(10), 1094–1102.

Robinson, D. N. (1984). Ethics and advocacy. *American Psychologist, 39*(7), 787–793.

Rosen, P. L. (1972). *The Supreme Court and social science.* Urbana, IL: University of Illinois Press.

Rosen, P. L. (1980). History and state of the art of applied social research in the courts. In M. Saks & C. Baron (Eds.), *The use/nonuse/misuse of applied social research in the courts* (pp. 9–15). Cambridge, MA: Abt Books.

Saks, M. J. (1978). Social psychological contributions to a legislative subcommittee on organ and tissue transplants. *American Psychologist, 33*(7), 680–690.

Sarason, S. B. (1972). *The creation of settings and the future societies.* San Francisco, CA: Jossey-Bass.

Sarason, S. B. (1975). Psychology *To the Finland Station* in *The Heavenly City of the Eighteenth Century Philosophers. American Psychologist, 30*(11), 1072–1080.

Sarason, S. B. (1976). Community psychology, networks, and Mr. Everyman. *American Psychologist, 31*(5), 317–328.

Sarason, S. B. (1978). The nature of problem solving in social action. *American Psychologist, 33*(4), 370–380.

Saunders, J. T., & Reppucci, N. D. (1977). Learning networks among administrators of human service institutions. *American Journal of Community Psychology, 5,* 269–276.

Saunders, J. T., & Reppucci, N. D. (1978). The social identity of behavior modification. In M. Hersen, R. Eisler, & P. Miller (Eds.), *Progress in behavior modification* (Vol. 6, pp. 143–158). New York: Academic Press.

Scriven, M. (1980). An evaluation of psychology. In R. Kasschau & F. Kessel (Eds.), *Psychology and society: In search of symbiosis* (pp. 62–77). New York: Holt, Rinehart & Winston.

Sechrest, L., West, S. G., Phillips, M., Redner, R., & Yeaton, W. (1979). Some neglected problems in evaluation research: Strength and integrity of treatments. In L. Sechrest, S. G. West, M. Phillips, R. Redner, & W. Yeaton (Eds.), *Evaluation studies: Review annual* (Vol. 4). Beverly Hills, CA: Sage.

Segall, M. (1976). *Human behavior and public policy: A political psychology.* New York: Pergamon Press.

Seidman, E. (1981). The route from the successful experiment to policy formation. In R. Roesch & R. Corrado (Eds.), *Evaluation and criminal justice policy.* Beverly Hills, CA: Sage.

Seidman, E. (1983). Unexamined premises of social problem solving. In E. Seidman (Ed.), *Handbook of social intervention* (pp. 48–67). Beverly Hills, CA: Sage.

Skinner, B. F. (1971). *Beyond freedom and dignity.* New York: Knopf.

Stephenson, G. M., & Davis, J. (Eds.). (1981). *Progress in applied social psychology* (Vol. 1). New York: Wiley.

Stern, P. C., & Gardner, G. T. (1981). Psychological research and energy policy. *American Psychologist, 36*(4), 329–342.

Stipek, D., Valentine, J., & Zigler, E. (1979). Project Head Start: A critique of theory and practice. In E. Zigler & J. Valentine (Eds.), *Project Head Start: A legacy of the War on Poverty.* New York: Free Press.

Tangri, S. S., & Strasburg, G. L. (1979). Can research on women be more effective in shaping policy? *Psychology of Women Quarterly, 3*(4), 321–343.

Toulmin, S. (1981). Toward reintegration: An agenda for psychology's second century. In R. Kasschau & C. Cofer (Eds.), *Psychology's second century: Enduring issues* (pp. 264–286). New York: Praeger.

Valentine, J., & Zigler, E. (1983). Head Start: A case study in the development of social policy for children and families. In E. Zigler, S. Kagan, & E. Klugmen (Eds.), *Children, families and government* (pp. 266–280). Cambridge, England: University of Cambridge Press.

Weiss, C. (1975). Evaluation research in the political context. In E. L. Struening & M. Guttentag (Eds.), *Handbook of evaluation research* (Vol. 1, pp. 13–26). Beverly Hills, CA: Sage.

Weiss, J. (1976). Using social science for social policy. *Policy Sciences Journal, 4,* 234–238.

Weiss, C. (Ed.). (1977). *Using social research in public policy making.* Lexington, MA: Heath.

Weiss, C., & Bucuvalas, M. (1977). The challenge of social research to decision making. In C. Weiss (Ed.), *Using social science research in public policy making.* Lexington, MA: Heath.

White, S. (1980). Psychology in all sorts of places. In R. Kasschau & F. Kessel (Eds.), *Psychology and society: In search of symbiosis* (pp. 105–131). New York: Holt, Rinehart & Winston.

Wolfgang, M. E. (1974). The social scientist in court. *Journal of Criminal Law and Criminology, 65,* 239–247.

Zigler, E., Kagan, S., & Klugman, E. (Eds.). (1983). *Children, families and government.* Cambridge, England: University of Cambridge Press.

Zigler, E., & Valentine, J. (Eds.). (1979). *Project Head Start: A legacy of the War on Poverty.* New York: Free Press.

Zilbergeld, B. (1983). *The shrinking of America: Myths of psychological change.* Boston: Little, Brown.

DOUGLAS W. BLOOMQUIST

TEACHING SENSATION AND PERCEPTION: ITS AMBIGUOUS AND SUBLIMINAL ASPECTS

DOUGLAS W. BLOOMQUIST

Douglas W. Bloomquist is associate professor and chair of psychology at Framingham State College in Massachusetts. He received his PhD in experimental psychology from Michigan State University. Previously, he earned his bachelor's and master's degrees at Bucknell University. In 1968–70 he was on active duty at the U.S. Army Natick Laboratories near Boston as a research psychologist and acting head of the Sensory Evaluation Laboratory. Subsequently, he taught at the State University College of New York at Oneonta for 3 years before going to Framingham State in 1973.

Bloomquist has participated in numerous sessions at national and regional meetings concerned with teaching approaches and career opportunities for bachelor's-level graduates. He is a past president of the Council of Undergraduate Psychology Departments. In 1981 he received honorable mention recognition for the American Psychological Association's (APA) Division Two Teaching Award. He wrote *A Guide to Preparing a Psychology Student Handbook* that is distributed by the APA Educational Affairs Office and is co-author with Harold O. Kiess of two texts on psychological research methods being published this year, *Psychological Research Methods: A Conceptual Approach* and *Understanding, Conducting, and Reporting Psychological Research: A Workbook for Students*.

DOUGLAS W. BLOOMQUIST

TEACHING SENSATION AND PERCEPTION: ITS AMBIGUOUS AND SUBLIMINAL ASPECTS

As introductory psychology textbooks tend to become more and more encyclopedic in their coverage of topics, I think instructors feel increasingly constrained when deciding what to present to students and how. In the typical introductory psychology course, approximately one week might be devoted to any one of the many areas represented in the textbook. Thus teaching the broad area of sensation and perception might be scheduled to take only one week, too. Many instructors feel pressured into providing more information in class with no increase in the time available to do so. This can be frustrating, as one wonders whether the information that students in an introductory-level course are asked to absorb is too overwhelming and whether the coverage in class presentations is too superficial.

I had similar apprehensions about this presentation in the G. Stanley Hall lecture series. A dilemma resides in the conflicting demands placed upon the lecturers as they try to fulfill the underlying purposes of the lecture series. We are asked to present the latest developments in the subject area we address and to suggest innovative and effective ways for teaching the subject matter as well. Accordingly, I sense that there may be conflicting expectations among the audience for this lecture: Some individuals are interested principally in learning of current developments in the field, I assume, whereas others are looking primarily for ideas on how to teach material relevant to the introductory psychology (or sensation and perception) course. In the very early stages of preparing this lecture, I realized just how difficult it would be to try to meet both needs.

Choosing which issues or topics to address in my presentation was not easy. It was important to keep in mind that the principal audience—those who teach the introductory psychology course—teach at different kinds of institutions and come to the course with different academic backgrounds and areas of interest within the discipline of psychology. Moreover, I know that it is unrealistic to expect that students and instructors will be equally enthusiastic about all areas covered in an introductory-level survey course. Accordingly, in this chapter I first identify some problems encountered in teaching sensation and perception—one being that the area does not inherently appeal to as many students as other areas in psychology do—and then I provide suggestions for dealing with the problems.

Subsequently, I address several specific areas that seem to vary widely in interest value and credibility among students and instructors. These include psychophysics, which is often greeted with yuks and yawns but includes methodological contributions that seem to be unappreciated; subliminal stimulation, a related issue that interests students considerably but which is often not regarded as a worthy topic by authors and instructors; and ambiguous figures, which fascinate everyone, I think. Specifically, then, this chapter deals with the following issues: (a) ways of introducing the area of sensation and perception in the introductory psychology course; (b) various kinds of ambiguous figures and some unfamiliar examples; (c) the contributions of S. S. Stevens to measuring sensation; and (d) subliminal advertising, for which reported effects, although dubious, are often eagerly accepted by students.

While researching these topics, I found it stimulating to discover (and rediscover) some of the old literature as well as to learn of new developments. Although I did not intentionally slight the more recent research, much of this presentation draws upon earlier work that is not usually discussed in introductory psychology textbooks, or even in sensation and perception textbooks. Throughout, I have tried to suggest ways to stimulate the interest of students (and instructors) in issues related to understanding how we perceive the external world.

The Relevance of Sensation and Perception to the Introductory Psychology Course

Is the Subject Matter Intimidating?

I know that sensation and perception, a standard area in the introductory psychology course, is not always enthusiastically received by students or sometimes even by instructors. This indifference is understandable, I think, for several reasons. What happens is that when students take a look at chapters on sensation and perception, they find structures of the eye and the ear illustrated in detail and discussion of the dimensions of light and auditory stimuli, such as wavelength in nanometers and intensity in decibels. Their first impression, therefore, is that sensation and perception involves a lot of physics, biology, and physiology. The question they raise, at least covertly, is, "What does this have to do with psychology?"

Similarly, an instructor may feel uncomfortable with the content related to sensory processes and perception, particularly if his or her own areas of specialization and interest are not in experimental psychology. Certainly most instructors feel more confident when discussing areas that lie closest to their training. It is understandable, then, that where choices have to be made, instructors will include or exclude some topics from the course syllabus on the basis of what they feel most knowledgeable about and comfortable with. Sensation and perception may be viewed by students and instructors as one of the less glamorous or interesting areas within psychology. In such instances, then, instructors may be inclined to exclude the area from the course or give it a cursory treatment at most.

I will document this observation briefly with an anecdote. A part-time instructor of an introductory course at a university in Massachusetts called a member of my department who was teaching the introductory course at the time. During their conversation, the caller asked my colleague, "You don't teach that physiological and perception junk, do you?" The point I want to make here is that the broad area of sensation and perception may need to be marketed more skillfully to students and instructors. Historically, of course, the area broadly defined as sensation and perception has been an important part of the discipline and therefore deserves to be included in an introductory psychology course. Indeed, instructors familiar with the history of psychology understand that the development of the science of psychology largely parallels the history of problems in sensation and perception.

Another, possibly pragmatic, reason for teaching sensation and perception in the introductory course is that there are many fascinating phenomena within the area that can be demonstrated in class. It can be fun to teach! And students do enjoy many of the demonstrations that are usually incorporated into the textbooks, such as negative afterimages, visual illusions, and so forth.

Sensations and Perceptions Are Psychological

I have already alluded to one problem in teaching sensation and perception: Students may not understand why perceptual phenomena are really psychological rather than biological or physical in nature. Although I am reluctant to make simplistic distinctions and to categorize subject matter by disciplines, I think students need to be convinced that sensory processes and perception relate to psychology. In introducing the area of sensation and perception to students, textbook authors properly point out that we obtain information about the external world through our senses. They go on to explain that the study of the sensory processes and perception examines how the representation of the external world is created and experienced and how well our perceptions correspond to reality (see, for example, Coren, Porac, & Ward, 1984, pp. 2–3). But still, I do not think that students initially appreciate why perceptual phenomena are psychological.

A sound is not a sound. If a tree falls in a forest and no one is around, does it make a sound? I often introduce sensation and perception with this proverbial question. When students respond, most of them predictably say, "Yes, it does." But I tell them that is not the answer psychologists provide; the answer is "No." I explain that a sound is a subjective experience that occurs only in the ear and brain of the listener. There are sound waves, of course, more specifically, cyclical air pressures created by air molecules alternately compressing or expanding that can be described in terms of frequencies and amplitudes. But no sound occurs unless this physical stimulus impinges upon a specialized receptor and produces neural impulses that go to a specific place in the brain and are experienced. In other words, a sound is not a sound unless it is heard.

This view is subject to debate, of course. The issue is periodically argued about by Johnny Carson and Ed McMahon on the "Tonight Show." I have found it fun to bait colleagues in the physics department at my college on the matter. I think, though, that they are inclined to dismiss my argument as a matter of semantics. But, then, it is interesting to observe that there is considerable overlap in the material on sound found in physics textbooks and the chapters on audition found in sensation and perception textbooks. Both kinds of books, for example, present psychophysical threshold functions, which show how the ability to detect the presence of a sound stimulus (psychological) is related to the characteristics of the sound stimulus (physical).

The whole question may be a moot issue, though. One viewer of the "Tonight Show" a year or so ago sent in an article from a scientific publication that addressed the issue on the basis of quantum physics. The point was made, as I recall, that whether a tree falls and makes a sound is irrelevant: The tree does not even have to fall, because there is no tree unless there is someone there to see it!

Does light contain color? This is another question that I pose to get students to understand the psychological nature of sensory experiences. I project a green light on a screen (through a green filter) and ask a series of related questions: Is color a property of light? Does the light contain the color? Where does the "greenness" come from? If students have been "set up" with the argument that a sound is not a sound unless it is heard, then they anticipate that the answer to the question posed here is "No, light does not contain color." To help students understand that color, too, is a subjective experience, it is useful to point out that most animals can respond to green light (or paint) but do not see it as green. Furthermore, people who are color blind experience green light or paint subjectively as yellow. The point, then, as was summarized by Geldard (1972) in his classic text on sensory processes, is that "a color is not a color until it is seen" (p. 22).

Sugar is not sweet. There are numerous related examples that may help students to understand the difference between the psychological and physical aspects of sensory experiences. It can be pointed out, for instance, that sugar tastes sweet, but that it is not sweet. Again, the sweetness is in the brain of the individual, not in the substance itself.

I raise these and other questions about sensory experiences to demonstrate why perceptual phenomena are really psychological. Subjective experiences are psychological, although they are initiated by physical stimuli, and physiological processes are prominently involved, of course. Indeed, McBurney and Collings (1984) emphasize the interdisciplinary nature of the area, "with people trained in physics, chemistry, and physiology all contributing to our knowledge of perception" (p. 1).

The Distinction Between Sensation and Perception

When teaching sensation and perception, it is appropriate to distinguish between the two terms. After all, instructors do identify two areas—sensation and perception. Introductory texts sometimes include separate chapters on the topics, one dealing essentially with sensory processes and the other with perception (usually visual perception). Where both topics are treated within a single chapter, sensory processes are usually discussed first, followed by traditional issues in perception. The fact that the two topics are treated separately suggests that there is a meaningful distinction between them. What is the difference? Table 1 presents definitions of the terms excerpted from several textbooks written for undergraduate-level sensation and perception courses. Although some of the authors suggest that meaningful distinctions are problematic—for example, "the distinction is blurry" (Goldstein, 1984)—most authors do differentiate between the two terms.

Table 1
Comparison of Textbook Definitions of *Sensation* and *Perception*

Sources	Definitions
Bennett (1978)	*Sensation:* "the means by which sensory information (that is, information about changes in the environment) is relayed to the brain." (p. 1)
	Perception: "refers to the ways in which we experience our sensory world. Perception occurs once sensory information has been conducted, via sensation, to the brain.... Perception is the process of extracting relevant information about the world from the influx of stimulation." (pp. 1–2)
	Note: Bennett stresses the importance of perception as an adaptive process and cites Gibson's description of perception as an "active process" that enables an organism to survive in its environment.
Schiff (1980)	*Perception:* "involves awareness of objects, events, scenes, and their representations in the environment and sometimes within our bodies, such awarenesses having arrived through the senses in the very recent past. Perception also involves searching for, obtaining, and sometimes processing information." (p. 6)
Levine & Shefner (1981)	*Sensation:* "refers to the process of detecting a stimulus (or some aspect of it) in the environment. It is the necessary collection of information about the world from which perceptions will be made." (p. 1)
	Perception: "refers to the way in which we interpret the information gathered (and processed) by the senses. In a word, we sense the presence of a stimulus, but we perceive what it is." (p. 1)
Schiffman (1982)	*Sensations:* "traditionally ... refer to certain immediate and direct qualitative experiences—qualities or attributes such as 'hard,' 'warm,' 'red,' and so on—produced by simple isolated physical stimuli. Moreover, the study of

Table 1, continued

Sources	Definitions
Schiffman, continued	sensations is primarily associated with structure, physiology, and general sense-receptor activity." (p. 1) *Perception:* "generally refers to psychological processes whereby meaning, past experience, or memory and judgment are involved. Perceptions are associated with the organization and integration of sensory attributes, that is, the awareness of 'things' and 'events' rather than mere attributes or qualities." (p. 1) Note: Schiffman states, "The distinction between the two is of greater historical relevance than of contemporary taxonomic utility." In addition, "there is a growing trend to view many of the 'perceptual' processes as part of a third, closely allied area—*cognition* or cognitive psychology" (p. 1).
Matlin (1983)	*Perception:* "is the study of the way you gather and interpret information about the world around you." (p. 2)
Goldstein (1984)	*Sensations:* "are usually thought to be simple, basic experiences elicited by simple stimuli.... Sensations are often linked to the activity of the sensory receptors." (p. 2) *Perceptions:* "are usually thought to be more complicated experiences elicited by complex, often meaningful stimuli" and "are often said to be the result of a higher-order process than sensations, being the result of an integration, or putting together, of the more simple sensations.... Perceptions are often linked to physiological activity in the brain." (p. 2) Note: Goldstein states, "Historically, a distinction has been made between sensations and perceptions ... In practice, the dividing line between the two is rather blurred." (p. 2)
Coren, Porac, and Ward (1984)	*Sensation:* "The study of sensation, or *sensory processes,* is concerned with the first contact

Table 1, continued

Sources	Definitions
Coren et al., continued	between the organism and the environment.... Such studies tend to focus on less complex (although not less complicated) aspects of our conscious experience" (e.g., brightness, loudness, or color). (p. 9)
	Perception: is concerned with "our conscious experience of objects and object relationships" (e.g., what an object is, where, how far away, how large).... The study of perception is concerned with "how we form a conscious representation of the outside environment and the accuracy of that representation." (p. 9)
	Note: Coren et al. state, "We recognize that it is difficult, perhaps impossible, and most certainly unwise to attempt to draw sharp lines separating one field of inquiry from another" (p. 9)

I summarize the definitions presented in Table 1 as follows: Sensations are relatively simple attributes or qualities such as brightness, loudness, redness, and so forth. Sensations result from a passive process in which an immediate qualitative experience reliably occurs when specialized receptors are stimulated. In contrast, perception is a more active process that involves complex experiences such as recognizing objects from an array of stimulation and identifying aspects such as the shape, size, and distance of things. Another distinction is that the study of the sensory processes and sensation emphasizes structure and activity at the receptor level, whereas perceptions involve more central processes such as memory, experience, and information processing.

A dramatic illustration of the complex nature of perceptions as opposed to sensations is given in Figure 1. Dallenbach (1951) introduced this "puzzle picture" in the *American Journal of Psychology,* which was founded by G. Stanley Hall. I know of only a couple of sensation and perception textbooks in which the figure has appeared (e.g., Goldstein, 1980; Levine & Shefner, 1981) and I have not seen it in any introductory psychology textbook. Accordingly, I assume that many instructors (and students) have not seen it before. The question, as the figure caption asks, is "What is it?"

Most first-time observers do not immediately perceive a meaningful configuration. Indeed, as Dallenbach states, the picture

SENSATION AND PERCEPTION

"appears when first scrutinized as an amorphous blotch without meaning or organization" (1951, p. 433). One reason for this inability to perceive what is there is that the picture is turned 90 degrees counterclockwise. When you orient it properly, however—so that it is turned horizontally with the figure caption on the left side and the predominantly white area in the lower right side—you most likely will still see it as meaningless. In other words, you are still looking at an array of stimulation, but a meaningless array of black, white, and gray.

The picture is actually a black-and-white photograph of something familiar to everyone. It is fun to ask students to relate initially what they do see. This request usually generates some predictable responses, such as a bird or turtle, and sometimes novel responses (e.g., a pilot). Upon seeing the photograph for the first time a few individuals will immediately recognize what it is. But most people have difficulty (as perhaps you do). One colleague suggested that inspecting the picture is akin to what William James described as a baby's first perceptual experience, that is, "one great, blooming, buzzing confusion" (James, 1890, p. 488). That is an apt description.

While looking at this so-called puzzle picture, one can readily appreciate that perception is an active process. Are you not struggling, for example, to impose some organization upon the meaningless array that you are in fact sensing? Do you not find yourself generating hypotheses about the figure and then testing them by searching for features in the picture that are congruent with the possibility? Moreover, if, after a few minutes of inspection, you cannot perceive the subject of the picture, you will probably experience some degree of frustration.

Figure 1. A photograph of something familiar to everyone. What is it? Reprinted from Dallenbach (1951) by permission.

The subject of the picture is a cow. The cow is not hidden in the figure; it is the principal subject. It is not a complete cow, however, with a head, body, four legs, and a tail. Instead, the photograph shows only a full front view of its head and forequarters. Everyone can eventually perceive it.

Why is it so difficult to perceive the cow? Dallenbach (1951, 1952) suggests that even when asked if he or she can see the cow, the observer adopts a set to perceive a complete figure, not part of one, and to perceive a figure hidden within the details of the picture. Dallenbach (1951) explained, "The chief principle of concealment in this puzzle picture is, as the writer believes, the set of the observer" (p. 433).

Newhall (1952) gave an alternate explanation for the obscurity of the cow: There are not sufficient contours present to readily differentiate the figure from the ground in the picture. Crowley (1952) made the same point: "The ground is made up of irregular spots of black and white, and so also is the figure" (p. 304). Both Dallenbach's and Newhall's explanations are based entirely on anecdotal evidence and speculation. Regardless of what makes it difficult for most observers to perceive the cow, the picture demonstrates compellingly that perception is a more complex process than students might initially appreciate, and that there is, in fact, much more to seeing than meets the eye. Whenever I present Dallenbach's puzzle picture to students in introductory courses, it is always well received. I do not understand, therefore, why it is not featured more often in textbooks for these courses.

Perceptual Issues and Demonstrations

In an introductory psychology course, I introduce sensation and perception by identifying and demonstrating some of the so-called problems in perception with which psychologists deal. By doing this, I hope to show students that they take their perceptual experiences for granted, and by illustrating phenomena that are not intuitively explained, I hope to stimulate their interest in this subject area. Essentially, then, I bring out the "toys"—apparatus and transparencies or slides—that I think provide thought-provoking demonstrations. If some of the demonstrations are discussed in the text being used, I may choose alternate examples, but I have found that students enjoy a wide variety of relevant demonstrations, whether they are described in their textbook or not. In my courses, I present the perceptual problems that follow. Subsequently in this chapter, I present information on topics related to these perceptual problems that instructors may wish to consider incorporating into class presentations.

1. *We cannot perceive all that is there.* We do not perceive or respond to all stimuli "out there." Many stimuli of which we are unaware impinge upon our sensory receptors. This is obvious, of course, but it leads to three basic questions addressed by the methodology of psychophysics. First, what stimuli are we capable of responding to? In other words, what are the boundaries to our sensory worlds? A stimulus must be present in some minimal amount in order to be experienced, but some animals and individuals have more sensitivity to weak stimuli than do others. Furthermore, some organisms can respond to visual stimuli that lie outside our visual spectrum or to high frequencies of auditory stimuli that are ultrasonic to us.

Second, how well can we respond to changes in stimulation? How much does a stimulus have to change before we are aware that it has changed? Although many instruments such as light meters, voltmeters, thermometers, and so forth precisely monitor the slightest changes in stimulation, we are not nearly so proficient at registering changes in stimulation psychologically.

Third, perhaps the most interesting psychophysical question is, How is the magnitude of psychological sensation related to the intensity of a stimulus? Contrary to the usual first guess, sensation magnitude is not directly proportional to the amount of stimulation. To illustrate, a perceived amount of brightness is not directly related to the intensity of light. A solution of two teaspoons of sugar and water does not taste twice as sweet as a solution with one teaspoon of sugar. What, then, is the relation, and how do we know? These three questions are fundamental to the study and methodology of sensation and perception; they deal with psychophysics.

2. *We can perceive what is not there.* Sometimes we perceive something even when no external stimulus exists to cause the perception. Negative and positive afterimages and subjective colors are examples of how we perceive something that does not actually exist "out there" when we experience it, and they do seem to intrigue students. Negative afterimages are usually described in introductory texts and are easily induced by stimuli provided in the texts. Positive afterimages, however, are infrequently mentioned.

The most familiar example of positive afterimages is the persistent image of a flashbulb that one experiences after looking directly at the flash when being photographed. More compelling positive afterimages cannot be easily demonstrated to students in a classroom, for they are best induced in a dark room. For example, when a highly-reflective object (e.g., a person's face or a light-colored shirt) is illuminated with a very intense light for about 1 msec or so (e.g., an electronic flash), and the observer closes his or her eyes immediately after the flash, a person or even a whole corner of a room will be perceived in the original colors, although they may seem frozen like a still photograph. The afterimage usually lasts only for a few seconds; its duration and vividness vary with the intensity of the light and the reflectance of the objects illuminated.

A recent article in a tabloid magazine reported that computer screens affect one's sense of color. The article pointed out that if a person looks for a long time at a green computer monitor, the screen will look amber. Without using the term, the article described the negative afterimage phenomenon but explained it merely as a "minor physiological curiosity." Students can be told that such color alterations are actually well understood.

3. *Perceptions mirror the external world.* What we perceive is different from what the sensory receptors receive. All visual perceptions, of course, are initiated by stimuli that are registered on the retina, no matter how impoverished these stimuli are. Often our perceptions do recreate external reality (as we know it) quite faithfully, despite the fact that the perceptions often do not necessarily correspond to the initiating image that is registered on the retina. I am referring here, obviously, to the problem of perceptual constancy.

The perceptual constancies such as shape, size, and color are examples of a general visual phenomenon that students take for granted. By pointing out that objects do not appear to grow or shrink when the size of the image registered on the retina changes in size, instructors invite the question, "Why not?" Similarly, why does the shape of a door not appear to change as one moves about a room even though the shape on the retina changes? So, perceptions are stable, and therefore we assume, understandably, that what we perceive is a faithful recreation of the external world, even though neither the perception nor the object corresponds to the retinal stimulation. Yet, we are also vulnerable to misperceptions of the external world.

4. *Perceptions are illusory.* We can be easily fooled into perceiving things the way they are not, even if they are represented accurately on the retina. In such instances, of course, our perceptions are not faithfully recreating the external world. Students will be familiar with many examples of so-called optical illusions, and textbooks invariably feature the best-known illusions, for example, the Müller-Lyer illusion.

The horizontal–vertical illusion is the simplest but perhaps most powerful of the so-called line illusions. It also lends itself to a persuasive demonstration of how susceptible we are to illusory perception. To illustrate the point, I present the horizontal–vertical illusion in reverse. I project a slide upon which I have drawn a vertical line 15 mm long that bisects a 20-mm-long horizontal line at a right angle. I tell my students that both lines appear to be about equally long, and they generally agree. They are surprised, then, when I explain that the vertical line is actually 25 percent shorter than the horizontal line. Then, I show a slide with both the horizontal and vertical lines drawn to equal lengths (20 mm), and the illusion is very evident.

The moon illusion is another powerful illusion that all students have seen, but they have probably not realized that it is a false perception. Common sense suggests that early in the evening the moon appears to be larger on the horizon than when it is higher in the sky because it must be closer to earth, and therefore to the observer. This is not the case, however. In either location the moon is the same distance from the observer and therefore forms the same-size retinal image. Many students are surprised to learn that it is an illusion. Several explanations of the illusion are summarized by Coren, Porac, and Ward (1984), Schiffman (1982), and in other textbooks on perception.

Students are intrigued when they learn that it is extremely difficult, if not impossible, to not experience these and other illusions—even when they know they are being fooled. Furthermore, having pointed out that perceptions, on the one hand, accurately represent the external world, but, on the other, are vulnerable to distortion, it is fun to ask (philosophical issues aside), How, then, can we ever be sure that what we perceive is really the way the world is?

5. *Perceptions can be ambiguous.* Sometimes our perceptual processes can be teased with a stimulus configuration that can be interpreted in more than one way. When alternative configurations readily lend themselves to equally good (or reasonable) interpretations, then the perceptual situation is ambiguous. Most introductory textbooks feature the classic examples of ambiguous figures—Rubin's vase–faces (or, chalice and faces) figure, the "wife and mother-in-law" figure, and the reversible Necker cube. Other examples of ambiguous figures commonly illustrated in textbooks include those found in the art work of Maurits Escher and Salvador Dali. But many other ambiguous figures that appear in the psychological literature are presented infrequently or not at all in textbooks. I present some of these figures to illustrate several types of ambiguous figures and to discuss their use in research in a following section.

Ambiguities in Perception

Ambiguous figures is an umbrella term that embraces different types of figures that generate alternative perceptions. These figures differ with respect to their stimulus features and the kinds of alternative perceptions they generate. Introductory textbooks generally do not distinguish among types of ambiguous figures. Because of their structural and functional differences, I think that a relatively simple taxonomy for classifying the variety of so-called ambiguous figures is useful.

Figure—Ground Reversals

A fundamental perceptual phenomenon in form perception is that a visual field can be differentiated into a distinct portion that stands out from the rest, that is, one part of the field is seen as figure and the remainder as ground. A common contour usually separates the figure and ground regions, but neither region overlaps or encloses the other. The factors that are presumed to determine the differentiation of figure from ground are often summarized in textbooks. In some visual configurations, however, figure and ground aspects can reverse, thereby making the configuration ambiguous. In such figures, the aspect of the configuration that initially represents the ground portion subsequently will be perceived as the meaningful figure portion. Whether a particular region is perceived as figure or ground will depend on the observer's focus of attention and how the shape of the contour is interpreted.

The classic example of this kind of ambiguous figure is Rubin's vase—faces figure in which one can alternately perceive either a vase (or chalice) or two faces in profile. As is characteristic of most ambiguous figures, one presumably cannot perceive both aspects at the same time; either one sees the two faces in profile or the vase, but

Figure 2. "Napoleon and tomb at St. Helena," a figure-ground reversal example. Reprinted from Fernberger (1950) by permission.

not both. Escher and Dali created some of the most interesting examples of figure–ground reversals in their art work.

Two less-familiar ambiguous figures that may involve figure–ground reversals are the hidden-figure drawings shown in Figures 2 and 3. The picture titled "Napoleon and Tomb at St. Helena" (Fig. 2) was introduced into the psychological literature by Fernberger (1950). Originally an etching that originated about 1830, the picture contains a full-length figure of Napoleon with arms folded, hidden between two trees. When the trees are perceived as prominent figure aspects of the scene, Napoleon is hidden in what appears to be the relatively formless ground portion between the two trees. But when attention is focused on this white ground portion, Napoleon becomes salient, and the trees then become less well defined. A similar kind of figure drawn by Currier and Ives is shown in Figure 3. "The Tomb and Shade of Washington" was introduced into the psychological literature by Carmichael (1951), who suggested that the hidden picture of Napoleon (Fig. 2) inspired Currier and Ives to create this American version in the 1860s.

Figure 3. "The tomb and shade of Washington," a figure-ground reversal example. Reprinted from Carmichael (1951) by permission.

Embedded Ambiguous Figures

In another category of ambiguous figures, two or more meaningful figure aspects are embedded within the contours of a stimulus configuration. The "wife and mother-in-law" figure (discussed in Boring, 1930) is perhaps the most familiar example. In this figure, created by Hill (1915) and published in *Puck* magazine, the aspects of both the young woman (wife) and the old woman (mother-in-law) are created by the same features. One aspect or the other is seen, depending on how the observer interprets the features in the configuration. For example, one contour in the figure can be seen as either the jaw of the wife or the nose of the mother-in-law.

Unlike reversible figure–ground figures, both meaningfully perceived aspects—either the young or the old woman—are embedded within common contours. In this type of figure, therefore, the ambiguity is not between figure and ground, but between which of the two possible aspects the figure actually represents. As in figure–ground reversals, both aspects cannot be perceived at the same time; here, one perceives either the young or the old woman, but not both simultaneously.

Boring (1930) clarified the distinction made between the two types of ambiguous figures that are illustrated by the "wife and mother-in-law" and vase–faces figures. He stated that in the former figure "the two alternating figures interpenetrate each other spatially and there is no definite division of the field by a contour" (p. 444). Attneave (1971) argued that in the case of embedded ambiguous figures, ambiguity exists because the stimulus input can be matched to different stored schemata. He explained that if two schemata match the stimulus configuration about equally well, then there is competition between them for the perceptual interpretation.

A less familiar example of an embedded ambiguous figure is the reversible silhouette shown in Figure 4. According to Crowley (1952), this figure is usually perceived initially as the profile of either a lady or the devil. Crowley stated, however, that after both aspects are seen, it is difficult to see the silhouette as either a lady or a devil; she said that one sees the lady and the devil aspects of a Janus head simultaneously. Although her statement is subject to dispute, this simple embedded ambiguous figure is an interesting example.

An amusing ambiguous figure was introduced by Kolers (1964). The figure was drawn by the caricaturist Al Hirschfeld to advertise the Broadway musical, "The Boys from Syracuse." In the figure, the boys' faces are embedded within the same contours. When either aspect is dominant, the nose and mouth of one boy forms the jaw of the other, and both boys share the same eye. The two aspects of the figure alternate spontaneously and readily.

SENSATION AND PERCEPTION

Figure 4. A reversible silhouette of a woman or a devil. Reprinted from Crowley (1952) by permission.

Reversible Perspective Figures

A third class of ambiguous figures is characterized by ambiguity in depth. The Necker cube, Schroeder's staircase, and reversible blocks are the most familiar examples of these reversible perspective figures. Although the figures are drawn in two dimensions, one sees very real three-dimensional perspectives when viewing them. A spontaneous reversal in depth occurs with continued inspection of the figure, particularly when one fixates on a feature rather than scans the figure. With the Necker cube, the square side that looks initially like the front of the figure reverses and becomes the back side. The orientation of the cube also then reverses. The front and back walls of Schroeder's staircase seem to reverse, and the staircase appears to be upside down. The tops of the reversible cubes shift perspective in such a way that the tops of the cubes in one perspective are clearly the bottom sides of the cubes after the reversal occurs. Depth reversals can also occur with real three-dimensional objects (see Attneave, 1971, for examples).

Ambiguous Figures in Art

Ambiguity has had a long history of deliberate use in art (Fisher, 1967a, 1968a). Among recent artists, Escher and Dali are well known for their ambiguous drawings. According to Teuber (1974), many of Escher's drawings were inspired by the research and writings of Gestalt psychologists Edgar Rubin and Kurt Koffka. Escher's work (1971) includes very creative examples of ambiguity, including figure–ground reversals (e.g., "Fish and Fowl") and reversible perspective figures (e.g., the "Metamorphosis I" woodcut). Seven of Dali's paintings incorporating ambiguous figures were discussed by Fisher (1967a), who suggested that Dali was probably inspired to use ambiguity, in part, by fishermen in a coastal village who taught Dali to perceive various rock formations as other objects.

A recent article by Kroy and Langerholc (1984) presented a fascinating line sketch by Hieronymus Bosch, a Dutch artist, whose work was produced in about 1500. The picture is titled "The Owl's Nest." Bosch's work is characterized by an extensive use of interlocking animal forms. According to the authors, these forms are so subtly incorporated within the picture that they have evidently not been noticed by art critics. The simple subject of the picture appears to be an owl perching on a tree, and two birds clinging to a branch are also apparent. But many other animal and human forms are concealed in the picture, some of them noticeable only when the picture is turned upside down. Bosch employed figure–ground reversals and embedded ambiguous figures to hide the animal and human forms within the picture. It is fun to try to identify all the hidden forms, and my students and I think we see some that are not described by the authors.

Research Using Ambiguous Figures

Although ambiguous figures can be fun, psychologists have also used them in research to better understand perceptual processes and the factors that influence the perception of alternative aspects in such figures. Reversible perspective figures, particularly the Necker cube, have generated the most experimental research. The early research in the 1930s up to the 1960s on ambiguous-figure perception examined the influence of variables such as age, sex, personality, and motivation (Fisher, 1967b). Individual difference factors in the perception of ambiguous figures have also been studied (Forsyth & Huber, 1976; Huber & Forsyth, 1972); the authors report that they were able to successfully differentiate individuals on the basis of age and clinical classification (i.e., college students vs. state-hospital patients) in terms of their responses to various ambiguous figure stimuli.

For obvious reasons, ambiguous figures have been used to examine the effect of set on perception. Leeper (1935), in a widely-cited series of studies, reported that the subjects seeing either the young- or the old-woman aspects of the "wife and mother-in-law" figure were influenced by prior visual exposure to a similar figure with features more clearly representing either the wife or the mother-in-law. Detailed verbal descriptions of the features of either aspect prior to exposure to the composite figure, however, did not influence the subsequent perception. The well-known "rat–psychologist" figure was created by Bugelski and Alampay (1961) to study the influence of cognitive set on perception. They regarded it as a unique ambiguous figure for such purposes, because the two aspects that can be perceived—either a likeness of a rat or of a bald man's head—belong to two different cognitive categories, that is, animals and humans. The researchers reported that subjects readily responded to either interpretation depending on their prior exposure to pictures of animals or humans.

Liu (1976) reported that playing taped auditory descriptions of rats before showing the ambiguous figure to subjects influenced the frequency of rat-aspect responses. He also found that listening to taped horror music before seeing the "wife and mother-in-law" figure influenced subjects to report seeing the old-woman aspect; Liu suggested that the perception of the witch-like mother-in-law aspect may have been influenced by a mood associated with a scary scene presumably induced by the horror music.

Reversible perspective figures, particularly the Necker cube, have generated considerable research and theoretical formulation over the years. Until recently, explanations for the reversals have fallen into two broad categories, one stressing neural fatigue mechanisms (e.g., Attneave, 1971) and the other, attentional factors (e.g., Gregory, 1970). Recent studies have examined the role of cognitive and personality style factors related to perceptual instability (high reversal rates) or stability (low reversal rates). Reversal rates have been found to be reliable among individuals (J. E. Bergum & B. O. Bergum, 1980), and factors found to be positively related to reversal rates include creativity (B. O. Bergum & J. E. Bergum, 1979; J. E. Bergum & B. O. Bergum, 1979) and original thinking (Klintman, 1984).

Ambiguous figures are not always truly ambiguous. Fisher (1967b, 1967c) pointed out that many of the commonly used ambiguous figures were not really ambiguous in that each meaningful aspect in a figure was not equally likely to be perceived. He argued that it is important to ensure that the probability of perceiving such aspect in a figure is the same, that is, that each mutually exclusive alternative aspect is equally probable when the figure is initially presented. If the probabilities are not equal, he explained, there will be problems in interpreting the results statistically and in generalizing from the results of studies using ambiguous figures.

The "wife and mother-in-law" figure did not meet this criterion of ambiguity. When he introduced the figure to American psychologists, Boring (1930) stated that it "seems to me to be the best of the puzzle-pictures in the sense that neither figure is favored over the other" (p. 445). Psychologists who subsequently used the figure found that it was indeed biased in favor of the young-woman aspect; in various studies the wife aspect was reported 65 percent to 94 percent of the time by subjects seeing the picture for the first time (Botwinick, 1961; Botwinick, Robbin, & Brinley, 1959; Leeper, 1935). These investigators then attempted to construct truly ambiguous figures for which neither aspect was likely to be perceived by a majority of subjects. Botwinick (1961), for example, published a "husband and father-in-law" figure (see Figure 5) that he regarded as ambiguous or balanced because about one-half (24 of 51) of a sample of subjects initially shown the figure saw the husband aspect (aspect A). Aspects B and C were strongly biased in favor of the young husband and older father-in-law aspects, respectively.

Constructing truly ambiguous figures. Fisher (1967b, 1967c) developed a technique for creating truly ambiguous figures in which neither of two aspects is more likely to be perceived when the figure is initially presented. The technique involved creating a series of 21 different drawings of a figure. In about half of the drawings the features are systematically changed to emphasize one aspect increasingly in the figure, whereas the other aspect is emphasized in the remaining drawings. The 21 drawings constitute a continuum, with one aspect highly biased on one end and the other aspect clearly emphasized on the other. Because the features that define each of the aspects of the figure are systematically varied, it is reasoned that

Figure 5. An alternative to the "wife and mother-in-law" ambiguous figure. Reprinted from Botwinick (1961) by permission.

one of the drawings, presumably somewhere in the middle of the series, will not be biased in favor of either aspect and therefore either aspect is equally likely to be perceived.

A group of "sophisticated" judges who are familiar with the purposes of the study are then asked to narrow this continuum to 15 drawings: They place the most ambiguous drawing at the center of the continuum, and the seven drawings placed at either side of this central drawing are those perceived as sequential modifications that emphasize one aspect increasingly.

Next, the 15 drawings are shown individually, in random order, to a relatively large sample of naive subjects. Each subject writes down what he or she sees first in the drawings, and the number of subjects who report seeing a particular aspect of the figure is tallied. Statistically, the best ambiguous figure drawing is defined as the one in which the frequency of subjects' responses correspond closest to the mean of the sampling distribution of two equally probable and mutually exclusive responses made independently. Simply, the drawing that comes closest to generating a 50-50 split in responses is statistically defined as ambiguous.

Using this procedure, Fisher (1967b) obtained equiprobable ambiguous versions of five well-known ambiguous figures—the "wife and mother-in-law," "husband and father-in-law," "duck and rabbit," "pirate and rabbit" (Leeper, 1935), and "chalice and faces" (vase–faces) figures. In addition, he constructed three new figures, including the "gypsy and girl" figure (Figure 6).

Of the 15 stimulus drawings that were used to measure the ambiguity of this figure, the seventh drawing was found to be most ambiguous. Of the 200 individuals in the sample used to measure the ambiguity of these drawings, 51.5 percent reportedly first saw the gypsy in this drawing. Only 39.5 percent initially identified the gypsy aspect in the eighth drawing, which had been selected as the center drawing among the original 21 pictures. Curiously, the "gypsy and girl" figure is not featured in introductory texts as an ambiguous figure. Another figure Fisher (1967c) created using the same technique, the "man and girl" figure in which one sees either a man's face or a woman's naked body, is often shown in textbooks, however.

A three-aspect figure developed by Fisher (1968b) is the "mother, father, and daughter" figure shown in Figure 7. Fisher asked subjects to identify what they saw in the drawing and then asked them to identify a second and then a third aspect if they could. Given the prominence of the "wife and mother-in-law" figure in psychology, I think it is worthwhile to present this unusual three-aspect figure, which is not usually included in introductory psychology textbooks. Fisher did not achieve his equiambiguity criterion with this figure; the daughter aspect is clearly most salient, as 71 percent of

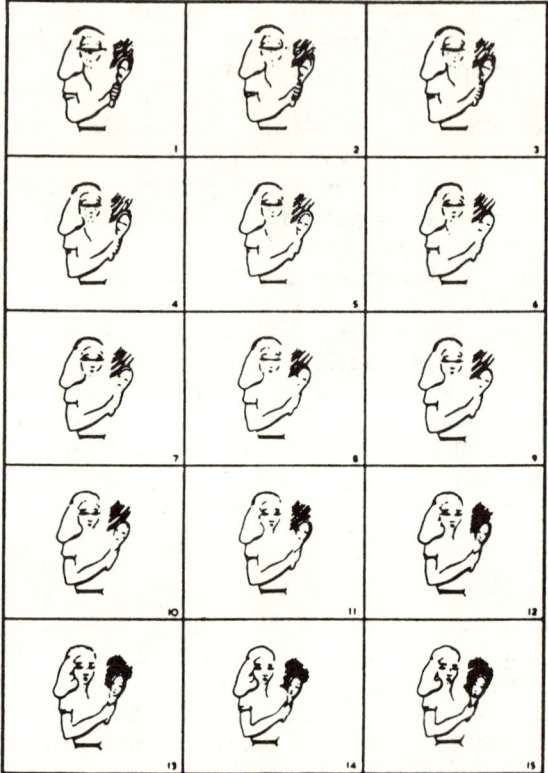

Figure 6. The set of stimuli used to create the "gypsy and girl" figure. Reprinted from Fisher (1967b) by permission.

179 subjects saw the daughter aspect initially, whereas 26 percent first saw the father, and only 3 percent identified the mother aspect.

Ambiguous Figures Without Real Contours

Most shapes or objects that we perceive, whether ambiguous or not, are usually formed by contours that exist physically. These real contours differentiate a portion of a figure from the ground in the visual field. But meaningful objects can also be perceived when no solid contours are present. Figure 8 consists merely of fragments. This figure, which appears frequently in introductory texts, is used to illustrate the Gestalt organizational principle of closure. By percep-

Figure 7. A three-aspect ambiguous figure. Reprinted from Fisher (1968b) by permission.

tually filling in gaps between fragments in the picture one can visualize a meaningful, organized figure; the array of fragments presumably represents a rider and horse.

One of my students pointed out, however, that there is another meaningful aspect to be perceived in this contourless figure—a snowman. Given this suggestion, most students readily report seeing this second aspect, in which the snowman appears to have a carrot nose and a scarf wrapped around its neck. Accordingly, this drawing

Figure 8. An ambiguous figure without contours that also employs the Gestalt principle of closure. The configuration is usually perceived as a rider on a horse, but it can also be seen as a snowman. Reprinted from Mednick, Higgins, and Kirschbaum (1975) by permission.

that illustrates the Gestalt closure principle is also an ambiguous figure with at least two aspects embedded within the fragments—a horse and rider and a snowman. But either meaningful form is perceived by constructing imaginary contours between fragments, a perceptual process that is analogous to what children do more concretely when forming figures in connect-the-dot drawings.

Subjective contour figures. In another class of figures, contours are actually and immediately perceived, not just imagined, even when no physical contours are present. The contours that are "seen" outline shapes of objects in completely homogeneous areas of stimulation. Most commonly called *subjective contours* (e.g., Kanizsa, 1976), they also are referred to as cognitive, fictional, anomalous, or apparent contours. Moreover, as I shall demonstrate, some of these figures are also ambiguous.

Subjective contours were first introduced to psychology by Schumann in 1904 (Parks, 1984). The so-called Schumann figure appears in some introductory textbooks, and in several articles (e.g., Coren, 1972; Parks, 1984). Most observers see a white square superimposed on a figure of alternating black-and-white concentric rings around a solid black circle. The subjective contour of a square is formed where only uniform white stimulation and no physical intensity gradient exists.

The most familiar example of a subjective contour figure was created by Kanizsa (1976). This figure seems to contain a triangle overlapping three black circles and an incomplete inverted triangle. The black circles overlapped by the corners of the triangle are actually sectored disks that have a distinct "Pac Man" resemblance (an observation that students readily report upon first seeing the figure.) Furthermore, the interior of the triangle bounded by the subjective contours appears to be brighter than the white ground in the remainder of the picture. Both the perceived contours and the enhanced whiteness of the triangle are illusory. The contours that are perceived between the white sectors of the disks are not real, as no intensity gradient exists, and the lightness of the visual areas within and outside the perceived triangle is the same. Other examples of subjective contour figures are presented by Parks (1984).

Several figures that induce ambiguous subjective contours, thereby inviting alternative perceptions, have been introduced by Bradley and his students (Bradley & Dumais, 1975; Bradley, Dumais, & Petry, 1976; Bradley & Petry, 1977). A striking example of such a figure is the subjective Necker cube created by H. M. Petry and presented in Figure 9 (ignore versions b, c, and d for the moment). According to Bradley, Dumais, and Petry (1976; and Bradley & Petry, 1977), most people report perceiving a Necker cube overlying eight black disks and the white background (a) first. With this organization, the white bars of the cube extend between the disks, and

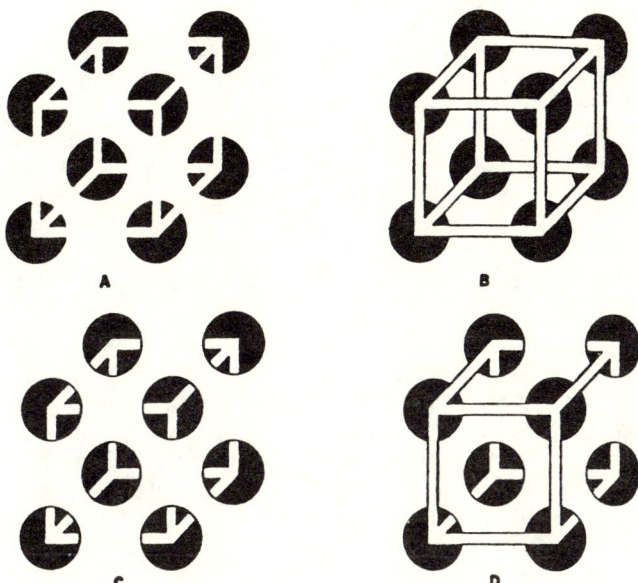

Figure 9. The subjective Necker cube (a) with illustrations of three possible organizations: cube in front (b), cube in back (c), and cube straddled (d). Reprinted from Bradley and Petry (1977) by permission.

the bars appear whiter than the white background. The edges of the bars that appear to reach between the disks, however, are subjective contours. This subjective Necker cube also reverses in depth. This "cube-in-front" organization of the figure is depicted in version b.

A second organization is also possible, although it is not as likely to be seen as quickly. Bradley and Petry stated that it is readily reported once the observer is shown the unambiguous organization diagrammed in version c, in which the cube appears to be behind a large white occluding surface with eight holes. Notice that the subjective contours now are formed at the interior edges of the holes of the front surface. I have been able to induce this alternative organization by describing it verbally rather than by showing version c to my students.

Adapting (and embellishing) the description given by Bradley and Petry (1977, p. 255), I ask the students to imagine that they are looking at a large white wall with eight round holes in it. They are standing at a distance from the wall and looking through the holes into a darkened room on the other side, and behind the wall they see glowing lines or bars of something. It takes a few moments for them to reorient their attention to the figure in accordance with the instructions, but when they "see" it, they are usually excited about their perceptual discovery. The cube, which can also reverse in perspective, appears exceptionally bright or even luminous. A third organization, shown in version d, also can be seen. This "straddled" organization, with part of the cube appearing in front and another part in back of the black disks, is not frequently reported by students. Students enjoy viewing the alternative organizations of this ambiguous figure with subjective contours, but it is not often presented in textbooks.

Why do subjective contours occur? Two major categories of theoretical explanations have been proposed. One approach has postulated that physiological mechanisms thought to be responsible for the perception of real contours may also explain how subjective contours are generated. The other approach has stressed the role of central or cognitive processes in the formation of subjective contours.

One physiological explanation suggests that subjective contours may arise from the activation of cortical feature detectors (see Smith & Over, 1975, 1979). When stimulated by specific features in the stimulus array (for instance, the sectored disks in Kanizsa's subjective triangle figure), the specialized contour-detector cells are activated and generate signals that are interpreted as continuous lines. But weaknesses with this hypothesis have been pointed out (e.g., Gregory, 1972; Kanizsa, 1976). It has been shown, for example, that when the straight-line edges of the sectored disks of the subjective triangle figure are misaligned, then curved subjective contours are created. Furthermore, under some circumstances, subjective contours forming a triangle can be produced with only three dots at the corners. More recently, it has been shown that after prolonged fixation, subjective contours fragment differently from real contours (Halpern & Warm, 1980, 1984).

Cognitive explanations propose that subjective contours occur only after the observer has derived a meaningful interpretation or organization from various elements in the stimulus array. The earliest explanation, by Schumann in 1904 (according to Coren, 1972), held that subjective contours were a manifestation of the Gestalt closure principle. Kanizsa (1976) favored a similar explanation. He stated that with the subjective triangle, for example, "the subjective contours are therefore the result of perceiving a surface and . . . the subjective surface in turn is generated by the tendency of the visual system to complete certain figural elements" (p. 52). Incidentally, when an explanation for subjective contours is provided in introductory textbooks, one based on the closure principle is most frequently given.

Subjective contours have also been attributed to implicit depth cues, such as interposition, that are typically present in a subjective contour figure. Coren (1972) suggested that the perception of depth of objects in the stimulus array due to the presence of depth cues was responsible for the subjective contours of figures; recently, however, Coren and Porac (1983) acknowledged that the consistent relations between depth cues and the occurrence of subjective contours does not necessarily imply a causal relation.

Other cognitive explanations that emphasize central as opposed to peripheral (i.e., physiological) processes have been suggested (e.g., Bradley & Petry, 1977; Gregory, 1972). In his comprehensive review of the research on subjective contours, Parks observed that "an explosion of both observation and theorizing has occurred," but he also concluded that "so little is firmly established about illusory figures themselves" (1984, p. 298).

Fun with Psychophysics: Perception Above and Below Threshold

I suggested earlier in this chapter that psychophysics, the study of the relation between physical stimuli and psychological responses, is not especially well received by students and instructors. Psychophysics deals with the methodology of the discipline—techniques for measuring detection thresholds, difference thresholds, and the subjective magnitude of sensations produced by stimuli above threshold. Admittedly, some of the concepts (e.g., signal detection theory, just noticeable differences, logarithmic and power functions) can be difficult to grasp readily. Unfortunately, psychophysics is also widely regarded as boring. No less an esteemed figure in the history of psychology than William James certainly thought so. About Gustave Fechner, the founder of psychophysics in 1850, James (1890) wrote in *The Principles of Psychology:*

> But it would be terrible if even such a dear old man as this could saddle our Science forever with his patient whimsies, and, in a world so full of more nutritious objects of attention, compel all future students to plow through the difficulties, not only of his own works, but of the still drier ones written in his refutation. Those who desire this dreadful literature can find it: it has a "disciplinary value;" But I will not even enumerate it in a footnote. (p. 549)

True, most people probably would be bored by Fechner's written works, but students are not asked to read them. Perhaps because of the perceived difficulty and dryness of some topics, instructors fear that students will be turned off by psychophysics. Even authors of sensation and perception textbooks sometimes defer to this supposed disinterest by relegating a detailed treatment of psychophysics to the last chapter or to an appendix of the book.

Discussing psychophysics in the introductory psychology course requires no apology by instructors. Indeed, there are many issues and applications in psychophysics that students should find interesting. This is particularly true of two psychophysical issues that I address in the remainder of this chapter, the late S. S. Stevens's work in psychophysical scaling and the applied aspects of subliminal perception.

Stevens's Law and Magnitude Estimation

Magnitude estimation is one of several methods developed by Stevens to establish the relation between sensation magnitude and stimulus intensity. Stevens asked observers to assign numbers to stimulus intensities that were proportional to one another. For example, if one stimulus was assigned a value of 20 by an observer, then another stimulus judged subjectively by the observer to be twice as intense (brighter, louder, sweeter, or whatever) was assigned the value 40. Using this direct scaling procedure to measure subjective experience, Stevens found that sensation magnitude is not directly proportional to the logarithm of stimulus intensity, as previously proposed by Fechner. Instead, Stevens's law states that sensation magnitude is proportional to the stimulus intensity raised to some power (Stevens, 1957).

An interesting and reliable relation that is not frequently cited in textbooks is that between subjective sweetness reported and the amount of sugar in the solution being tasted. Sweetness has been found to increase more rapidly than sugar concentration; specifically, doubling the amount of sucrose in solution results in the solution tasting more than twice as sweet, usually about 2.5 times sweeter (Moskowitz, 1970a; Stevens, 1969). The artificial sweetener saccharin is inherently a sweeter substance than sucrose, of course, for it can be detected in much smaller amounts. Most students, therefore, are surprised to learn that the sweetness of saccharin, unlike that of sucrose, lags behind increases in intensity; a solution of two 0.25-grain tablets and water does not taste twice as sweet as one 0.25-grain tablet in water, but rather, tastes about 1.7 times as sweet (Moskowitz, 1970b; Stevens, 1969).

Magnitude estimation has been applied to a wide variety of sensory and nonsensory stimulus continua. It has been used to scale the characteristics of food substances, for example, including the perceived strength of coffee (Stone & Harder, 1969), the chunkiness of hamburger grind, the amount of mayonnaise in tuna salad (Moskowitz, Kluter, Westerling & Jacobs, 1974), and the ingredients that yield the optimal taste in processed foods such as spaghetti sauce (see Rice, 1978). Imagery of nouns (Elmes & Thompson, 1976), perception of the horizontal–vertical illusion (Masin & Vidotto, 1983), effort in sniffing (Teghtsoonian & Teghtsoonian, 1982), and color sensations of normal and color-weak individuals (Hemminger & Georgi, 1982) indicate the diversity of subjective experiences measured with the method.

Stevens also measured social phenomena with magnitude estimation. The relation between the desirability of wrist watches and perceived fair price, seriousness of thefts and dollar amounts taken, and seriousness of criminal acts and penalties are examples of applications of the method to social psychophysics (see Stevens, 1972, 1975).

Stevens is noted for his engaging writing style, which was particularly evident when he refuted his critics. He minced no words and defended the power law vigorously: "In other words, the sensory power law takes precedence over the results of any particular experiment" (Stevens, 1971, p. 448). To those who suggested that the uniqueness of the individual prevails and that there is no general law to be found, Stevens replied in his typical, feisty fashion: "My own guess is that even a phenomenological existentialist would cherish a natural law if he found one" (Stevens, 1962, p. 2).

Stevens died in 1972, but his legacy continues in certain refinements made to his approach. One method that has emerged is *magnitude matching* (J. C. Stevens & Marks, 1980). This method essentially combines magnitude estimation with cross-modality matching; the latter method (see Stevens, 1962) requires observers to adjust the intensity of one stimulus (e.g., force of handgrip with a hand dynamometer) so that it is proportional to the apparent intensity of another stimulus (e.g., brightness of a light or loudness of a tone).

In magnitude matching, a range of stimulus intensities from two modalities (e.g., light and sound) are alternately presented. Subjects are asked to assign magnitude estimates on "a common scale of intensity" in order to obtain an "absolute match" of numbers and sensation intensities (J. C. Stevens & Marks, 1980). The method was used to scale loudness and exertion in bicycle pedaling in one recent experiment (Marks, Borg, & Ljunggren, 1983). Stevens and Marks outlined the advantages of magnitude matching over the usual cross-modality matching procedure. They suggested, too, that the most promising advantage is its potential use in identifying sensory pathologies.

If the relevance of a topic can be measured by its coverage in *Time* magazine, then psychophysics is relevant. The entire "Living" section of the June 4, 1984 issue, was devoted to the psychophysics of taste perception and featured magnitude matching (Sheraton, 1984). Moreover, I was delighted to see the imposing term *psychophysicists* appear prominently in the heading of the article. Even if it seems gimmicky, illustrations in the popular media of academic topics can provide credibility in the minds of students and help to stimulate their interest.

Subliminal Stimulation: Commercial Applications

Psychophysical scaling techniques such as magnitude estimation measure responses to supraliminal stimuli—stimuli at intensities well above the detection threshold. What about stimuli below an individual's threshold? There has been substantial interest in whether stimuli too weak to be reported can influence behavior. Subliminal stimuli, by definition, lie below an individual's level of conscious awareness (Dixon, 1971, 1981; Henley, 1984; Shevrin & Dickman, 1980).

Students' interests in subliminal advertising. In introductory psychology textbooks, the commercial applications of subliminal stimulation, particularly in advertising, are largely ignored. Given the false promises and failures of those who sought to exploit subliminal techniques for commercial reasons, the omission is understandable. Yet this issue generates considerable interest among students, and I suggest that it warrants attention in introductory courses for several reasons.

First, many students have heard about subliminal advertising. They know, for example, that the message "Drink Coke" was flashed "invisibly" on the screen in a movie theater some years ago and that the sales of Coca Cola increased dramatically. But the information they have about this "study" is usually fragmented and distorted. In some cases, there is even some doubt about whether such an attempt to manipulate people's behavior was undertaken at all. I was surprised to learn from one student, for instance, that her professor in a media communications course at a large university insisted that reports about the "Drink Coke" study were fabricated, that somehow the rumor got started and has been passed on through the years. The movie theater incident did indeed take place, but the facts are generally not well understood, principally because no scientific report of the study was ever published.

A second, pragmatic reason to discuss applications of subliminal stimulation is that it provides an attention-getting framework for introducing the so-called boring concepts related to psychophysical thresholds—their definitions, classical methods for measuring them, the contributions of signal detection theory, and so forth. I suggest, therefore, that discussing subliminal advertising, which sensationalizes the broader issue of subliminal perception, may generate more interest in psychophysics among students.

Subliminal perception has had a very controversial history, but it is now regarded as a valid phenomenon (Dixon, 1971, 1981; Henley, 1984; Moore, 1982; Shevrin & Dickman, 1980). There is, however, absolutely no compelling empirical evidence that supports the claims made about the effects of subliminal advertising. Furthermore, there is no documentation to substantiate the claims of companies that market products by promising self-help through subliminal stimulation. Videotapes, software cartridges for personal computers, and audiotapes that are now available provide subliminal messages that allegedly help people to achieve a variety of personal goals. Supposedly, one can gain confidence, lose weight, stop smoking or drinking, and improve one's sex life through exposure to subliminal suggestions flashed on a screen or recorded on tape.

Many students, it seems to me, want to believe in extraordinary phenomena such as extrasensory perception, astrology, and, I would add, subliminal stimulation effects. In this respect, students are somewhat impressionable and lack skepticism about unusual phenomena. A third, pedagogical reason for discussing subliminal advertising, therefore, is that a presentation of the issues related to subliminal advertising (and, more generally, to subliminal perception) may stimulate critical and skeptical thinking among students.

Subliminal stimulation in the media. It was inevitable that research interest in subliminal perception, which began with the so-called dirty words experiments of the 1940s (e.g., McGinnies, 1949), would lead to applications of the phenomenon outside the laboratory. And so it was that in the 1950s the first attempts to commercialize subliminal stimulation took place. Movie producers, assisted by consulting psychologists, introduced subliminal stimuli into motion pictures to enhance entertainment. For example, during the frightening scenes in a horror film titled *My World Dies Screaming*, emotion-charged words (e.g., *blood*) and images (e.g., a skull) were superimposed on single frames of the film (Brean, 1958). Presumably, the $1/30$-second (33.3-msec) exposure (one out of the 30 frames projected per second) was too brief to allow the word or image to register consciously.

In another movie based on Henry James's story, *The Turn of the Screw*, there were plans to present subliminal ghost images in the film. I am not certain, however, that either motion picture was released, with or without the subliminal gimmicks. No mention is made of either of these film experiments in more recent articles on subliminal perception. Furthermore, neither movie is listed among the 12,000 titles in Maltin's (1978) comprehensive guide to movies shown on television.

Subliminal commercials and other kinds of messages were reportedly used in the television, magazine, and radio media (Brean, 1958; Key, 1980/1981; Moore, 1982). In the 1950s, for example, subliminal auditory messages were broadcast by several radio stations. A Chicago radio station charged advertisers for airing subaudible commercials. Disc jockeys at a Seattle radio station challenged listeners to detect subliminal messages such as "How about a cup of coffee?" In the late 1970s, subliminal auditory messages were broadcast in Toronto department stores to deter shoplifters (Moore, 1982). Public service messages (e.g., "Drive safely") and other messages were aired as subliminal flashes in the 1950s by television stations in Los Angeles and in Bangor, Maine (Brean, 1958). As recently as 1978, a station in a midwestern city inserted subliminal messages in news film at the request of police investigators searching for a murderer (Moore, 1982).

Hungry? Eat popcorn. A movie theater in Fort Lee, New Jersey, was the site of the demonstration that pioneered the commercial applications of subliminal techniques in the United States and that also provoked the subsequent furor that led to curtailing such practices. In 1956 popcorn sales in that theater increased by 18 percent and Coca Cola sales rose by an astonishing 58 percent during a six-week period. According to psychologist and marketing researcher James M. Vicary, the theater audiences were unknowingly influenced by secret messages flashed on the screen during the movie, *Picnic.* Vicary made this startling announcement at a press conference in September, 1957, at which he described the experiment that he and his associates had conducted on audiences using a technique he termed subliminal advertising (Brean, 1958; Moore, 1982).

The study was never reported in a scientific journal. Details of Vicary's research are available only from reports appearing in the popular press. Brean's (1958) *Life* magazine article provides one such account. According to Brean, the messages "Hungry? Eat popcorn" and "Drink Coca Cola" were alternately projected on the screen for a mere $1/3000$ of a second (less than 1 msec) by special equipment developed by Vicary's firm, the Subliminal Projection Company, Inc. The extremely brief messages were therefore superimposed upon the images in the movie being projected on the screen; they were not embedded within single frames of the film, as was done with the films mentioned previously.

An indignant public reacted immediately and strongly to Vicary's announcement. According to Brean (1958), Moore (1982), and other sources, there was concern that such techniques could be used to influence voters by promoting or denigrating the character of politicians. Temperance proponents wondered what would happen if breweries were allowed to use subliminal advertising. Consumers feared that they would be manipulated into buying gadgets and appliances that they did not need or want. Newspaper editors fretted that government officials might possibly use invisible messages for spreading propaganda.

In a forceful editorial in *The Saturday Review,* Norman Cousins proposed that the only suitable solution was to "take this invention and everything connected to it and attach it to the center of the next nuclear explosive scheduled for testing" (Cousins, 1957, p. 20). The unconscious mind, he added, "is not to be smudged, sullied, or twisted in order to boost the sales of popcorn or anything else. It does not exist for the convenience of ingenious and invisible pitchmen" (p. 20).

In response to the public outcry, radio and television network organizations prohibited the use of subliminal stimulation by their stations, and state legislatures passed bills banning its use. The skeptic might ask, however, how prohibitions against subliminal techniques could be adequately monitored if one cannot consciously perceive such stimuli.

Validity of Vicary's experiment. It appears that there was much ado about nothing (or, at most, very little) with respect to the proclaimed effects of subliminal advertising. Certainly the information available from the press reports was insufficient for evaluating Vicary's results critically. The theater owners would not even release to the Federal Communications Commission (FCC) data to support the contention of increased popcorn and Coke sales. Numerous criticisms and questions about Vicary's Fort Lee demonstration were raised by various skeptics (e.g., Goldiamond, 1958, 1966; McConnell, Cutler, & McNeil, 1958; Moore, 1982; Senders, 1959), including the following:

• There were no adequate controls. The conditions that prevailed during the period that baseline figures were determined are unknown. What were the weather conditions? What films were shown in the theater then? Were audiences exposed to any advertising while in the theater? How large were the previous audiences? The percentage increase in sales would be misleading if baseline figures were based on small sales.

• The $1/3000$-second exposure time reported for each message is extremely fast. Was it possible to produce repeated exposures reliably without technical difficulties? Did the equipment induce an afterimage that raised the effective stimulation to above-threshold levels? On the other hand, would not the movie images on the screen effectively mask the subliminal stimulus?

• Assuming that the subliminal messages were solely responsible for the increased popcorn or Coca Cola buying, how did it occur? Did members of the audience develop a sudden craving for popcorn, or did it elevate an existing but weak need? When did the patrons buy it—before the movie started, during the feature presentation, or after they had seen the film? Did people who normally do not eat popcorn buy it? Or did others consume more than they usually do?

Vicary's company was serious about putting subliminal stimulation to commercial use in television advertising. Vicary argued that the television viewer would benefit for the amount of time that one spent consciously viewing commercials could decrease (Brean, 1958). Goldiamond (1966), for one, approved of this use: "It would be welcome because it can render obnoxious advertising less effective" (p. 277). Goldiamond's sarcastic remark was based in part on the experimental research that consistently shows that more intense stimuli are generally more effective than are weak stimuli, a point made by numerous reviewers of the subliminal stimulation literature. The logic of using weak, subthreshold stimuli that observers cannot verbally report is not well founded.

Can subliminal stimulation work? Is there any evidence to support the promise of commercial applications of subliminal stimulation? Can behavior changes of practical importance be induced by subliminal stimulation? Evidently Vicary's enthusiastic claims in 1957 were premature. At least McConnell et al. (1958) thought so:

> Anyone who wishes to utilize subliminal stimulation for commercial or other purposes can be likened to a stranger entering into a misty, confused countryside where there are but few landmarks. Before this technique is used in the marketplace, if it is to be used at all, a tremendous amount of research should be done, and by competent experimenters (p. 237).

McConnell et al. (1958) and Senders (1959) formulated questions that, they suggested, needed to be answered by careful experimentation. For example,

- What type of subliminal stimulus is more effective—words or pictures?
- How frequently should the subliminal stimulus be repeated?
- What is the optimal exposure duration?
- What parameters of the message are most effective? That is, how many words? What size? Should they be familiar or unfamiliar?
- On what type of background should the stimuli be presented: when the screen is momentarily blank, or when an image is on the screen?
- What should be the affective situation when the message is presented? That is, should the stimulus be presented only during pleasant scenes in order to induce a positive effect? Can unpleasant scenes produce negative attitudes toward the product being advertised?
- What demographic and personality factors of the targeted audience need to be taken into account?

Research on some of these issues has been conducted, but there is little evidence that subliminal stimuli exert any compelling influence on behavior that would encourage advertisers to use the technique pioneered by Vicary. The results of the few applied studies using flashed messages (e.g., Byrne, 1959; Hawkins, 1970) suggest that hunger and thirst drives may be aroused by subliminal word stimuli (e.g., the words "beef," "Coke," and "drink Coke"). But these and other studies are methodologically flawed (see Saegert, 1979), and Moore (1982) dismisses the results as having minimal relevance to advertising.

Sex in Ritz crackers. To the contrary, according to Key, subliminal advertising is more widespread than ever and has powerful effects on individuals and society. Author of three books on the subject, Key maintains that subliminal techniques are used extensively in all mass media. Everyone "has been victimized and manipulated by the use of subliminal stimuli directed into his unconscious mind by the mass merchandisers of media" (1980/1981, p. 1). He uses the terms "assaults," "bombardment," and "mind-bending media saturation," among others, to emphasize the pervasiveness of subliminal manipulation. Virtually all of the advertising for some products (e.g., alcohol) employs subliminal stimuli, Key (1976/1977) asserts. He warns that subliminal stimulation is dangerous to our society and suggests that the cumulative effects of this exploitation may even be responsible for drug dependency, divorce, and alienation between the sexes in our society (Key, 1980/1981).

The principal technique Key describes is the use of subliminal visual embeds in the pictorial content of printed advertisements—words or symbolic images that usually deal with sex or death. These concealed pictures-within-pictures are not consciously perceived under normal viewing conditions, according to Key, but feelings are unconsciously associated with the product being advertised (Key, 1973/1974).

Subliminal embeds can be consciously perceived, but only after intensive examination, and then usually with some difficulty, Key says. He describes, illustrates, and interprets numerous examples that have appeared in national magazines. Virtually no product is exempt from such hidden messages in their advertisements, whether it be alcohol, cigarettes, deodorants, swimsuits, toothpaste, margarine, or crackers, Key asserts. Here is one analysis by Key:

> In a Gilbey's London Dry Gin ad the letters S, E, and X are hidden within ice cubes in a tall glass obviously containing gin and tonic with a slice of lime. Reflections of the gin bottle and bottle cap on the table can be interpreted as a man's legs and penis. The space between the bottle and the glass standing next to it suggest a vagina into which the penis has been inserted, for the melting ice on the bottle may symbolize seminal fluid. Accordingly, the scene may unconsciously indicate that *coitus interruptus* just occurred, reinforcing the message in the printed copy in the ad which advises, "and keep your tonics dry!" (Key, 1973/1974).

Subliminal embeds are even contained in the consumer products themselves, according to Key. Ritz crackers, says Key (1976/1977), have a mosaic of the word, *SEX*, baked into both sides of each cracker! Key contends that anyone, if relaxed, will be able to see these hidden words in about 10 seconds. To aid the reader, Key presents a photograph that outlines the capitalized SEXes on a cracker. (I have photographed Ritz crackers and found that a felt-tip pen writes satisfactorily on them. The problem, though, is that I have not been able to determine where the pen should be used; even with prolonged inspection of various crackers, I was unable to detect a single facsimile of SEX. Perhaps I was not sufficiently relaxed.) Key sees nothing sinister about Nabisco baking the word SEX into the crackers. In fact, he states, "Embedding really makes the damned things taste better" (p. 10).

How and why do subliminal embeds work? Key is not very explicit on the matter. Presumably, the important requirement is that the advertiser's message be laden with emotional content—words like *sex* and *death*, erotic images of male and female sex organs, sexual activity, skulls, knives dripping blood, and so forth. It is not clear, though, how the printed embedded messages are perceived subliminally. Key implies that the observer receives a tachistoscope-like exposure to them (Key, 1973/1974).

The pictorial matter in advertisements is designed to be perceived for only one or two seconds, Key insists. A longer exposure is likely to enhance conscious recall of the ad, thereby subjecting it to critical judgment. Advertisers, he says, do not want their products evaluated consciously and objectively. Messages that are implanted subliminally will not be subjected to critical evaluation in the unconscious; they will have only affective associations with the product. Key purports that emotionally-loaded taboo words and images that are subliminally perceived will register in unconscious memory and be stored indefinitely. The information stored unconsciously emerges as a "favorable attitudinal predisposition" when a decision to purchase the product arises (Key, 1973/1974, p. 48).

Recall, though, that the consumer is exposed to subliminal embeds in virtually all ads for some products. How then, I wonder, does a favorable attitude toward one particular liquor, for instance, emerge to influence the consumer's choice? It seems to me that the consumer should be utterly confused when so many unconscious messages compete to sway his or her conscious choice.

Critics have not responded favorably to Key's contentions. Moore (1982) and Schulman (1981) point out that those who persevere in a search for embedded sexual imagery in ads probably will find it, whether it is there or not. However, as Moore points out, the relevant issue is not whether the embeds exist, but whether they have any effect on the consumer who is exposed to them. Nowhere in his three books does Key present any evidence of the alleged "powerful" effects of subliminal messages. Indeed, he suggests that subliminal advertising probably has only "marginal effects upon changing brand market shares" (1980/1981, p. 181). Somewhat surprisingly, given the fervent presentation of his thesis, he also candidly admits he has no specific proof that subliminal messages affect behavior, although he believes that the techniques have a "significant potential to change human behavior in measurable ways" (1980/1981, p. 27).

Key reasons that advertising agencies would not spend billions of dollars collectively on advertisements using such techniques if there were no basis for using them. Moreover, Key has not been impressed by any denials of its use. The results of research done by advertising firms are not likely to be shared with their competitors or the public for obvious reasons, he suggests.

I do not doubt that embeds with sexual imagery are contained in some ads. But given the lack of evidence and theoretical bases for their impact on the consumer, why would they be used? I think that they are intentionally created by commercial artists and photographers who possess a sense of humor and do it for their own amusement. Advertising executives may also think there is no harm in using the technique, even if they are uncertain about the alleged efficacy of embeds.

There still is no reason to take subliminal advertising seriously. Surely, if persuasive evidence existed for the viability of the techniques or if they were knowingly used by the media, then the issue would not be ignored in psychology textbooks. But students do not necessarily know that flashing subliminal messages are no longer regarded as effective means of advertising in the motion picture and television media. Furthermore, students who read Key's books or listen to him lecture often find his arguments persuasive. The fact that the FCC ruled that the use of subliminal techniques is inconsistent with their guidelines against deception in broadcasts (Key, 1980/1981) may only reinforce the belief that the public is vulnerable to subliminal mind control.

Students should understand, therefore, that no empirical evidence exists to demonstrate that any subliminal advertising technique—flashing messages or embedded taboo words and images—has an impact on consumers' purchasing behavior. Because of students' fascination with the issue, subliminal perception and its applications merit some attention in the introductory psychology course. Ignoring the topic altogether will not dispel any misunderstanding that students bring to the course.

Subliminal Psychodynamic Activation

Subliminal stimulation has emerged recently in another applied area. A method termed subliminal psychodynamic activation has been used to test a major aspect of psychoanalytic theory, the relations between psychopathology and unconscious conflict. According to Silverman (1976), studies have shown that a subliminal stimulus related to an unconscious conflict underlying a psychopathology can trigger an increase or a decrease in symptoms. The method involves presenting 4-msec exposures of verbal and pictorial stimuli that are either conflict-related or neutral.

Silverman, Ross, Adler, and Lustig (1978), for instance, used the method to manipulate oedipal conflict in a sample of normal college males. Dart-throwing accuracy was measured. Messages designed to intensify (e.g., "beating dad is wrong") or alleviate (e.g., "beating dad is ok") the oedipal conflict were presented subliminally and paired with a picture that conveyed feelings congruent with the verbal message. Dart-throwing scores improved or decreased, as expected, when the subliminal messages either sanctioned or condemned "beating Dad." Silverman et al. concluded that the subjects' ability to perform in the competitive task was influenced by the degree of unconscious oedipal conflict being experienced at the time.

The basic subliminal psychodynamic activation paradigm has been used in numerous studies with mixed results. Failures to find effects using Silverman's technique have been reported (e.g., Condon & Allen, 1980; Haspel & Harris, 1982; Heilbrun, 1980; Oliver & Burkham, 1982). A recent comment by Silverman (1982a) initiated a lively exchange of replies and rejoinders on subliminal psychodynamic activation studies (Allen & Condon, 1982; Heilbrun, 1982; Silverman, 1982b).

What Now?

Despite the myths about subliminal advertising and the uncertainty over the usefulness of subliminal techniques in dealing with psychopathology, the broader issue of subliminal perception is gaining acceptance. Intense skepticism and enthusiasm have accompanied its development in psychology. Informative reviews of the early history, methodological problems, and controversial issues in subliminal perception research are found in various articles (e.g., Bevan, 1964; Erdelyi, 1974; Eriksen, 1958, 1960; Goldiamond, 1958; McConnell et al., 1958). Although the phenomenon was widely discredited, recent work summarized in two books by Dixon (1971, 1981) has given the problem renewed credibility.

Numerous studies, for example, have shown that some stimuli too weak to be verbally reported evoke cortical responses and alter EEG patterns. Furthermore, specific neurophysiological activities have been correlated with unconscious processes that are presumably related to subliminal stimuli (Shevrin & Dickman, 1980). Henley (1984) briefly cites these and a variety of other research areas that have provided evidence for unconscious perception. Given the ongoing research on neurophysiological processing of subliminal stimulation and the use of subliminal techniques in psychopathology, it is possible that subliminal perception may work its way into introductory psychology courses again—at supraliminal levels.

References

Allen, G. J., & Condon, T. J. (1982). Whither subliminal psychodynamic activation? A reply to Silverman. *Journal of Abnormal Psychology, 91,* 131–133.

Attneave, F. (1971). Multistability in perception. *Scientific American, 225,* 62–71.

Bennett, T. L. (1978). *The sensory world: An introduction to sensation and perception.* Monterey, CA: Brooks/Cole.

Bergum, B. O., & Bergum, J. E. (1979). Creativity, perceptual stability, and self-perception. *Bulletin of the Psychonomic Society, 14,* 61–63.

Bergum, J. E., & Bergum, B. O. (1979). Self-perceived creativity and ambiguous figure reversal rates. *Bulletin of the Psychonomic Society, 14,* 373–374.

Bergum, J. E., & Bergum, B. O. (1980). Reliability of reversal rates as a measure of perceptual stability. *Perceptual and Motor Skills, 50,* 1038.

Bevan, W. (1964). Subliminal stimulation: A pervasive problem for psychology. *Psychological Bulletin, 61,* 81–99.

Boring, E. G. (1930). A new ambiguous figure. *American Journal of Psychology, 42,* 444–445.

Botwinick, J. (1961). Husband and father-in-law—a reversible figure. *American Journal of Psychology, 74,* 312–313.

Botwinick, J., Robbin, J. S., & Brinley, J. F. (1959). Reorganization of perceptions with age. *Journal of Gerontology, 14,* 85–88.

Bradley, D. R., & Dumais, S. T. (1975). Ambiguous cognitive contours *Nature, 257,* 582–584.

Bradley, D. R., Dumais, S. T., & Petry, H. M. (1976). [Reply to Cavonius]. *Nature, 261,* 78.

Bradley, D. R., & Petry, H. M. (1977). Organizational determinants of subjective contour: The subjective Necker cube. *American Journal of Psychology, 90,* 253–262.

Brean, H. (1958, March 31). "Hidden sell" technique is almost here. *Life,* pp. 102–104, 107–108, 110, 113–114.

Bugelski, B. R., & Alampay, D. A. (1961). The role of frequency in developing perceptual sets. *Canadian Journal of Psychology, 15,* 205–211.

Byrne, D. (1959). The effect of a subliminal food stimulus on verbal responses. *Journal of Applied Psychology, 43,* 249–251.

Carmichael, L. (1951). Another "hidden-figure" picture. *American Journal of Psychology, 64,* 137–138.

Condon, T. J., & Allen, G. J. (1980). The role of psychoanalytic merging fantasies in systematic desensitization: A rigorous methodological examination. *Journal of Abnormal Psychology, 89,* 437–443.

Coren, S. (1972). Subjective contours and apparent depth. *Psychological Review, 79,* 359–367.

Coren, S., & Porac, C. (1983). Subjective contours and apparent depth: A direct test. *Perception & Psychophysics, 33,* 197–200.

Coren, S., Porac, C., & Ward, L. M. (1984). *Sensation and perception* (2nd ed.). New York: Academic Press.

Cousins, N. (1957, October 5). Smudging the subconscious. *Saturday Review*, p. 20.
Crowley, M. E. (1952). A puzzle-picture in silhouette. *American Journal of Psychology, 65*, 302–304.
Dallenbach, K. M. (1951). A puzzle-picture with a new principle of concealment. *American Journal of Psychology, 64*, 431–433.
Dallenbach, K. M. (1952). More about the 'cow' puzzle-picture. *American Journal of Psychology, 65*, 304–306.
Dixon, N. F. (1971). *Subliminal perception: The nature of a controversy*. London: McGraw-Hill.
Dixon, N. F. (1981). *Preconscious processing*. New York: Wiley.
Elmes, D. G., & Thompson, J. B. (1976). Magnitude estimation of imagery. *Bulletin of the Psychonomic Society, 8*, 343–344.
Erdelyi, M. H. (1974). A new look at the New Look: Perceptual defense and vigilance. *Psychological Review, 81*, 1–25.
Eriksen, C. W. (1958). Unconscious processes. In M. R. Jones (Ed.), *Nebraska Symposium on Motivation: 1958*. Lincoln: University of Nebraska Press.
Eriksen, C. W. (1960). Discrimination and learning without awareness: A methodological survey and evaluation. *Psychological Review, 67*, 279–300.
Escher, M. C. (1971). *The graphic work of M. C. Escher*. New York: Ballantine.
Fernberger, S. W. (1950). An early example of a "hidden-figure" picture. *American Journal of Psychology, 63*, 448–449.
Fisher, G. H. (1967a). Ambiguous figure treatments in the art of Salvador Dali. *Perception & Psychophysics, 2*, 328–330.
Fisher, G. H. (1967b). Measuring ambiguity. *American Journal of Psychology, 80*, 541–557.
Fisher, G. H. (1967c). Preparation of ambiguous stimulus materials. *Perception & Psychophysics, 2*, 421–422.
Fisher, G. H. (1968a). Ambiguity of form: Old and new. *Perception & Psychophysics, 4*, 189–192.
Fisher, G. H. (1968b). 'Mother, father, and daughter': A three-aspect ambiguous figure. *American Journal of Psychology, 81*, 274–277.
Forsyth, G. A., & Huber, R. J. (1976). Selective attention in ambiguous-figure perception: An individual differences analysis. *Bulletin of the Psychonomic Society, 7*, 498–500.
Geldard, F. A. (1972). *The human senses* (2nd ed.). New York: Wiley.
Goldiamond, I. (1958). Indicators of perception: I. Subliminal perception, subception, unconscious perception: An analysis in terms of psychophysical indicator methodology. *Psychological Bulletin, 55*, 373–411.
Goldiamond, I. (1966). Statement on subliminal advertising. In R. Ulrich, T. Stachnik, & J. Mabry (Eds.), *Control of human behavior: Vol. I. Expanding the behavioral laboratory* (pp. 277–279). Glenview, IL: Scott, Foresman.
Goldstein, E. B. (1980). *Sensation and perception*. Belmont, CA: Wadsworth.
Goldstein, E. B. (1984). *Sensation and perception* (2nd ed.). Belmont, CA: Wadsworth.
Gregory, R. L. (1970). *The intelligent eye*. New York: McGraw-Hill.
Gregory, R. L. (1972). Cognitive contours. *Nature, 238*, 51–52.
Halpern, D. F., & Warm, J. S. (1980). The disappearance of real and subjective contours. *Perception & Psychophysics, 28*, 229–235.

Halpern, D. F., & Warm, J. S. (1984). The disappearance of dichoptically presented real and subjective contours. *Bulletin of the Psychonomic Society, 22*, 433–436.
Haspel, K. C., & Harris, R. S. (1982). Effect of tachistoscopic stimulation of subconscious oedipal wishes on competitive performance: A failure to replicate. *Journal of Abnormal Psychology, 91*, 437–443.
Hawkins, D. (1970). The effects of subliminal stimulation on drive level and brand preference. *Journal of Marketing Research, 7*, 322–326.
Heilbrun, K. S. (1980). Silverman's subliminal psychodynamic activation: A failure to replicate. *Journal of Abnormal Psychology, 89*, 560–566.
Heilbrun, K. S. (1982). Reply to Silverman. *Journal of Abnormal Psychology, 91*, 134–135.
Hemminger, H., & Georgi, W. (1982). Color sensation of normal and anomalous trichromats measured by magnitude estimation. *Psychological Research, 44*, 147–163.
Henley, S. H. A. (1984). Unconscious perception re-revisited: A comment on Merikle's (1982) paper. *Bulletin of the Psychonomic Society, 22*, 121–124.
Hill, W. E. (1915, November 6). My wife and my mother-in-law. *Puck*, p. 11.
Huber, R. J., & Forsyth, G. A. (1972). Selective attention and social interest. *Journal of Individual Psychology, 28*, 51–59.
James, W. (1890). *The principles of psychology.* New York: Henry Holt.
Kanizsa, G. (1976). Subjective contours. *Scientific American, 234*, 48–52.
Key, W. B. (1974). *Subliminal seduction: Ad media's manipulation of a not so innocent America.* New York: Signet. (Original work published 1973.)
Key, W. B. (1977). *Media sexploitation.* New York: Signet. (Original work published 1976.)
Key, W. B. (1981). *The clam-plate orgy and other subliminal techniques for manipulating your behavior.* New York: Signet. (Original work published 1980.)
Klintman, H. (1984). Original thinking and ambiguous figure reversal rates. *Bulletin of the Psychonomic Society, 22*, 129–131.
Kolers, P. A. (1964). The boys from Syracuse: Another ambiguous figure. *American Journal of Psychology, 77*, 671–672.
Kroy, W., & Langerholc, J. (1984). Ambiguous figures by Bosch. *Perception & Psychophysics, 35*, 402–404.
Leeper, R. (1935). A study of a neglected portion of the field of learning—the development of sensory organization. *Journal of Genetic Psychology, 46*, 41–75.
Levine, M. W., & Shefner, J. M. (1981). *Fundamentals of sensation and perception.* Reading, MA: Addison-Wesley.
Liu, An-Yen (1976). Cross-modality set effect on the perception of ambiguous pictures. *Bulletin of the Psychonomic Society, 7*, 331–333.
Maltin, L. (Ed.). (1978). *TV movies: 1979–80 edition.* New York: Signet.
Marks, L. E., Borg, G., & Ljunggren, G. (1983). Individual differences in perceived exertion assessed by two new methods. *Perception & Psychophysics, 34*, 280–288.
Masin, S. C., & Vidotto, G. (1983). A magnitude estimation study of the inverted-T illusion. *Perception & Psychophysics, 33*, 582–584.
Matlin, M. W. (1983). *Perception.* Boston: Allyn and Bacon.
McBurney, D. H., & Collings, V. B. (1984). *Introduction to sensation/perception* (2nd ed.). Englewood Cliffs, NJ: Prentice-Hall.

McConnell, J. V., Cutler, R. L., & McNeil, E. B. (1958). Subliminal stimulation: An overview. *American Psychologist, 13,* 229–242.
McGinnies, E. (1949). Emotionality and perceptual defense. *Psychological Review, 56,* 244–251.
Mednick, S. A., Higgins, J., & Kirschbaum, J. (1975). *Psychology: Explorations in behavior and experience.* New York: Wiley.
Moore, T. E. (1982). Subliminal advertising: What you see is what you get. *Journal of Marketing, 46,* 38–47.
Moskowitz, H. R. (1970a). Ratio scales of sugar sweetness. *Perception & Psychophysics, 7,* 315–320.
Moskowitz, H. R. (1970b). Sweetness and intensity of artificial sweeteners. *Perception & Psychophysics, 8,* 40–42.
Moskowitz, H. R., Kluter, R. A., Westerling, J., & Jacobs, H. L. (1974). Sugar sweetness and pleasantness: Evidence for different psychological laws. *Science, 184,* 583–585.
Newhall, S. M. (1952). Hidden cow puzzle-picture. *American Journal of Psychology, 65,* 110.
Oliver, J. M., & Burkham, R. (1982). Subliminal psychodynamic activation in depression: A failure to replicate. *Journal of Abnormal Psychology, 91,* 337–342.
Parks, T. E. (1984). Illusory figures: A (mostly) atheoretical review. *Psychological Bulletin, 95,* 282–300.
Rice, B. (1978, November). Cooking with psychophysics. *Psychology Today,* pp. 80–83, 89, 122.
Saegert, J. (1979). Another look at subliminal perception. *Journal of Advertising Research, 19,* 55–57.
Schiff, W. (1980). *Perception: An applied approach.* Boston: Houghton Mifflin.
Schiffman, H. R. (1982). *Sensation and perception: An integrated approach* (2nd ed.). New York: Wiley.
Schulman, M. (1981). The great conspiracy. *Journal of Communication, 31,* 209–210.
Senders, V. L. (1959). A still, small voice—subliminally perceived. In *Controlling human behavior: A report to the people* (pp. 23–29). Minneapolis, MN: University of Minnesota, Social Science Research Center of the Graduate School.
Sheraton, M. (1984, June 4). You can argue with taste. *Time,* pp. 74–75.
Shevrin, H. & Dickman, S. (1980). The psychological unconscious: A necessary assumption for all psychological theory? *American Psychologist, 35,* 421–434.
Silverman, L. H. (1976). Psychoanalytic theory: "The reports of my death are greatly exaggerated." *American Psychologist, 31,* 621–637.
Silverman, L. H. (1982a). A comment on two subliminal psychodynamic activation studies. *Journal of Abnormal Psychology, 91,* 126–130.
Silverman, L. H. (1982b). Rejoinder to Allen and Condon's and Heilbrun's replies. *Journal of Abnormal Psychology, 91,* 136–138.
Silverman, L. H., Ross, D. L., Adler, J. M., & Lustig, D. A. (1978). Simple research paradigm for demonstrating subliminal psychodynamic activation: Effects of oedipal stimuli on dart-throwing accuracy in college males. *Journal of Abnormal Psychology, 87,* 341–357.
Smith, A., & Over, R. (1975). Tilt aftereffects with subjective contours. *Nature, 257,* 581–582.

Smith, A. T., & Over, R. (1979). Motion aftereffect with subjective contours. *Perception & Psychophysics, 25,* 95–98.
Stevens, J. C., & Marks, L. E. (1980). Cross-modality matching functions generated by magnitude estimation. *Perception & Psychophysics, 27,* 379–389.
Stevens, S. S. (1957). On the psychophysical law. *Psychological Review, 64,* 153–181.
Stevens, S. S. (1962). The surprising simplicity of sensory metrics. *American Psychologist, 17,* 29–39.
Stevens, S. S. (1969). Sensory scales of taste intensity. *Perception & Psychophysics, 6,* 302–308.
Stevens, S. S. (1971). Issues in psychophysical measurement. *Psychological Review, 78,* 426–450.
Stevens, S. S. (1972). *Psychophysics and social scaling.* Morristown, NJ: General Learning Press, pp. 1–26.
Stevens, S. S. (1975). *Psychophysics: Introduction to its perceptual, neural, and social prospects* (Edited by G. Stevens). New York: Wiley.
Stone, L. A., & Harder, R. E. (1969). Subjective intensity of a familiar liquid substance—coffee. *Psychonomic Science, 15,* 105–106.
Teghtsoonian, R., & Teghtsoonian, M. (1982). Perceived effort in sniffing: The effects of sniff pressure and resistance. *Perception & Psychophysics, 31,* 324–329.
Teuber, M. L. (1974). Sources of ambiguity in the prints of Maurits C. Escher. In W. H. Freeman (1976), *Readings from Scientific American: Recent progress in perception* (pp. 153–167). San Francisco: Author.

BF
1
G111
v. 5

99980

DATE DUE

WITHDRAWN
From Library Collection

Ireton Library
Marymount University
Arlington, VA 22207